Modular Programming with PHP 7

Utilize the power of modular programming to improve code readability, maintainability, and testability

Branko Ajzele

[PACKT] open source ❋
PUBLISHING
community experience distilled

BIRMINGHAM - MUMBAI

Modular Programming with PHP 7

First published: September 2016

Production reference: 1020916

Published by Packt Publishing Ltd.
Livery Place
35 Livery Street
Birmingham B3 2PB, UK.

ISBN 978-1-78646-295-4

www.packtpub.com

Credits

Author
Branko Ajzele

Reviewer
Tomislav Sudmak

Commissioning Editor
Kunal Parikh

Acquisition Editor
Chaitanya Nair

Content Development Editor
Priyanka Mehta

Technical Editor
Ravikiran Pise

Copy Editor
Safis Editing

Project Coordinator
Izzat Contractor

Proofreader
Safis Editing

Indexer
Tejal Daruwale Soni

Graphics
Abhinash Sahu

Production Coordinator
Aparna Bhagat

Cover Work
Aparna Bhagat

About the Author

Branko Ajzele was born in January 1983 and lives in Osijek, Croatia. He is a husband, father of two, book author, and software developer. He holds a faculty degree in electrical engineering. He loves all things digital and makes a living out of software development.

Branko has years of hands-on experience in full-time software development and team management and specializes in e-commerce platforms. He has worked with Magento since 2008, knee-deep since its very first beta version. He is regularly in touch with modern software development technologies.

He has strong technical knowledge and is able to communicate technicalities clearly with strong direction. He feels comfortable proposing alternatives to demands that he feels can be improved, even when this means pulling a late shift to meet deadlines.

Branko holds several IT certifications such as Zend Certified Engineer (ZCE PHP), Magento Certified Developer (MCD), Magento Certified Developer Plus (MCD+), and Magento Certified Solution Specialist (MCSS).

Instant E-Commerce with Magento: Build a Shop by Packt Publishing was his first Magento-related book oriented toward Magento newcomers, after which he decided to write *Getting Started with Magento Extension Development* for developers. His third book, *Magento 2 Developer's Guide*, covers Magento 2 e-commerce platform development.

He currently works as a full-time contractor for Lab Lateral Ltd.—an award-winning team of innovative thinkers, artists, and developers, specializing in customer-centric websites, digital consultancy, and marketing—as the lead Magento developer and head of the Lab's Croatia office.

Branko was crowned E-commerce Developer of the Year by Digital Entrepreneur Awards in October 2014 for his excellent knowledge and expertise in e-commerce development. His work is second to none, and is truly dedicated to helping the Lab Lateral Ltd. team and fellow developers across the world.

About the Reviewer

Tomislav Sudmak is a software developer with an interest in all things digital. He developed an interest in programming during his college life while participating at the Start Up Academy, and he has been in love with various software technologies since then.

He has a master's degree in electrical engineering. Through his education, he crafted his skills with PHP and the Laravel framework, after which he became interested in e-commerce and Magento. He has also worked with Symfony, WordPress, Drupal, and other PHP-related frameworks.

During and after college, he worked as a freelancer on various web-related projects.

He has years of hands-on experience with full-time software development related with PHP, which is his main programming language.

Currently, he works as a backend developer in an award-winning digital agency, Lab Lateral Ltd.

During his free time and when he is not doing anything related to IT, Tomislav enjoys going to the gym, riding his bike, and visiting places he has never been to.

www.PacktPub.com

eBooks, discount offers, and more

Did you know that Packt offers eBook versions of every book published, with PDF and ePub files available? You can upgrade to the eBook version at www.PacktPub.com and as a print book customer, you are entitled to a discount on the eBook copy. Get in touch with us at customercare@packtpub.com for more details.

At www.PacktPub.com, you can also read a collection of free technical articles, sign up for a range of free newsletters and receive exclusive discounts and offers on Packt books and eBooks.

https://www2.packtpub.com/books/subscription/packtlib

Do you need instant solutions to your IT questions? PacktLib is Packt's online digital book library. Here, you can search, access, and read Packt's entire library of books.

Why subscribe?

- Fully searchable across every book published by Packt
- Copy and paste, print, and bookmark content
- On demand and accessible via a web browser

Table of Contents

Preface

Building modular applications is a challenging task. It involves a wide spectrum of knowledge, ranging from design patterns and principles to the ins and outs of the chosen technology stack. The PHP ecosystem has quite a selection of tools, libraries, frameworks, and platforms to assist us with our goal of modular application development.

PHP 7 brings a lot of improvements that can further assist achieving that goal. We will start our journey by looking into some of these improvements. By the end of this book, our final delivery will be a modular web shop application built by the Symfony framework.

What this book covers

Chapter 1, *Ecosystem Overview*, gives a gentle introduction to the current state of the PHP ecosystem. It looks into the latest features of PHP 7, some of which open a door to the new concepts of use in modular development. Furthermore, this chapter glosses over the popular PHP frameworks.

Chapter 2, *GoF Design Patterns*, describes recurring solutions to common problems in software design. Practical PHP examples are given for each of the following patterns: creation pattern types, structural patterns, and behavioral patterns.

Chapter 3, *SOLID Design Principles*, dives into the five basic principles of object-oriented programming and design under the acronym SOLID (single responsibility, open-closed, Liskov substitution, Interface Segregation, and dependency inversion). It gives practical examples and explains the importance of these principles in modular development.

Chapter 4, Requirement Specification for a Modular Web Shop App, guides a reader through the process of defining overall application requirements. It starts by defining actual application feature requirements and progresses all the way to the technology stack selection.

Chapter 5, Symfony at a Glance, gives a high-level overview of Symfony as a framework, a set of tools, and a development methodology. It focuses on the building blocks that we will need to build our modular application.

Chapter 6, Building the Core Module, guides you through setting up a core module based on the Symfony bundle. The core module is then used to set the structure and dependencies for other modules to use.

Chapter 7, Building the Catalog Module, guides us through building a self-sufficient module that matches the web shop catalog-only feature set. It shows us how to set up entities relevant to the module functionality and how to manage those entities and their interactions using the existing framework.

Chapter 8, Building the Customer Module, guides us through building a self-sufficient module that matches the web shop customer-related feature set. It shows us how to set up entities relevant to the module's functionality and how to manage those entities and their interactions using the existing framework. It further shows us how to create a register and login systems.

Chapter 9, Building the Payment Module, guides us through building a self-sufficient module that matches the web shop payment-related feature set. It shows us how to integrate with a third-party payment provider. It further shows us how to expose a payment provider as service for other modules to use.

Chapter 10, Building the Shipment Module, guides us through building a self-sufficient module that matches the web shop shipment-related feature set. It shows us how to define several flat methods that yield different shipment pricing based on various cart product attributes. It further shows us how to expose a shipment method as service for other modules to use.

Chapter 11, Building the Sales Module, guides us through building a self-sufficient module that matches the web shop sales-only feature set. It shows us how to set up cart, cart item, order, and order item entities relevant to the module functionality and how to manage those entities and their interactions using the existing framework.

Chapter 12, Integrating and Distributing Modules, integrates all the modules built in the preceding chapters into a single functioning application. Moving on, it guides us through the modern PHP module distribution techniques. These include Git and Composer, which in turn indirectly include GitHub and Packagist.

What you need for this book

In order to successfully run all the examples provided in this book, you will need either your own web server or a third-party web-hosting solution. The high-level technology stack includes PHP 7.0 or greater, Apache/Nginx, and MySQL.

The Symfony framework itself comes with a detailed list of system requirements that can be found at `http://symfony.com/doc/current/reference/requirements.html`.

This book assumes that the reader is familiar with setting up the complete development environment.

Who this book is for

This book is primarily intended for intermediate-level PHP developers, with little to no knowledge of modular programming who want to understand design patterns and principles in order to better utilize the existing framework for modular application development.

The modular web-shop application developed as a part of this book uses the Symfony framework. However, no previous knowledge of the Symfony framework is assumed or required.

Conventions

In this book, you will find a number of text styles that distinguish between different kinds of information. Here are some examples of these styles and an explanation of their meaning.

Code words in text, database table names, folder names, filenames, file extensions, pathnames, dummy URLs, user input, and Twitter handles are shown as follows: "We can include other contexts through the use of the `include` directive."

A block of code is set as follows:

```
function hint (int $A, float $B, string $C, bool $D)
{
    var_dump($A, $B, $C, $D);
}
```

Any command-line input or output is written as follows:

```
sudo curl -LsS https://symfony.com/installer -o /usr/local/bin/
  symfony
sudo chmod a+x /usr/local/bin/symfony
```

New terms and **important words** are shown in bold. Words that you see on the screen, for example, in menus or dialog boxes, appear in the text like this: "Clicking the **Next** button moves you to the next screen."

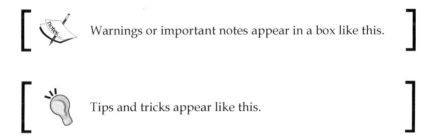

Warnings or important notes appear in a box like this.

Tips and tricks appear like this.

Reader feedback

Feedback from our readers is always welcome. Let us know what you think about this book—what you liked or disliked. Reader feedback is important for us as it helps us develop titles that you will really get the most out of.

To send us general feedback, simply e-mail feedback@packtpub.com, and mention the book's title in the subject of your message.

If there is a topic that you have expertise in and you are interested in either writing or contributing to a book, see our author guide at www.packtpub.com/authors.

Customer support

Now that you are the proud owner of a Packt book, we have a number of things to help you to get the most from your purchase.

Downloading the example code

You can download the example code files for this book from your account at http://www.packtpub.com. If you purchased this book elsewhere, you can visit http://www.packtpub.com/support and register to have the files e-mailed directly to you.

You can download the code files by following these steps:

1. Log in or register to our website using your e-mail address and password.
2. Hover the mouse pointer on the **SUPPORT** tab at the top.
3. Click on **Code Downloads & Errata**.
4. Enter the name of the book in the **Search** box.
5. Select the book for which you're looking to download the code files.
6. Choose from the drop-down menu where you purchased this book from.
7. Click on **Code Download**.

You can also download the code files by clicking on the **Code Files** button on the book's webpage at the Packt Publishing website. This page can be accessed by entering the book's name in the **Search** box. Please note that you need to be logged in to your Packt account.

Once the file is downloaded, please make sure that you unzip or extract the folder using the latest version of:

- WinRAR / 7-Zip for Windows
- Zipeg / iZip / UnRarX for Mac
- 7-Zip / PeaZip for Linux

The code bundle for the book is also hosted on GitHub at https://github.com/ PacktPublishing/Modular-Programming-with-PHP7. We also have other code bundles from our rich catalog of books and videos available at https://github. com/PacktPublishing/. Check them out!

Downloading the color images of this book

We also provide you with a PDF file that has color images of the screenshots/ diagrams used in this book. The color images will help you better understand the changes in the output. You can download this file from https://www.packtpub. com/sites/default/files/downloads/ModularProgrammingwithPHP7_ ColorImages.pdf.

Errata

Although we have taken every care to ensure the accuracy of our content, mistakes do happen. If you find a mistake in one of our books—maybe a mistake in the text or the code—we would be grateful if you could report this to us. By doing so, you can save other readers from frustration and help us improve subsequent versions of this book. If you find any errata, please report them by visiting http://www.packtpub.com/submit-errata, selecting your book, clicking on the **Errata Submission Form** link, and entering the details of your errata. Once your errata are verified, your submission will be accepted and the errata will be uploaded to our website or added to any list of existing errata under the Errata section of that title.

To view the previously submitted errata, go to https://www.packtpub.com/books/content/support and enter the name of the book in the search field. The required information will appear under the **Errata** section.

Piracy

Piracy of copyrighted material on the Internet is an ongoing problem across all media. At Packt, we take the protection of our copyright and licenses very seriously. If you come across any illegal copies of our works in any form on the Internet, please provide us with the location address or website name immediately so that we can pursue a remedy.

Please contact us at copyright@packtpub.com with a link to the suspected pirated material.

We appreciate your help in protecting our authors and our ability to bring you valuable content.

Questions

If you have a problem with any aspect of this book, you can contact us at questions@packtpub.com, and we will do our best to address the problem.

1
Ecosystem Overview

It has been more than two decades now since the birth of PHP. Originally created by Rasmus Lerdorf in 1994, the PHP acronym initially stood for **Personal Home Page**. Back then, PHP was merely a few **Common Gateway Interface (CGI)** programs in C, used to power a simple web page.

Though PHP was not intended to be a new programming language, the idea caught on. During the late nineties Zeev Suraski and Andi Gutmans, co-founders of Zend Technologies, continued the work on PHP by rewriting its entire parser, giving birth to PHP 3. The PHP language name acronym now stood for **PHP: Hypertext Preprocessor**.

PHP positions itself among the top ten programming languages in the world. According to TIOBE, the software quality company, it currently holds sixth place. For the last decade, especially since the release of PHP 5 in July 2004, PHP has been recognized as the popular solution for building web applications.

Though PHP still presents itself as a scripting language, it's safe to say that as of PHP 5 it is far more than that. Some of the world web's most popular platforms like WordPress, Drupal, Magento, and PrestaShop are built in PHP. It is projects like these that played a role in further raising the popularity of PHP. Some of them stretch the boundaries of PHP by implementing complex OOP (Object Oriented Programming) design patterns found in other programming languages like Java, C#, and their frameworks.

Even though PHP 5 had decent OOP support, lots of things were still left to be dreamed of. Work on PHP 6 was planned to give more support for the PHP Unicode strings. Sadly, its development came to a halt and PHP 6 was canceled in 2010.

That same year, Facebook announced its HipHop compiler. Their compiler was converting PHP code into C++ code. The C++ code was further compiled into native machine code via a C++ compiler. This concept brought major performance improvements for PHP. However, this approach was not very practical, because it took too long to compile PHP scripts all the way to native machine code.

Shortly after, Dmitry Stogov, Zend Technologies Chief Performance Engineer, announced a project called **PHPNG**, which became the basis for the next PHP version, PHP 7.

In Dec 2015, PHP 7 was released, bringing numerous improvements and new features:

- New version of the Zend Engine
- Improved performance (twice as fast as PHP 5.6)
- Significantly reduced memory usage
- Abstract Syntax Tree
- Consistent 64-bit support
- Improved exception hierarchy
- Many fatal errors converted to exceptions
- Secure random number generator
- Removed old and unsupported SAPIs and extensions
- The null coalescing operator
- Return and Scalar type declarations
- Anonymous classes
- Zero cost asserts

In this chapter, we will look at the following topics:

- Getting ready for PHP 7
- Frameworks

Getting ready for PHP 7

PHP 7 comes with quite a big list of changes. These changes affect both the PHP interpreter and the various extensions and libraries. Though most of the PHP 5 code will continue to operate normally on the PHP 7 interpreter, it is worth getting up to speed with the newly available features.

Moving forward, we will look into some of these features and the benefits they provide.

Scalar type hints

Scalar type hints are not an entirely new feature in PHP. With the introduction of PHP 5.0 we were given the ability to type hint classes and interfaces. PHP 5.1 extended this by introducing array type hinting. Later on, with PHP 5.4, we were additionally given the ability to type hint callable. Finally, PHP 7 introduced scalar type hints. Extending the type hints to scalars makes this probably one of the most exciting features added to PHP 7.

The following scalar type hints are now available:

- `string`: Strings (for example, `hello`, `foo`, and `bar`)
- `int`: Integer numbers (for example, `1`, `2`, and `3`)
- `float`: Floating point numbers (for example, `1.2`, `2.4`, and `5.6`)
- `bool`: Boolean values (for example, `true` or `false`)

By default, PHP 7 works in weak *type-checking* mode, and will attempt to convert to the specified type without complaint. We can control this mode using the `strict_types`declare() directive.

The `declare(strict_types=1);` directive must be the first statement in a file, or else it will generate a compiler error. It only affects the specific file it is used in, and does not affect other included files. The directive is entirely compile-time and cannot be controlled at runtime:

```
declare(strict_types=0); //weak type-checking
declare(strict_types=1); // strict type-checking
```

Let's assume the following simple function that accepts hinted scalar types.

```
function hint (int $A, float $B, string $C, bool $D)
{
    var_dump($A, $B, $C, $D);
}
```

The weak type-checking rules for the new scalar type declarations are mostly the same as those of extensions and built-in PHP functions. Because of this automated conversion we might unknowingly lose data when passing it into a function. One simple example is passing a float into a function that requires an int; in which case conversion would simply strip away decimals.

Assuming the weak type-checking is on, as by default, the following can be observed:

```
hint(2, 4.6, 'false', true);
/* int(2) float(4.6) string(5) "false" bool(true) */

hint(2.4, 4, true, 8);
/* int(2) float(4) string(1) "1" bool(true) */
```

We can see that the first function call passes on parameters as they are hinted. The second function call does not pass the exact types of parameters but still the function manages to execute as parameters go through conversion.

Assuming the weak type-checking is off, by using the `declare(strict_types=1);` directive, the following can be observed:

```
hint(2.4, 4, true, 8);

Fatal error: Uncaught TypeError: Argument 1 passed to hint() must
be of the type integer, float given, called in php7.php on
line 16 and defined in php7.php:8 Stack trace: #0 php7.php(16):
hint(2.4, 4, true, 8) #1 {main} thrown in php7.php on line 8
```

The function call broke on the first argument resulting in the `\TypeError` exception. The `strict_types=1` directive does not allow any type juggling. The parameter has to be of the same type, as hinted by the function definition.

Return type hints

In addition to type hinting, we can also type hint the return *values*. All of the type hints that can be applied to function parameters can be applied to function return values. This also implies to the weak type-checking rules.

To add a return type hint, simply follow the parameter list with a colon and the return type, as shown in the following example:

```
function divide(int $A, int $B) : int
{
    return $A / $B;
}
```

The preceding function definition says that the `divide` function expects two parameters of the `int` type, and is supposed to return a parameter of the `int` type.

Assuming the *weak type-checking* is on, as by default, the following can be observed:

```
var_dump(divide(10, 2)); // int(5)
var_dump(divide(10, 3)); // int(3)
```

Though the actual result of `divide(10, 3)` should be a float, the return type hint triggers conversion into an integer.

Assuming the weak type-checking is off, by using the `declare(strict_types=1);` directive, the following can be observed:

```
int(5)
Fatal error: Uncaught TypeError: Return value of divide() must be
of the type integer, float returned in php7.php:10 Stack trace:
#0php7.php(14): divide(10, 3) #1 {main} thrown in php7.php on
line 10
```

With the `strict_types=1` directive in place, the `divide(10, 3)` fails with the `\TypeError` exception.

 Using scalar type hints and return type hints can improve our code readability as well as auto-complete features of IDE editors like NetBeans and PhpStorm.

Anonymous classes

With the addition of anonymous classes, PHP objects gained closure-like capabilities. We can now instantiate objects through nameless classes, which brings us closer to object literal syntax found in other languages. Let's take a look at the following simple example:

```
$object = new class {
    public function hello($message) {
        return "Hello $message";
    }
};

echo$object->hello('PHP');
```

The preceding example shows an `$object` variable storing a reference to an instance of an anonymous class. The more likely usage would be to directly pass the new class to a function parameter, without storing it as a variable, as shown here:

```
$helper->sayHello(new class {
    public function hello($message) {
```

```
            return "Hello $message";
        }
    });
```

Similar to any normal class, anonymous classes can pass arguments through to their constructors, extend other classes, implement interfaces, and use traits:

```php
class TheClass {}
interface TheInterface {}
trait TheTrait {}

$object = new class('A', 'B', 'C') extends TheClass implements
    TheInterface {

    use TheTrait;

    public $A;
    private $B;
    protected $C;

    public function __construct($A, $B, $C)
    {
        $this->A = $A;
        $this->B = $B;
        $this->C = $C;
    }
};

var_dump($object);
```

The above example would output:

```
object(class@anonymous)#1 (3) { ["A"]=> string(1) "A"
["B":"class@anonymous":private]=> string(1) "B"
["C":protected]=> string(1) "C" }
```

The internal name of an anonymous class is generated with a unique reference based on its address.

There is no definitive answer as to when to use anonymous classes. It depends almost entirely on the application we are building, and the objects, depending on their perspective and usage.

Some of the benefits of using anonymous classes are as follows:

- Mocking application tests becomes trivial. We can create on-the-fly implementations for interfaces, avoiding using complex mocking APIs.
- Avoid invoking the autoloader every so often for simpler implementations.
- Makes it clear to anyone reading the code that this class is used here and nowhere else.

Anonymous classes, or rather objects instantiated from anonymous classes, cannot be serialized. Trying to serialize them results in a fatal error as follows:

```
Fatal error: Uncaught Exception: Serialization of
   'class@anonymous' is not allowed in php7.php:29 Stack trace: #0
   php7.php(29): serialize(Object(class@anonymous)) #1 {main}
   thrown in php7.php on line 29
```

Nesting an anonymous class does not give it access to private or protected methods and properties of the outer class. In order to use the outer class protected methods and properties, the anonymous class can extend the outer class. Ignoring methods, private or protected properties of the outer class can be used in the anonymous class if passed through its constructor:

```php
class Outer
{
    private $prop = 1;
    protected $prop2 = 2;

    protected function outerFunc1()
    {
        return 3;
    }

    public function outerFunc2()
    {
        return new class($this->prop) extends Outer
        {
            private $prop3;

            public function __construct($prop)
            {
                $this->prop3 = $prop;
            }

            public function innerFunc1()
            {
```

```
                return $this->prop2 + $this->prop3 + $this
                   ->outerFunc1();
            }
        };
    }
}

echo (new Outer)->outerFunc2()->innerFunc1(); //6
```

Though we labeled them as anonymous classes, they are not really anonymous in terms of the internal name the PHP engine assigns to objects instantiated from these classes. The internal name of an anonymous class is generated with a unique reference based on its address.

The statement `get_class(new class{});` would result in something like `class@anonymous/php7.php0x7f33c22381c8`, where `0x7f33c22381c8` is the internal address. If we were to define the exact same anonymous class elsewhere in the code, its class name would be different as it would have a different memory address assigned. The resulting object in that case might have the same property values, which means they will be equal (`==`) but not identical (`===`).

The Closure::call() method

PHP introduced the Closure class in the 5.3 version. Closure class is used to represent anonymous functions. Anonymous functions, implemented in PHP 5.3, yield objects of this type. As of PHP 5.4, the Closure class got several methods (`bind`, `bindTo`) that allow further control of the anonymous function after it has been created. These methods basically duplicate the Closure with a specific bound object and class scope. PHP 7 introduced the call method on a Closure class. The `call` method does not duplicate the closure, it temporarily binds the closure to new this (`$newThis`), and calls it with any given parameters. It then returns the return value of the closure.

The `call` function signature looks like the following:

```
function call ($newThis, ...$parameters) {}
```

`$newThis` is the object to bind the closure for the duration of the `call`. The parameters, which will be given as `$parameters` to the closure are optional, meaning zero or more.

Let's take a look at the following example of a simple `Customer` class and a `$greeting` closure:

```php
class Customer {
    private $firstname;
    private $lastname;

    public function __construct($firstname, $lastname)
    {
        $this->firstname = $firstname;
        $this->lastname = $lastname;
    }
}

$customer = new Customer('John', 'Doe');

$greeting = function ($message) {
    return "$message $this->firstname $this->lastname!";
};

echo $greeting->call($customer, 'Hello');
```

Within the actual `$greeting` closure, there is no `$this`, it does not exist until the actual binding occurs. We could easily confirm this by directly calling a closure like `$greeting('Hello');`. However, we assume `$this` will come in to existence when we bind the closure to a given object instance via its `call` function. In which case, `$this` within the closure becomes `$this` of the `customer` object instance. The preceding example shows binding of `$customer` to the closure using a `call` method call. The resulting output displays **Hello John Doe!**

Generator delegation

Generators provide a simple way to implement *iterators* without the overhead of implementing a class that implements the **Iterator** interface. They allow us to write code which uses `foreach` to iterate over a set of data without needing to build an array in memory. This eliminates the exceeds memory limit errors. They were not new to PHP, as they were added in PHP 5.5.

However, PHP 7 brings several new improvements to generators, one of which is generator delegation.

Generator delegation allows a generator to yield other generators, arrays, or objects that implement the **Traversable** interface. In another words, we might say that generator delegation is yielding **subgenerators**.

Let's take a look at the following example with three generator type functions:

```php
function gen1() {
    yield '1';
    yield '2';
    yield '3';
}

function gen2() {
    yield '4';
    yield '5';
    yield '6';
}

function gen3() {
    yield '7';
    yield '8';
    yield from gen1();
    yield '9';
    yield from gen2();
    yield '10';
}

// output of the below code: 123
foreach (gen1() as $number) {
echo $number;
}

//output of the below code: 78123945610
foreach (gen3() as $number) {
    echo $number;
}
```

Yielding other generators requires using the `yield from <expression>` syntax.

Generator return expressions

Prior to PHP 7, generator functions were not able to return expressions. The inability of generator functions to specify return values limited their usefulness for multitasking in co-routine contexts.

PHP 7 made it possible for generators to return expressions. We can now call
`$generator->getReturn()` to retrieve the `return` expression. Calling `$generator->getReturn()` when the generator has not yet returned, or has thrown an uncaught
exception, will throw an exception.

If the generator has no return expression defined and has completed yielding, null is
returned.

Let's take a look at the following example:

```
function gen() {
    yield 'A';
    yield 'B';
    yield 'C';

    return 'gen-return';
}

$generator = gen();

//output of the below code: object(Generator)#1 (0) { }
var_dump($generator);

// output of the below code: Fatal error
// var_dump($generator->getReturn());

// output of the below code: ABC
foreach ($generator as $letter) {
    echo $letter;
}

// string(10) "gen-return"
var_dump($generator->getReturn());
```

Looking at the `gen()` function definition and its `return` expression, one might
expect the value of the `$generator` variable to be equal to the `gen-return` string.
However, this is not the case, as the `$generator` variable becomes the instance of the
`\Generator` class. Calling the `getReturn()` method on the generator while it is still
open (not iterated over) will result in a fatal error.

If the code is structured in such a way that it is not obvious if the generator has been
closed, we can use the `valid` method to check, before fetching the return value:

```
if ($generator->valid() === false) {
    var_dump($generator->getReturn());
}
```

The null coalesce operator

In PHP 5 we had the ternary operator which tests a value and then returns the second element if that value is `true`, or third element if that value is `false`, as shown in the following code block:

```
$check = (5 > 3) ? 'Correct!' : 'Faulty!'; // Correct!
$check = (5 < 3) ? 'Correct!' : 'Faulty!'; // Faulty!
```

While processing user-provided data in web-centered languages such as PHP, it is common to check for variable existence. If a variable doesn't exist, then set it to some default value. A ternary operator makes this easy for us, as shown here:

```
$role = isset($_GET['role']) ? $_GET['role'] : 'guest';
```

However, easy is not always quick or elegant. With that in mind, PHP 7 set out to resolve one of the most common usage patterns, by introducing the null coalesce operator(`??`).

The null coalesce operator enables us to write even shorter expressions, as in the following code block:

```
$role = $_GET['role'] ??'guest';
```

The coalesce operator(`??`) is added right after the `$_GET['role']` variable, which returns the result of its first operand if it exists and is not `NULL`, or else its second operand. This means the `$_GET['role'] ?? 'guest'` is completely safe and will not raise an `E_NOTICE`.

We can also nest the coalesce operator:

```
$A = null; // or not set
$B = 10;

echo $A ?? 20; // 20
echo $A ?? $B ?? 30; // 10
```

Reading from left to right, the first value which exists and is not null is the value that will be returned. The benefit of this construct is that it enables a clean and effective way to achieve safe fallback to the desired value.

 The code bundle for the book is also hosted on GitHub at `https://github.com/PacktPublishing/Modular-Programming-with-PHP7`. We also have other code bundles from our rich catalog of books and videos available at `https://github.com/PacktPublishing/`. Check them out!

The Spaceship operator

The three-way comparison operator, also known as the Spaceship operator, was introduced in PHP 7. Its syntax goes as follows:

```
(expr) <=> (expr)
```

The operator returns 0 if both operands are equal, 1 if the left is greater, and -1 if the right is greater.

It uses the same comparison rules as other existing comparison operators: <, <=, ==, >=, and >:

```
operator<=> equivalent
$a < $b($a <=> $b) === -1
$a <= $b($a <=> $b) === -1 || ($a <=> $b) === 0
$a == $b($a <=> $b) === 0
$a != $b($a <=> $b) !== 0
$a >= $b($a <=> $b) === 1 || ($a <=> $b) === 0
$a > $b($a <=> $b) === 1
```

The following are some examples of Spaceship operator behavior:

```php
// Floats
echo 1.5 <=> 1.5; // 0
echo 1.5 <=> 2.5; // -1
echo 2.5 <=> 1.5; // 1

// Strings
echo "a"<=>"a"; // 0
echo "a"<=>"b"; // -1
echo "b"<=>"a"; // 1

echo "a"<=>"aa"; // -1
echo "zz"<=>"aa"; // 1

// Arrays
echo [] <=> []; // 0
echo [1, 2, 3] <=> [1, 2, 3]; // 0
echo [1, 2, 3] <=> []; // 1
echo [1, 2, 3] <=> [1, 2, 1]; // 1
echo [1, 2, 3] <=> [1, 2, 4]; // -1

// Objects
$a = (object) ["a" =>"b"];
$b = (object) ["a" =>"b"];
```

```
echo $a <=> $b; // 0

$a = (object) ["a" =>"b"];
$b = (object) ["a" =>"c"];
echo $a <=> $b; // -1

$a = (object) ["a" =>"c"];
$b = (object) ["a" =>"b"];
echo $a <=> $b; // 1

// only values are compared
$a = (object) ["a" =>"b"];
$b = (object) ["b" =>"b"];
echo $a <=> $b; // 0
```

One practical use case for this operator is for writing callbacks used in sorting functions like `usort`, `uasort`, and `uksort`:

```
$letters = ['D', 'B', 'A', 'C', 'E'];

usort($letters, function($a, $b) {
return $a <=> $b;
});

var_dump($letters);

// array(5) { [0]=> string(1) "A" [1]=> string(1) "B" [2]=>
  string(1) "C" [3]=> string(1) "D" [4]=> string(1) "E" }
```

Throwables

Though PHP 5 introduced the exception model, overall errors and error handling remained somewhat unpolished. Basically PHP had two error handling systems. Traditional errors still popped out and were not handled by `try...catch` blocks.

Take the following E_RECOVERABLE_ERROR as an example:

```
class Address
{
    private $customer;
    public function __construct(Customer $customer)
    {
        $this->customer = $customer;
    }
}
```

```
$customer = new stdClass();

try {
    $address = new Address($customer);
} catch (\Exception $e) {
    echo 'handling';
} finally {
echo 'cleanup';
}
```

The `try...catch` block has no effect here, as the error is not interpreted as an exception, rather a catchable fatal error:

```
Catchable fatal error: Argument 1 passed to Address::__construct()
must be an instance of Customer, instance of stdClass given,
called in script.php on line 15 and defined in script.php on
line 6.
```

A possible workaround involves setting a user-defined error handler by using the `set_error_handler` function as follows:

```
set_error_handler(function($code, $message) {
    throw new \Exception($message, $code);
});
```

The error handler, as written above, would now transform every error into an exception, therefore making it catchable with `try...catch` blocks.

PHP 7 made fatal and catchable fatal errors part of engine exceptions, therefore catchable with `try...catch` blocks. This excludes warnings and notices which still do not pass through the exception system, which makes sense for backward compatibility reasons.

It also introduced a new exception hierarchy via the `\Throwable` interface. `\Exception` and `\Error` implement the `\Throwable` interface.

Standard PHP fatal and catchable fatal are now thrown as `\Error` exceptions, though they will continue to trigger traditional fatal error if they are uncaught.

Throughout our application we must use `\Exception` and `\Error`, as we cannot implement the `\Throwable` interface directly. We could, however, use the following block to catch all errors, regardless of whether it is the `\Exception` or `\Error` type:

```
try {
// statements
} catch (\Throwable $t) {
    // handling
```

```
} finally {
// cleanup
}
```

The \ParseError

The **ParseError** is a nice PHP 7 addition to error handling. We can now handle parse errors triggered by `eval()`, `include` and `require` statements, as well as those thrown by `\ParseError` exceptions. It extends `\Error`, which in turn implements a `\Throwable` interface.

The following is an example of a broken PHP file, because of a missing `","` inbetween between array items:

```
<?php

$config = [
'host' =>'localhost'
'user' =>'john'
];

return $config;
```

The following is an example of a file including `config.php`:

```
<?php

try {
include 'config.php';
} catch (\ParseError $e) {
// handle broken file case
}
```

We can now safely catch possible parse errors.

Level support for the dirname() function

The `dirname` function has been with us since PHP 4. It's probably one of the most often used functions in PHP. Up until PHP 7, this function only accepted the `path` parameter. With PHP 7, the new levels parameter was added.

Let's take a look at the following example:

```
// would echo '/var/www/html/app/etc'
echo dirname('/var/www/html/app/etc/config/');

// would echo '/var/www/html/app/etc'
echo dirname('/var/www/html/app/etc/config.php');

// would echo '/var/www/html/app'
echo dirname('/var/www/html/app/etc/config.php', 2);

// would echo '/var/www/html'
echo dirname('/var/www/html/app/etc/config.php', 3);
```

By assigning the `levels` value, we indicate how many levels to go up from the assigned path value. Though small, the addition of the `levels` parameter will certainly make it easier to write some of the code that deals with paths.

The integer division function

The `intdiv` is a new integer division function introduced in PHP 7. The function accepts dividend and divisor as parameters and returns the integer quotient of their division, as shown here by the function description:

```
int intdiv(int $dividend, int $divisor)
```

Let's take a look at the following few examples:

```
intdiv(5, 3); // int(1)
intdiv(-5, 3); // int(-1)
intdiv(5, -2); // int(-2)
intdiv(-5, -2); // int(2)
intdiv(PHP_INT_MAX, PHP_INT_MAX); // int(1)
intdiv(PHP_INT_MIN, PHP_INT MIN); // int(1)

// following two throw error
intdiv(PHP_INT_MIN, -1); // ArithmeticError
intdiv(1, 0); // DivisionByZeroError
```

If the `dividend` is `PHP_INT_MIN` and the divisor is `-1`, then an `ArithmeticError` exception is thrown. If the divisor is `0`, then the `DivisionByZeroError` exception is thrown.

Constant arrays

Prior to PHP 7, constants defined with `define()` could only contain scalar expressions, but not arrays. As of PHP 5.6, it is possible to define an array constant by using `const` keywords, and as of PHP 7, array constants can also be defined using `define()`:

```
// the define() example
define('FRAMEWORK', [
'version' => 1.2,
'licence' =>'enterprise'
]);

echo FRAMEWORK['version']; // 1.2
echo FRAMEWORK['licence']; // enterprise

// the class const example
class App {
    const FRAMEWORK = [
'version' => 1.2,
'licence' =>'enterprise'
    ];
}

echo App::FRAMEWORK['version']; // 1.2
echo App::FRAMEWORK['licence']; // enterprise
```

Constants may not be redefined or undefined once they have been set.

Uniform variable syntax

To make PHP's parser more complete for various variable dereferences, PHP 7 introduced a uniform variable syntax. With uniform variable syntax all variables are evaluated from left to right.

Unlike various functions, keywords, or settings being removed, changes in semantics like this one can be quite impacting for the existing code base. The following code demonstrates the syntax, its old meaning and new:

```
// Syntax
$$foo['bar']['baz']
// PHP 5.x:
// Using a multidimensional array value as variable name
${$foo['bar']['baz']}
// PHP 7:
```

```
// Accessing a multidimensional array within a variable-variable
($$foo)['bar']['baz']

// Syntax
$foo->$bar['baz']
// PHP 5.x:
// Using an array value as a property name
$foo->{$bar['baz']}
// PHP 7:
// Accessing an array within a variable-property
($foo->$bar)['baz']

// Syntax
$foo->$bar['baz']()
// PHP 5.x:
// Using an array value as a method name
$foo->{$bar['baz']}()
// PHP 7:
// Calling a closure within an array in a variable-property
($foo->$bar)['baz']()

// Syntax
Foo::$bar['baz']()
// PHP 5.x:
// Using an array value as a static method name
Foo::{$bar['baz']}()
// PHP 7:
// Calling a closure within an array in a static variable
(Foo::$bar)['baz']()
```

Aside from previously rewritten examples of old-to-new syntax, there are now a few newly supported syntax combinations.

PHP 7 now supports nested double colons, : : , and following is an example of it:

```
// Access a static property on a string class name
// or object inside an array
$foo['bar']::$baz;
// Access a static property on a string class name or object
// returned by a static method call on a string class name
// or object
$foo::bar()::$baz;
// Call a static method on a string class or object returned by
// an instance method call
$foo->bar()::baz();
```

We can also nest methods and function calls — or any callables — by doubling up on parentheses as shown in the following code examples:

```
// Call a callable returned by a function
foo()();
// Call a callable returned by an instance method
$foo->bar()();
// Call a callable returned by a static method
Foo::bar()();
// Call a callable return another callable
$foo()();
```

Furthermore, we can now dereference any valid expression enclosed with parentheses:

```
// Access an array key
(expression)['foo'];
// Access a property
(expression)->foo;
// Call a method
(expression)->foo();
// Access a static property
(expression)::$foo;
// Call a static method
(expression)::foo();
// Call a callable
(expression)();
// Access a character
(expression){0};
```

Secure random number generator

PHP 7 introduced two new **CSPRNG** functions. CSPRNG is an acronym for **cryptographically secure pseudo-random number generator**.

The first, `random_bytes`, generates an arbitrary length string of cryptographic random bytes that are suitable for cryptographic use, such as when generating *salts*, *keys*, or *initialization* vectors. The function accepts only one (`length`) parameter, representing the length of the random string that should be returned in bytes. It returns a string containing the requested number of cryptographically secure random bytes, or, optionally, it throws an exception if an appropriate source of randomness cannot be found.

The following is an example of `random_bytes` usage:

```
$bytes = random_bytes(5);
```

The second, `random_int`, generates cryptographic random integers that are suitable for use where unbiased results are critical, such as when shuffling a deck of cards for a poker game. The function accepts two (`min`, `max`) parameters, representing the lowest value to be returned (must be `PHP_INT_MIN` or higher) and the highest value to be returned (must be less than or equal to `PHP_INT_MAX`). It returns a cryptographically secure random integer in the range min to max (inclusive).

The following is an example of `random_int` usage:

```
$int = random_int(1, 10);
$int = random_int(PHP_INT_MIN, 500);
$int = random_int(20, PHP_INT_MAX);
$int = random_int(PHP_INT_MIN, PHP_INT_MAX);
```

Filtered unserialize()

Serialized data can include objects. These objects can further include functions like destructors, `__toString`, and `__call`. In order to increase security when unserializing objects on unstructured data, PHP 7 introduced the optional `options` parameter to the existing `unserialize` function.

The `options` parameter is of type array that currently only accepts the `allowed_classes` key.

The `allowed_classes` can have one of three values:

- `true`: This is a default value and allows all objects just as before
- `false`: Here no objects allowed
- array of allowed class names, lists the allowed classes for unserialized objects

The following is an example of using the `allowed_classes` option:

```php
class Customer{
    public function __construct(){
        echo '__construct';
    }

    public function __destruct(){
        echo '__destruct';
    }
```

```php
    public function __toString(){
        echo '__toString';
        return '__toString';
    }

    public function __call($name, $arguments) {
        echo '__call';
    }
}

$customer = new Customer();

$s = serialize($customer); // triggers: __construct, __destruct

$u = unserialize($s); // triggers: __destruct
echo get_class($u); // Customer

$u = unserialize($s, ['allowed_classes'=>false]); // does not
    trigger anything
echo get_class($u); // __PHP_Incomplete_Class
```

We can see that the object of that class which is not accepted is instantiated as `__PHP_Incomplete_Class`.

Context sensitive lexer

According to the `http://php.net/manual/en/reserved.keywords.php` list, PHP has over 60 reserved keywords. These make up for language constructs, like names for properties, methods, constants within classes, interfaces, and traits.

Sometimes these reserved words end up clashing with user defined API declarations.

To resolve the issue, PHP 7.0 introduced the context sensitive lexer. With the context sensitive lexer, we may now use keywords for property, function, and constant names within our code.

The following are a few practical examples related to the impact of context sensitive lexer:

```php
class ReportPool {
    public function include(Report $report) {
//
    }
}
```

```
$reportPool = new ReportPool();
$reportPool->include(new Report());

class Collection extends \ArrayAccess, \Countable,
  \IteratorAggregate {

    public function forEach(callable $callback) {
//
    }

    public function list() {
//
    }

    public static function new(array $items) {
        return new self($items);
    }
}

Collection::new(['var1', 'var2'])
->forEach(function($index, $item){ /* ... */ })
->list();
```

The only exception being the `class` keyword, which remains reserved in *class constant context*, as shown here:

```
class Customer {
  const class = 'Retail'; // Fatal error
}
```

Group use declarations

The *group use declarations* are introduced in PHP 7 as a way to cut verbosities when importing multiple classes from a common namespace. They enable shorthand syntax as follows:

```
use Library\Group1\Group2\{ ClassA, ClassB, ClassC as Classy };
```

Let's take a look at the following examples where class names within the *same namespace* are group used:

```
// Current use syntax
use Doctrine\Common\Collections\Expr\Comparison;
use Doctrine\Common\Collections\Expr\Value;
use Doctrine\Common\Collections\Expr\CompositeExpression;
```

```
// Group use syntax
use Doctrine\Common\Collections\Expr\{ Comparison, Value,
  CompositeExpression };
```

We can also use the *group use declarations* on part of namespaces, as shown in the following example:

```
// Current use syntax
use Symfony\Component\Console\Helper\Table;
use Symfony\Component\Console\Input\ArrayInput;
use Symfony\Component\Console\Output\NullOutput;
use Symfony\Component\Console\Question\Question;
use Symfony\Component\Console\Input\InputInterface;
use Symfony\Component\Console\Output\OutputInterface;
use Symfony\Component\Console\Question\ChoiceQuestion as Choice;
use Symfony\Component\Console\Question\ConfirmationQuestion;

// Group use syntax
use Symfony\Component\Console\{
  Helper\Table,
  Input\ArrayInput,
  Input\InputInterface,
  Output\NullOutput,
  Output\OutputInterface,
  Question\Question,
  Question\ChoiceQuestion as Choice,
  Question\ConfirmationQuestion,
};
```

We can further use `group use` for importing functions and constants as shown in the following lines of code:

```
use Framework\Component\{
SubComponent\ClassA,
function OtherComponent\someFunction,
const OtherComponent\SOME_CONSTANT
};
```

Unicode enhancements

Unicode, and UTF-8 in particular, have grown increasingly popular in PHP applications.

PHP 7 adds the new escape sequence for *double-quoted strings* and *heredocs*, with the syntax as follows:

```
\u{code-point}
```

It produces the UTF-8 encoding of a Unicode code point, specified with hexadecimal digits. It is worth noting that the length of the code-point within curly braces is arbitrary. This means that we can use \u{FF} or the more traditional \u{00FF}.

The following is a simple listing of the four most traded currencies, their symbols, and their UTF-8 code points:

```
Euro€U+20AC
Japanese Yen¥U+00A5
Pound sterling£U+00A3
Australian dollar$U+0024
```

Some of these symbols usually exist directly on a keyboard, so it's easy to write them down as shown here:

```
echo "the € currency";
echo "the ¥ currency";
echo "the £ currency";
echo "the $ currency";
```

However, the majority of other symbols are not as easily accessible via the keyboard as single keystrokes, and therefore need to be written in the form of code-points, shown as follows:

```
echo "the \u{1F632} face";
echo "the \u{1F609} face";
echo "the \u{1F60F} face";
```

In older versions of PHP, the resulting output of preceding statements would be the following:

```
the \u{1F632} face
the \u{1F609} face
the \u{1F60F} face
```

This obviously did not parse code-points, as it was outputting them literally.

PHP 7 introduced Unicode code-point escape sequence syntax to string literals, making previous statements result in the following output:

```
the □ face
the □ face
the □ face
```

Assertions

Assertions is a debug feature, used to check the given assertion and take appropriate action if its result is `false`. They have been part of PHP for years, ever since PHP 4.

Assertions differ from error handling in a way that assertions cover for impossible cases, whereas errors are possible and need to be handled.

Using assertions as a general-purpose error handling mechanism should be avoided. Assertions do not allow for recovery from errors. Assertion failure will normally halt the execution of a program.

With modern debugging tools like Xdebug, not many developers use assertions for debugging.

Assertions can be easily enabled and disabled using the `assert_options` function or the `assert.active` INI setting.

To use assertions, we pass in either an expression or a string as shown in the following function signature:

```
// PHP 5
bool assert ( mixed $assertion [, string $description ] )

// PHP 7
bool assert ( mixed $assertion [, Throwable $exception ] )
```

These two signatures differ in the second parameter. PHP 7 can accept either string `$description` or `$exception`.

If the expression result or the result of evaluating the string evaluates to `false`, then a warning is raised. If the second parameter is passed as `$exception`, then an exception will be thrown instead of failure.

In regards to `php.ini` configuration options, the `assert` function has been expanded to allow for so-called *zero-cost assertions*:

```
zend.assertions = 1 // Enable
zend.assertions = 0 // Disable
zend.assertions = -1 // Zero-cost
```

With zero-cost settings, assertions have zero impact on performance and execution as they are not compiled.

Finally, the `Boolean assert.exception` option was added to the **INI** setting. Setting it to `true`, results in `AssertionError` exceptions for the failed assertions.

Changes to the list() construct

In PHP 5, `list()` assigns the values starting with the right-most parameter. In PHP 7, `list()` starts with the left-most parameter. Basically, values are now assigned to variables in the order they are defined.

However, this only affects the case where `list()` is being used in conjunction with the `array []` operator, as discussed in the following code block:

```php
<?php

list($color1, $color2, $color3) = ['green', 'yellow', 'blue'];
var_dump($color1, $color2, $color3);

list($colors[], $colors[], $colors[]) = ['green', 'yellow',
    'blue'];
var_dump($colors);
```

Output of the preceding code in PHP 5 would result in the following:

```
string(5) "green"
string(6) "yellow"
string(4) "blue"

array(3) {
[0]=> string(5) "blue"
[1]=> string(6) "yellow"
[2]=> string(4) "green"
}
```

Output of the preceding code in PHP 7 would result in the following:

```
string(5) "green"
string(6) "yellow"
string(4) "blue"

array(3) {
[0]=> string(5) "green"
[1]=> string(6) "yellow"
[2]=> string(4) "blue"
}
```

The order of assignment might change again in the future, so we should not rely heavily on it.

Session options

Prior to PHP 7, the `session_start()` function did not directly accept any configuration options. Any configuration options we wanted to set on the session, needed to come from `php.ini`:

```
// PHP 5
ini_set('session.name', 'THEAPP');
ini_set('session.cookie_lifetime', 3600);
ini_set('session.cookie_httponly', 1);
session_start();

// PHP 7
session_start([
'name' =>'THEAPP',
'cookie_lifetime' => 3600,
'cookie_httponly' => 1
]);
```

Driven by the goal of performance optimization, a new `lazy_write` runtime configuration was added in PHP 7. When `lazy_write` is set to `1`, the session data is only rewritten if it changes. This is the default behavior:

```
session_start([
'name' =>'THEAPP',
'cookie_lifetime' => 3600,
'cookie_httponly' => 1,
'lazy_write' => 1
]);
```

While changes listed here might not look impressive at first, being able to override session options directly via the `session_start` function gives certain flexibility to our code.

Deprecated features

Globally accepted, major versions of software have the luxury of breaking backward compatibility. Ideally, not much, but in order to keep the software moving forward, some old ideas need to be left behind. These changes don't come overnight. Certain features are first flagged as deprecated to warn developers that it will be removed in future versions of the language. Sometimes this period of deprecation takes years.

Throughout PHP 5.x, a number of features have been marked as deprecated, and in PHP 7.0, they have all been removed.

The **POSIX-compatible** regular expressions have been deprecated in PHP 5.3, and now completely removed in PHP 7.

The following functions are no longer available for use:

- `ereg_replace`
- `ereg`
- `eregi_replace`
- `eregi`
- `split`
- `spliti`
- `sql_regcase`

We should instead use **Perl Compatible Regular Expressions (PCRE)**. The `http://php.net/manual/en/book.pcre.php` is a great source of documentation for these functions.

The `mysql` extension, which had been deprecated in PHP 5.5, has now been removed. None of the `mysql_*` functions are available anymore. We should instead use the `mysqli` extension. The good thing is that moving from `mysql` to `mysqli` functions is mostly simple, as when adding `i` to our code, the `mysql_*` function calls and passes the database handle (returned by `mysqli_connect`) as the first parameter. The `http://php.net/manual/en/book.mysqli.php` is a great source of documentation for these functions.

The PHP script and ASP tags are no longer available:

```
<!-- PHP script tag example -->
<script language="php">
// Code here
</script>

<!-- PHP ASP tag example -->
<%
// Code here
%>
<%=$varToEcho; %>
```

Frameworks

Application frameworks are a collection of functions, classes, configurations, and conventions all designed to support the development of web applications, services, and APIs. Some applications are embracing an API first approach, whereas server-side REST and SOAP APIs are built via PHP, and client side in other technologies like JavaScript.

When building a web application, we usually have three obvious choices:

- We can build everything ourselves, from scratch. This way, our development process might be slow, but we can achieve architecture built entirely per our standards. Needless to say, this is a highly unproductive approach.

- We can use one of the existing frameworks. This way, our development process is fast, but we need to be happy that our application is built on top of other things.

- We can use one of the existing frameworks but also try to abstract it to the level where our application looks independent of it. This is a painful and slow approach, to say the least. It involves writing numerous adapters, wrappers, interfaces, and so on.

In a nutshell, frameworks are here to make it easier and quicker for us to build our software. A great deal of programming languages out there have popular frameworks. PHP is no exception to this.

Given the popularity of PHP as a go-to web programming language, it is no surprise that dozens of frameworks have sprouted over the years. Choosing the "right" framework is a daunting task, even so more for fresh starters. What is right for one project or a team might not be right for another.

However, there are some general, high level segments each modern framework should encompass. These account for:

- **Modular**: It supports modular application development, allowing us to neatly separate our code into functional building blocks, whereas it is built in a modular manner.

- **Secure**: It provides various cryptographic and other security tooling expected of a modern web application. Provides seamless support for things like authentication, authorization, and data encryption.

- **Extensible**: Manages to easily adopt our application needs, allowing us to extend it according to our application needs.

- **Community**: It is actively developed and supported by a vibrant and active community.

- **High performing**: Built with performance in mind. Many frameworks brag about performance, but there are many variables to it. We need to be specific as to what we are evaluating here. Measuring cached performance against raw performance is often the misleading evaluation, as caching proxies can be put in front of many frameworks.

- **Enterprise ready**: Depending on the type of project at hand, most likely we would want to target a framework which flags itself as enterprise ready. Making us confident enough of running critical and high-usage business applications on top of it.

While it's perfectly alright to code an entire web application in pure PHP without using any framework, the majority of today's projects do use frameworks.

The benefits of using frameworks outweigh the purity of doing it all from scratch. Frameworks are usually well supported and documented, which makes it easier for teams to catch up with libraries, project structure, conventions, and other things.

When it comes to PHP frameworks, it is worth pointing out a few popular ones:

- **Laravel**: `https://laravel.com`
- **Symfony**: `http://symfony.com`
- **Zend Framework**: `http://framework.zend.com`
- **CodeIgniter**: `https://www.codeigniter.com`
- **CakePHP**: `http://cakephp.org`
- **Slim**: `http://www.slimframework.com`
- **Yii**: `http://www.yiiframework.com`
- **Phalcon**: `https://phalconphp.com`

This is by no means a complete or even a popularity sorted list.

Laravel framework

Laravel is released under an MIT license, and can be downloaded from `https://laravel.com/`.

Aside from the usual routing, controllers, requests, responses, views, and (blade) templates, out of the box Laravel provides a large amount of additional services such as authentication, cache, events, localization, and many others.

Another neat feature of Laravel, is **Artisan**, the command line tool, that provides a number of useful commands that we can use during development. Artisan can further be extended by writing our own console commands.

Laravel has a pretty active and vibrant community. Its documentation is simple and clear, which makes it easy for newcomers to get started. Furthermore, there is also `https://laracasts.com`, which extends out beyond Laravel in terms of documentation and other content. Laracasts is a web service providing a series of expert screencasts, some of which are free.

All of these features make Laravel a choice worth evaluating when it comes to the selection of a framework.

Symfony

Symfony is released under an MIT license, and can be downloaded from `http://symfony.com`.

Over time, Symfony introduced the concept of **Long-term Support(LTS)** releases. This release process has been adopted as of Symfony 2.2, and strictly followed as of Symfony 2.4. The standard version of Symfony is maintained for eight months. Long-term Support versions are supported for three years.

One other interesting thing about new releases is the time-based release model. All of the new versions of Symfony releases come out every six months: one in May and one in November.

Symfony has great community support via mailing lists, IRC, and StackOverflow. Furthermore, SensioLabs professional support provides a full range of solutions from consulting, training, coaching, to certification.

Lots of Symfony components are used in other web applications and frameworks, such as Laravel, Silex, Drupal 8, Sylius, and others.

What made Symfony such a popular framework is its interoperability. The idea of "Don't lock yourself up within Symfony!" made it popular with developers as it allowed for building applications that precisely meet our needs.

By embracing the "don't reinvent the wheel" philosophy, Symfony itself makes heavy use of existing PHP open-source projects as part of the framework, including:

- Doctrine (or Propel): Object-relational mapping layer
- PDO database abstraction layer (Doctrine or Propel)
- PHPUnit: A unit testing framework
- Twig: A templating engine
- Swift Mailer: An e-mail library

Depending on our project needs, we can choose to use a full-stack Symfony framework, the Silex micro-framework, or simply some of the components individually.

Out of the box, Symfony provides a lot of structural ground for new web applications. It does so via its bundle system. Bundles are sort of like micro-applications inside our main application. Within them, the entire app is nicely structured into models, controllers, templates, configuration files, and other building blocks. Being able to fully separate logic from different domains helps us to keep a clean separation of concerns and autonomously develop every single feature of our domain.

Symfony is one of the PHP pioneers when it comes to embracing the dependency injection across the framework, allowing it to achieve decoupled components and to keep high flexibility of code.

Documented, modular, highly flexible, performant, supported, those are the attributes that make Symfony a choice worth evaluating.

Zend Framework

Zend Framework is released under a new BSD license, and can be downloaded from `http://framework.zend.com`.

Zend Framework features include:

- Fully object-oriented PHP components
- Loosely coupled components
- Extensible MVC supporting layouts and templates
- Support for multiple database systems MySQL, Oracle, MS SQL, and so on
- E-mail handling via mbox, Maildir, POP3, and IMAP4
- Flexible caching system

Aside from a free Zend Framework, Zend Technologies Ltd provides its own commercial version of a PHP stack called Zend Server, and Zend Studio IDE that includes features specifically to integrate with Zend Framework. While Zend Framework is perfectly fine running on any PHP stack, Zend Server is advertised as an optimized solution for running Zend Framework applications.

By its architectural design, Zend Framework is merely a collection of classes. There is no strictly imposed structure our application needs to follow. This is one of the features that makes it so appealing to a certain range of developers. We could either utilize Zend MVC components to create a fully-functional Zend Framework project, or we can simply load the components we need.

The so called full-stack frameworks impose structure, ORM implementations, code-generation, and other fixed things onto your projects. Zend Framework, on the other hand, with its decoupled nature, classifies for a glue type of framework. We can easily glue it to an existing application, or use it to build a new one.

The latest versions of Zend Framework follow the **SOLID object oriented design** principle. The so called "use-at-will" design allows developers to use whichever components they want.

Though the main driving force behind Zend Framework is Zend Technologies, many other companies have contributed significant features to the framework.

Furthermore, Zend Technologies provides excellent Zend Certified PHP Engineer certifications. Quality community, official company support, education, hosting, and development tools make the Zend Framework choice worth evaluating.

CodeIgniter

CodeIgniter is released under an MIT license, and can be downloaded from `https://www.codeigniter.com`.

CodeIgniter prides itself in being lightweight. The core system requires only a handful of small libraries, which is not always the case with other frameworks.

The framework uses the simple **Model-View-Control** approach, allowing for clean separation between logic and presentation. The View layer does not impose any special template language, so it uses native PHP out of the box.

Here are some of the outstanding features of CodeIgniter:

- Model-View-Control-based system
- Extremely light weight
- Full featured database classes with support for several platforms
- Query builder database support
- Form and data validation
- Security and XSS filtering
- Localization

- Data encryption
- Full page caching
- Unit testing class
- Search-engine friendly URLs
- Flexible URI routing
- Support for hooks and class extensions
- Large library of helper functions

CodeIgniter has an active community gathered around `http://forum. codeigniter.com`.

Small footprint, flexibility, exceptional performance, near-zero configuration, and thorough documentation are what makes this framework choice worth evaluating.

CakePHP

CakePHP is released under an MIT license, and can be downloaded from `http://cakephp.org`.

The CakePHP framework was greatly inspired by **Ruby on Rails**, using many of its concepts. It values conventions over configuration.

It comes with "batteries included". Most of the things we need for modern web applications are already built-in. Translations, database access, caching, validation, authentication, and much more are all built-in.

Security is another big part of the CakePHP philosophy. CakePHP comes with built-in tools for input validation, CSRF protection, form tampering protection, SQL injection prevention, and XSS prevention, helping us to secure our application.

CakePHP supports a variety of database storage engines, such as MySQL, PostgreSQL, Microsoft SQL Server, and SQLite. The built-in CRUD feature is very handy for database interaction.

It counts on a big community behind it. It also has a big list of plugins, available at `http://plugins.cakephp.org`.

CakePHP provides a certification exam, whereby developers are tested in their knowledge of the CakePHP framework, MVC principles, and standards used within CakePHP. Certification is geared towards real world scenarios and intimate CakePHP specifics.

Commercial support, consultation, code review, performance analysis, security audits, and even development services are provided by the Cake Development Corporation `http://www.cakedc.com`. The Cake Development Corporation is the commercial entity behind the framework, established in 2007 by Larry Masters, a founder of CakePHP.

Slim

Slim is released under an MIT license, and can be downloaded from `http://www.slimframework.com`.

While frameworks with the "batteries included" mindset provide robust libraries, directory structures, and configurations, micro frameworks get us started with a few lines of code.

Micro frameworks usually lack even the basic framework features such as:

- Authentication and authorization
- ORM database abstraction
- Input validation and sanitation
- Template engine

This limits their use, but also makes them a great tool for rapid prototyping.

Slim supports any PSR-7 HTTP message implementation. An HTTP message is either a request from a client to a server or a response from a server to a client. Slim functions like a dispatcher that receives an HTTP request, invokes an appropriate callback routine, and returns an HTTP response.

The good thing about Slim is that it plays nicely with middleware. The middleware is basically a callable that accepts three arguments:

- `\Psr\Http\Message\ServerRequestInterface`: The PSR7 request object
- `\Psr\Http\Message\ResponseInterface`: The PSR7 response object
- `callable`: The next middleware callable

Middlewares are free to manipulate request and response objects, as long as they return an instance of `\Psr\Http\Message\ResponseInterface`. Furthermore, each middleware needs to invoke the next middleware and pass it to request and response objects as arguments.

This simple concept gives Slim the power of extensibility, through various possible third party middlewares.

Even though Slim provides good documentation, a vibrant community, and the project is being actively developed to date, its usage is limited. Micro frameworks are hardly a choice for robust enterprise applications. Still, they have their place in development.

Yii

Yii is released under a BSD License, and can be downloaded from `http://www.yiiframework.com`.

Yii's focus on performance optimization makes it a perfect choice for almost any type of project, including the enterprise type of applications.

Some of the outstanding Yii features include:

- The MVC design pattern
- Automatic generation of complex service WSDL
- Translation, localization, locale-sensitive formatting of dates, time, and numbers
- Data caching, fragment caching, page caching, and HTTP caching
- Error handler that displays errors based on the nature of the errors and the mode the application runs in
- Security measures to help prevent SQL injection, **Cross-site scripting** (**XSS**), **Cross-site request forgery** (**CSRF**), and cookie tampering
- Unit and functional testing based on **PHPUnit** and **Selenium**

One of the neat features of Yii is a tool called **Gii**. It's an extension that provides a web-based code generator. We can use Gii's graphical interface to quickly set up generate models, forms, modules, CRUD, and so on. There is also a command line version of Gii for those who prefer consoles over GUI.

Yii's architecture allows it to play nicely with third-party code, like PEAR libraries, Zend Framework, and the like. It adopts the MVC architecture, allowing for clean separation of concerns.

Yii provides an impressive library of extensions available at `http://www.yiiframework.com/extensions`. The majority of extensions are distributed as composer packages. They empower us with accelerated development. We can easily package our code as extensions and share it with others. This makes Yii even more interesting for modular application development.

Official documentation is quite comprehensive. There are also several books available.

Rich documentation, a vibrant community, active releases, performance optimization, security emphasis, feature richness, and flexibility make Yii a choice worth evaluating.

Phalcon

Phalcon is released under a BSD License, and can be downloaded from `https://phalconphp.com`.

Phalcon was originally released in 2012, by Andres Gutierrez and collaborators. The goal of the project was to find a new approach to traditional web application frameworks written in PHP. This new approach came in the form of C language extensions. The entire Phalcon framework is developed as a C extension.

The benefits of C-based frameworks lies in the fact that an entire PHP extension is loaded during runtime. This greatly reduces I/O operations massively since there is no need to load `.php` files any more. Furthermore, compiled C language code executes faster than PHP bytecode. Since C extensions are loaded together with PHP one time during the web server daemon start process, their memory footprint is small. The downside of C-based frameworks is that the code is compiled, so we cannot easily debug it and patch it as we would with PHP classes.

Low-level architecture and optimizations make Phalcon one of the lowest overheads for MVC-based applications.

Phalcon is a full-stack, loosely coupled framework. While it does provide full MVC structure to our application, it also allows us to use its objects as glue components based on the needs of our application. We can choose if we want to create a full blown MVC application, or the minimal style micro application. Micro applications are suitable to implement small applications, APIs, and prototypes in a practical way.

All of the frameworks we mentioned so far enable some form of extensions, where we can add new libraries or entire packages to a framework. Since Phalcon is a C-code framework, contributions to the framework doesn't come in the form of PHP code. On the other hand, writing and compiling C language code can be somewhat challenging for an average PHP developer.

Zephir project `http://zephir-lang.com` addresses these challenges by introducing high-level Zephir language. Zephir is designed to ease the creation and maintainability of C extensions for PHP with a focus on type and memory safety.

When communicating with databases, Phalcon uses **Phalcon Query Language**, **PhalconQL**, or simply **PHQL** for short. PHQL is a high-level, object-oriented SQL dialect that allows us to write queries using SQL-like language that works with objects instead of tables.

View templates are handled by Volt, Phalcon's own templating engine. It is highly integrated with other components, and can be used independently in our applications.

Phalcon is pretty easy to pick up. Its documentation covers both the MVC and micro applications style of using a framework, with practical examples. The framework itself is rich enough to support the structure and libraries we need for most of today's applications. On top of that, there is an official Phalcon website called **Phalconist** `https://phalconist.com` which provides additional resources to framework.

Though there is no official company behind it, no certifications, no commercial support, and similar enterprise looking things, Phalcon does a great job of positioning itself as a choice worth evaluating even with a robust enterprise application development.

Summary

Looking back on the release of PHP 5 and its support to OOP programming, we can see the enormous positive impact it had on the PHP ecosystem. A large number of frameworks and libraries have sprawled out, offering enterprise level solutions to web application development.

The release of PHP 7 is likely to be another leap forward for the PHP ecosystem. Though none of the new features are revolutionary as such, as they can be found in other programming languages from years ago, they impact PHP greatly. We are yet to see how its new features will reshape existing and future frameworks and the way we write applications.

The introduction of more advanced *errors to exceptions* handling, scalar type hints, and function return type hints will surely bring much awaited stability to applications and frameworks using them. The speed improvements compared to PHP 5.6 are significant enough to cut down the hosting costs for higher load sites. Thankfully, the PHP development team minimized backward incomparability changes, so they should not stand in the way of swift PHP 7 adoption.

Choosing the right framework is all but an easy task. What classifies a framework as an enterprise class framework is more than just collection of classes. It has an entire ecosystem around it.

One should never be driven by hype when evaluating a framework for a project. Questions like the following should be taken into consideration:

- Is it company or community driven?
- Does it provide quality documentation?
- Does it have a stable and frequent release cycle?
- Does it provide some official form of certification?
- Does it provide free and commercial support?
- Does it have occasional seminars we can attend?
- Is it open towards community involvement, so we can submit functionalities and patches?
- Is it a full-stack or glue type of framework?
- Is it convention or configuration driven?
- Does it provide enough libraries to get you started (security, validation, templating, database abstractions, ORMs, routing, internationalization, and so on)?
- Can the core framework be extended and overridden enough to make it more future proof with possible changes?

There are a number of established PHP frameworks and libraries out there, so the choice is all but easy. Most of these frameworks and libraries are still to fully catch up with the latest features added in PHP 7.

Moving forward, in the next chapter, we will look into common design patterns and how to integrate them in PHP.

2
GoF Design Patterns

There are a handful of things that make a great software developer. Knowledge and usage of design patterns is one of them. Design patterns empower developers to communicate using well-known names for various software interactions. Whether someone is a PHP, Python, C#, Ruby, or any other language developer, design patterns provide language agnostic solutions for frequently occurring software problems.

The concept of design patterns emerged in 1994 as part of the *Elements of Reusable Object-Oriented Software* book. Detailing 23 different design patterns, the book was written by four authors Erich Gamma, Richard Helm, Ralph Johnson, and John Vlissides. The authors are often referred to as the **Gang of Four (GoF)**, and the presented design patterns are sometimes referred to as GoF design patterns. In Today, more than two decades later, designing software that is extensible, reusable, maintainable, and adaptable is near to impossible without embracing design patterns as part of implementation.

There are three types of design patterns which we will cover in this chapter:

- Creational
- Structural
- Behavioral

Throughout this chapter we will not go deep into the theory of each of them, as that alone is an entire book's worth of material. Moving forward, we will focus more on simple PHP implementation examples for each of the patterns, just so we get a more visual sense of things.

Creational patterns

Creational patterns, as the name suggests, create *objects* for us, so we do not have to instantiate them directly. Implementing creation patterns gives our application a level of flexibility, where the application itself can decide what objects to instantiate at a given time. The following is a list of patterns we categorize as creational patterns:

- Abstract factory pattern
- Builder pattern
- Factory method pattern
- Prototype pattern
- Singleton pattern

 See https://en.wikipedia.org/wiki/Creational_pattern for more information about creational design patterns.

Abstract factory pattern

Building portable applications requires a great level of dependencies encapsulation. The abstract factory facilitates this by *abstracting the creation of families of related or dependent objects*. Clients never create these platform objects directly, the factory does it for them, making it possible to interchange concrete implementations without changing the code that uses them, even at runtime.

The following is an example of possible abstract factory pattern implementation:

```
interface Button {
    public function render();
}

interface GUIFactory {
    public function createButton();
}

class SubmitButton implements Button {
    public function render() {
        echo 'Render Submit Button';
    }
}
```

```
class ResetButton implements Button {
    public function render() {
        echo 'Render Reset Button';
    }
}

class SubmitFactory implements GUIFactory {
    public function createButton() {
        return new SubmitButton();
    }
}

class ResetFactory implements GUIFactory {
    public function createButton() {
        return new ResetButton();
    }
}

// Client
$submitFactory = new SubmitFactory();
$button = $submitFactory->createButton();
$button->render();

$resetFactory = new ResetFactory();
$button = $resetFactory->createButton();
$button->render();
```

We started off by creating an interface `Button`, which is later implemented by our `SubmitButton` and `ResetButton` concrete classes. `GUIFactory` and `ResetFactory` implement the `GUIFactory` interface, which specifies the `createButton` method. The client then simply instantiates factories and calls for `createButton`, which returns a proper button instance that we call the `render` method.

Builder pattern

The builder pattern separates the construction of a complex object from its representation, making it possible for the same construction process to create different representations. While some creational patterns construct a product in one call, builder pattern does it step by step under the control of the director.

The following is an example of builder pattern implementation:

```
class Car {
    public function getWheels() {
        /* implementation... */
    }

    public function setWheels($wheels) {
        /* implementation... */
    }

    public function getColour($colour) {
        /* implementation... */
    }

    public function setColour() {
        /* implementation... */
    }
}

interface CarBuilderInterface {
    public function setColour($colour);
    public function setWheels($wheels);
    public function getResult();
}

class CarBuilder implements CarBuilderInterface {
    private $car;

    public function __construct() {
        $this->car = new Car();
    }

    public function setColour($colour) {
        $this->car->setColour($colour);
        return $this;
    }

    public function setWheels($wheels) {
        $this->car->setWheels($wheels);
        return $this;
    }
}
```

```php
        public function getResult() {
            return $this->car;
        }
    }

    class CarBuildDirector {
        private $builder;

        public function __construct(CarBuilder $builder) {
            $this->builder = $builder;
        }

        public function build() {
            $this->builder->setColour('Red');
            $this->builder->setWheels(4);

            return $this;
        }

        public function getCar() {
            return $this->builder->getResult();
        }
    }

    // Client
    $carBuilder = new CarBuilder();
    $carBuildDirector = new CarBuildDirector($carBuilder);
    $car = $carBuildDirector->build()->getCar();
```

We started off by creating a concrete Car class with several methods defining some base characteristics of a car. We then created a CarBuilderInterface that will control some of those characteristics and get the final result (car). The concrete class CarBuilder then implemented the CarBuilderInterface, followed by the concrete CarBuildDirector class, which defined build and the getCar method. The client then simply instantiated a new instance of CarBuilder, passing it as a constructor parameter to a new instance of CarBuildDirector. Finally, we called the build and getCar methods of CarBuildDirector to get the actual car Car instance.

Factory method pattern

The factory method pattern deals with the problem of creating objects without having to specify the exact class of the object that will be created.

The following is an example of factory method pattern implementation:

```
interface Product {
    public function getType();
}

interface ProductFactory {
    public function makeProduct();
}

class SimpleProduct implements Product {
    public function getType() {
        return 'SimpleProduct';
    }
}

class SimpleProductFactory implements ProductFactory {
    public function makeProduct() {
        return new SimpleProduct();
    }
}

/* Client */
$factory = new SimpleProductFactory();
$product = $factory->makeProduct();
echo $product->getType(); //outputs: SimpleProduct
```

We started off by creating a ProductFactory and Product interfaces. The SimpleProductFactory implements the ProductFactory and returns the new product instance via its makeProduct method. The SimpleProduct class implements Product, and returns the product type. Finally, the client creates the instance of SimpleProductFactory, calling the makeProduct method on it. The makeProduct returns the instance of the Product, whose getType method returns the SimpleProduct string.

Prototype pattern

The prototype pattern replicates other objects by use of cloning. What this means is that we are not using the new keyword to instantiate new objects. PHP provides a clone keyword which makes a shallow copy of an object, thus providing pretty much straight forward prototype pattern implementation. Shallow copy does not copy references, only values to the new object. We can further utilize the magic __clone method on our class in order to implement more robust clone behavior.

The following is an example of prototype pattern implementation:

```php
class User {
    public $name;
    public $email;
}

class Employee extends User {
    public function __construct() {
        $this->name = 'Johhn Doe';
        $this->email = 'john.doe@fake.mail';
    }

    public function info() {
        return sprintf('%s, %s', $this->name, $this->email);
    }

    public function __clone() {
        /* additional changes for (after)clone behavior? */
    }
}

$employee = new Employee();
echo $employee->info();

$director = clone $employee;
$director->name = 'Jane Doe';
$director->email = 'jane.doe@fake.mail';
echo $director->info(); //outputs: Jane Doe, jane.doe@fake.mail
```

We started off by creating a simple User class. The Employee then extends the User, while setting name and email in its constructor. The client then instantiates the Employee via the new keyword, and clones it into the director variable. The $director variable is now a new instance, one made not by the new keyword, but with cloning, using the clone keyword. Changing name and email on $director, does not affect $employee.

Singleton pattern

The purpose of singleton pattern is to restrict instantiation of class to a *single* object. It is implemented by creating a method within the class that creates a new instance of that class if one does not exist. If an object instance already exists, the method simply returns a reference to an existing object.

The following is an example of singleton pattern implementation:

```
class Logger {
    private static $instance;

    public static function getInstance() {
        if (!isset(self::$instance)) {
            self::$instance = new self;
        }

        return self::$instance;
    }

    public function logNotice($msg) {
        return 'logNotice: ' . $msg;
    }

    public function logWarning($msg) {
        return 'logWarning: ' . $msg;
    }

    public function logError($msg) {
        return 'logError: ' . $msg;
    }
}

// Client
echo Logger::getInstance()->logNotice('test-notice');
echo Logger::getInstance()->logWarning('test-warning');
echo Logger::getInstance()->logError('test-error');
// Outputs:
// logNotice: test-notice
// logWarning: test-warning
// logError: test-error
```

We started off by creating a `Logger` class with a static `$instance` member, and the `getInstance` method that always returns a single instance of the class. Then we added a few sample methods to demonstrate the client executing various methods on a single instance.

Structural patterns

Structural patterns deal with class and object composition. Using interfaces or abstract classes and methods, they define ways to compose objects, which in turn obtain new functionality. The following is a list of patterns we categorize as structural patterns:

- Adapter
- Bridge
- Composite
- Decorator
- Facade
- Flyweight
- Proxy

See `https://en.wikipedia.org/wiki/Structural_pattern` for more information about structural design patterns.

Adapter pattern

The adapter pattern allows the interface of an existing class to be used from another interface, basically, helping two incompatible interfaces to work together by converting the interface of one class into an interface expected by another class.

The following is an example of adapter pattern implementation:

```
class Stripe {
    public function capturePayment($amount) {
        /* Implementation... */
    }

    public function authorizeOnlyPayment($amount) {
        /* Implementation... */
    }
```

```
        public function cancelAmount($amount) {
            /* Implementation... */
        }
    }

    interface PaymentService {
        public function capture($amount);
        public function authorize($amount);
        public function cancel($amount);
    }

    class StripePaymentServiceAdapter implements PaymentService {
        private $stripe;

        public function __construct(Stripe $stripe) {
            $this->stripe = $stripe;
        }

        public function capture($amount) {
            $this->stripe->capturePayment($amount);
        }

        public function authorize($amount) {
            $this->stripe->authorizeOnlyPayment($amount);
        }

        public function cancel($amount) {
            $this->stripe->cancelAmount($amount);
        }
    }

    // Client
    $stripe = new StripePaymentServiceAdapter(new Stripe());
    $stripe->authorize(49.99);
    $stripe->capture(19.99);
    $stripe->cancel(9.99);
```

We started off by creating a concrete Stripe class. We then defined the
PaymentService interface with some basic payment handling methods. The
StripePaymentServiceAdapter implements the PaymentService interface,
providing concrete implementation of payment handling methods. Finally, the
client instantiates the StripePaymentServiceAdapter and executes the payment
handling methods.

Bridge pattern

The bridge pattern is used when we want to decouple a class or abstraction from its implementation, allowing them both to change independently. This is useful when the class and its implementation vary often.

The following is an example of bridge pattern implementation:

```
interface MailerInterface {
    public function setSender(MessagingInterface $sender);
    public function send($body);
}

abstract class Mailer implements MailerInterface {
    protected $sender;

    public function setSender(MessagingInterface $sender) {
        $this->sender = $sender;
    }
}

class PHPMailer extends Mailer {
    public function send($body) {
        $body .= "\n\n Sent from a phpmailer.";
        return $this->sender->send($body);
    }
}

class SwiftMailer extends Mailer {
    public function send($body) {
        $body .= "\n\n Sent from a SwiftMailer.";
        return $this->sender->send($body);
    }
}

interface MessagingInterface {
    public function send($body);
}

class TextMessage implements MessagingInterface {
    public function send($body) {
        echo 'TextMessage > send > $body: ' . $body;
    }
}
```

```
class HtmlMessage implements MessagingInterface {
    public function send($body) {
        echo 'HtmlMessage > send > $body: ' . $body;
    }
}

// Client
$phpmailer = new PHPMailer();
$phpmailer->setSender(new TextMessage());
$phpmailer->send('Hi!');

$swiftMailer = new SwiftMailer();
$swiftMailer->setSender(new HtmlMessage());
$swiftMailer->send('Hello!');
```

We started off by creating a `MailerInterface`. The concrete `Mailer` class then implements the `MailerInterface`, providing a base class for `PHPMailer` and `SwiftMailer`. We then define the `MessagingInterface`, which gets implemented by the `TextMessage` and `HtmlMessage` classes. Finally, the client instantiates `PHPMailer` and `SwiftMailer`, passing on instances of `TextMessage` and `HtmlMessage` prior to calling the `send` method.

Composite pattern

The composite pattern is about treating the hierarchy of objects as a single object, through a common interface. Where the objects are composed into three structures and the client is oblivious to changes in the underlying structure because it only consumes the common interface.

The following is an example of composite pattern implementation:

```
interface Graphic {
    public function draw();
}

class CompositeGraphic implements Graphic {
    private $graphics = array();

    public function add($graphic) {
        $objId = spl_object_hash($graphic);
        $this->graphics[$objId] = $graphic;
    }
```

```php
        public function remove($graphic) {
            $objId = spl_object_hash($graphic);
            unset($this->graphics[$objId]);
        }

        public function draw() {
            foreach ($this->graphics as $graphic) {
                $graphic->draw();
            }
        }
    }

    class Circle implements Graphic {
        public function draw()
        {
            echo 'draw-circle';
        }
    }

    class Square implements Graphic {
        public function draw() {
            echo 'draw-square';
        }
    }

    class Triangle implements Graphic {
        public function draw() {
            echo 'draw-triangle';
        }
    }

    $circle = new Circle();
    $square = new Square();
    $triangle = new Triangle();

    $compositeObj1 = new CompositeGraphic();
    $compositeObj1->add($circle);
    $compositeObj1->add($triangle);
    $compositeObj1->draw();

    $compositeObj2 = new CompositeGraphic();
    $compositeObj2->add($circle);
    $compositeObj2->add($square);
    $compositeObj2->add($triangle);
    $compositeObj2->remove($circle);
    $compositeObj2->draw();
```

We started off by creating a `Graphic` interface. We then created the `CompositeGraphic`, `Circle`, `Square`, and `Triangle`, all of which implement the `Graphic` interface. Aside from just implementing the `draw` method from the `Graphic` interface, the `CompositeGraphic` adds two more methods, used to track internal collection of graphics added to it. The client then instantiates all of these `Graphic` classes, adding them all to the `CompositeGraphic`, which then calls the `draw` method.

Decorator pattern

The decorator pattern allows behavior to be added to an individual object instance, without affecting the behavior of other instances of the same class. We can define multiple decorators, where each adds new functionality.

The following is an example of decorator pattern implementation:

```php
interface LoggerInterface {
    public function log($message);
}

class Logger implements LoggerInterface {
    public function log($message) {
        file_put_contents('app.log', $message, FILE_APPEND);
    }
}

abstract class LoggerDecorator implements LoggerInterface {
    protected $logger;

    public function __construct(Logger $logger) {
        $this->logger = $logger;
    }

    abstract public function log($message);
}

class ErrorLoggerDecorator extends LoggerDecorator {
    public function log($message) {
        $this->logger->log('ERROR: ' . $message);
    }

}

class WarningLoggerDecorator extends LoggerDecorator {
    public function log($message) {
```

```
            $this->logger->log('WARNING: ' . $message);
        }
    }

    class NoticeLoggerDecorator extends LoggerDecorator {
        public function log($message) {
            $this->logger->log('NOTICE: ' . $message);
        }
    }

    $logger = new Logger();
    $logger->log('Resource not found.');

    $logger = new Logger();
    $logger = new ErrorLoggerDecorator($logger);
    $logger->log('Invalid user role.');

    $logger = new Logger();
    $logger = new WarningLoggerDecorator($logger);
    $logger->log('Missing address parameters.');

    $logger = new Logger();
    $logger = new NoticeLoggerDecorator($logger);
    $logger->log('Incorrect type provided.');
```

We started off by creating a LoggerInterface, with a simple log method. We then defined Logger and LoggerDecorator, both of which implement the LoggerInterface. Followed by ErrorLoggerDecorator, WarningLoggerDecorator, and NoticeLoggerDecorator which implement the LoggerDecorator. Finally, the client part instantiates the logger three times, passing it different decorators.

Facade pattern

The facade pattern is used when we want to simplify the complexities of large systems through a simpler interface. It does so by providing convenient methods for most common tasks, through a single wrapper class used by a client.

The following is an example of facade pattern implementation:

```
class Product {
    public function getQty() {
        // Implementation
    }
}
```

```php
class QuickOrderFacade {
    private $product = null;
    private $orderQty = null;

    public function __construct($product, $orderQty) {
        $this->product = $product;
        $this->orderQty = $orderQty;
    }

    public function generateOrder() {
        if ($this->qtyCheck()) {
            $this->addToCart();
            $this->calculateShipping();
            $this->applyDiscount();
            $this->placeOrder();
        }
    }

    private function addToCart() {
        // Implementation...
    }

    private function qtyCheck() {
        if ($this->product->getQty() > $this->orderQty) {
            return true;
        } else {
            return true;
        }
    }

    private function calculateShipping() {
        // Implementation...
    }

    private function applyDiscount() {
        // Implementation...
    }

    private function placeOrder() {
        // Implementation...
    }
}

// Client
$order = new QuickOrderFacade(new Product(), $qty);
$order->generateOrder();
```

We started off by creating a `Product` class, with a single `getQty` method. We then created a `QuickOrderFacade` class that accepts `product` instance and quantity via a `constructor` and further provides the `generateOrder` method that aggregates all of the order generating actions. Finally, the client instantiates the `product`, which it passes onto the instance of `QuickOrderFacade`, calling the `generateOrder` on it.

Flyweight pattern

The flyweight pattern is about performance and resource reduction, sharing as much data as possible between similar objects. What this means is that instances of a class which are identical are shared in an implementation. This works best when a large number of same class instances are expected to be created.

The following is an example of flyweight pattern implementation:

```
interface Shape {
    public function draw();
}

class Circle implements Shape {
    private $colour;
    private $radius;

    public function __construct($colour) {
        $this->colour = $colour;
    }

    public function draw() {
        echo sprintf('Colour %s, radius %s.', $this->colour,
          $this->radius);
    }

    public function setRadius($radius) {
        $this->radius = $radius;
    }
}

class ShapeFactory {
    private $circleMap;

    public function getCircle($colour) {
        if (!isset($this->circleMap[$colour])) {
            $circle = new Circle($colour);
            $this->circleMap[$colour] = $circle;
```

```
        }

        return $this->circleMap[$colour];
    }
}

// Client
$shapeFactory = new ShapeFactory();
$circle = $shapeFactory->getCircle('yellow');
$circle->setRadius(10);
$circle->draw();

$shapeFactory = new ShapeFactory();
$circle = $shapeFactory->getCircle('orange');
$circle->setRadius(15);
$circle->draw();

$shapeFactory = new ShapeFactory();
$circle = $shapeFactory->getCircle('yellow');
$circle->setRadius(20);
$circle->draw();
```

We started off by creating a Shape interface, with a single draw method. We then defined the Circle class implementing the Shape interface, followed by the ShapeFactory class. Within the ShapeFactory, the getCircle method returns an instance of a new Circle, based on the color option. Finally, the client instantiates several ShapeFactory objects, passing in different colors to the getCircle method call.

Proxy pattern

The proxy design pattern functions as an interface to an original object behind the scenes. It can act as a simple forwarding wrapper or even provide additional functionality around the object it wraps. Examples of extra added functionality might be lazy loading or caching that might compensate for resource intense operations of an original object.

The following is an example of proxy pattern implementation:

```
interface ImageInterface {
    public function draw();
}
```

```
class Image implements ImageInterface {
    private $file;

    public function __construct($file) {
        $this->file = $file;
        sleep(5); // Imagine resource intensive image load
    }

    public function draw() {
        echo 'image: ' . $this->file;
    }
}

class ProxyImage implements ImageInterface {
    private $image = null;
    private $file;

    public function __construct($file) {
        $this->file = $file;
    }

    public function draw() {
        if (is_null($this->image)) {
            $this->image = new Image($this->file);
        }

        $this->image->draw();
    }
}

// Client
$image = new Image('image.png'); // 5 seconds
$image->draw();

$image = new ProxyImage('image.png'); // 0 seconds
$image->draw();
```

We started off by creating an ImageInterface, with a single draw method. We then defined the Image and ProxyImage classes, both of which extend the ImageInterface. Within the __construct of the Image class, we simulated the **resource intense** operation with the sleep method call. Finally, the client instantiates both Image and ProxyImage, showing the execution time difference between the two.

Behavioral patterns

Behavioral patterns tackle the challenge of communication between various objects. They describe how different objects and classes send messages to each other to make things happen. The following is a list of patterns we categorize as behavioral patterns:

- Chain of responsibility
- Command
- Interpreter
- Iterator
- Mediator
- Memento
- Observer
- State
- Strategy
- Template method
- Visitor

Chain of responsibility pattern

The chain of responsibility pattern decouples the sender of a request from its receiver, by enabling more than one object to handle requests, in a chain manner. Various types of handling objects can be added dynamically to the chain. Using a recursive composition chain allows for an unlimited number of handling objects.

The following is an example of chain of responsibility pattern implementation:

```
abstract class SocialNotifier {
    private $notifyNext = null;

    public function notifyNext(SocialNotifier $notifier) {
        $this->notifyNext = $notifier;
        return $this->notifyNext;
    }

    final public function push($message) {
        $this->publish($message);

        if ($this->notifyNext !== null) {
            $this->notifyNext->push($message);
```

```
            }
        }

    abstract protected function publish($message);
}

class TwitterSocialNotifier extends SocialNotifier {
    public function publish($message) {
        // Implementation...
    }
}

class FacebookSocialNotifier extends SocialNotifier {
    protected function publish($message) {
        // Implementation...
    }
}

class PinterestSocialNotifier extends SocialNotifier {
    protected function publish($message) {
        // Implementation...
    }
}

// Client
$notifier = new TwitterSocialNotifier();

$notifier->notifyNext(new FacebookSocialNotifier())
    ->notifyNext(new PinterestSocialNotifier());

$notifier->push('Awesome new product available!');
```

We started off by creating an abstract `SocialNotifier` class with the abstract
method `publish`, `notifyNext`, and `push` method implementations. We
then defined `TwitterSocialNotifier`, `FacebookSocialNotifier`, and
`PinterestSocialNotifier`, all of which extend the abstract `SocialNotifier`.
The client starts by instantiating the `TwitterSocialNotifier`, followed by two
`notifyNext` calls, passing it instances of two other `notifier` types before it calls
the final `push` method.

Command pattern

The command pattern decouples the object that executes certain operations from objects that know how to use it. It does so by encapsulating all of the relevant information needed for later execution of a certain action. This implies information about object, method name, and method parameters.

The following is an example of command pattern implementation:

```php
interface LightBulbCommand {
    public function execute();
}

class LightBulbControl {
    public function turnOn() {
        echo 'LightBulb turnOn';
    }

    public function turnOff() {
        echo 'LightBulb turnOff';
    }
}

class TurnOnLightBulb implements LightBulbCommand {
    private $lightBulbControl;

    public function __construct(LightBulbControl
      $lightBulbControl) {
        $this->lightBulbControl = $lightBulbControl;
    }

    public function execute() {
        $this->lightBulbControl->turnOn();
    }
}

class TurnOffLightBulb implements LightBulbCommand {
    private $lightBulbControl;

    public function __construct(LightBulbControl
      $lightBulbControl) {
        $this->lightBulbControl = $lightBulbControl;
    }
```

```
    public function execute() {
        $this->lightBulbControl->turnOff();
    }
}

// Client
$command = new TurnOffLightBulb(new LightBulbControl());
$command->execute();
```

We started off by creating a `LightBulbCommand` interface. We then defined the `LightBulbControl` class that provides two simple `turnOn` / `turnOff` methods. Then we defined the `TurnOnLightBulb` and `TurnOffLightBulb` classes which implement the `LightBulbCommand` interface. Finally, the client is instantiating the `TurnOffLightBulb` object with an instance of `LightBulbControl`, and calling the `execute` method on it.

Interpreter pattern

The interpreter pattern specifies how to evaluate language grammar or expressions. We define a representation for language grammar along with an interpreter. Representation of language grammar uses composite class hierarchy, where rules are mapped to classes. The interpreter then uses the representation to interpret expressions in the language.

The following is an example of interpreter pattern implementation:

```
interface MathExpression
{
    public function interpret(array $values);
}

class Variable implements MathExpression {
    private $char;

    public function __construct($char) {
        $this->char = $char;
    }

    public function interpret(array $values) {
        return $values[$this->char];
    }
}
```

```php
class Literal implements MathExpression {
    private $value;

    public function __construct($value) {
        $this->value = $value;
    }

    public function interpret(array $values) {
        return $this->value;
    }
}

class Sum implements MathExpression {
    private $x;
    private $y;

    public function __construct(MathExpression $x, MathExpression
      $y) {
        $this->x = $x;
        $this->y = $y;
    }

    public function interpret(array $values) {
        return $this->x->interpret($values) + $this->y->
          interpret($values);
    }
}

class Product implements MathExpression {
    private $x;
    private $y;

    public function __construct(MathExpression $x, MathExpression
      $y) {
        $this->x = $x;
        $this->y = $y;
    }

    public function interpret(array $values) {
        return $this->x->interpret($values) * $this->y->
          interpret($values);
    }
}
```

```
// Client
$expression = new Product(
    new Literal(5),
    new Sum(
        new Variable('c'),
        new Literal(2)
    )
);
```

```
echo $expression->interpret(array('c' => 3)); // 25
```

We started off by creating a `MathExpression` interface, with a single `interpret` method. We then add `Variable`, `Literal`, `Sum`, and `Product` classes, all of which implement the `MathExpression` interface. The client then instantiates from the `Product` class, passing it instances of `Literal` and `Sum`, finishing with an `interpret` method call.

Iterator pattern

The iterator pattern is used to traverse a container and access its elements. In other words, one class becomes able to traverse the elements of another class. The PHP has a native support for the iterator as part of built in `\Iterator` and `\IteratorAggregate` interfaces.

The following is an example of iterator pattern implementation:

```
class ProductIterator implements \Iterator {
    private $position = 0;
    private $productsCollection;

    public function __construct(ProductCollection
      $productsCollection) {
        $this->productsCollection = $productsCollection;
    }

    public function current() {
        return $this->productsCollection->getProduct($this->
          position);
    }

    public function key() {
        return $this->position;
    }
```

```php
        public function next() {
            $this->position++;
        }

        public function rewind() {
            $this->position = 0;
        }

        public function valid() {
            return !is_null($this->productsCollection->
              getProduct($this->position));
        }
    }

    class ProductCollection implements \IteratorAggregate {
        private $products = array();

        public function getIterator() {
            return new ProductIterator($this);
        }

        public function addProduct($string) {
            $this->products[] = $string;
        }

        public function getProduct($key) {
            if (isset($this->products[$key])) {
                return $this->products[$key];
            }
            return null;
        }

        public function isEmpty() {
            return empty($products);
        }
    }

    $products = new ProductCollection();
    $products->addProduct('T-Shirt Red');
    $products->addProduct('T-Shirt Blue');
    $products->addProduct('T-Shirt Green');
    $products->addProduct('T-Shirt Yellow');
```

```
foreach ($products as $product) {
    var_dump($product);
}
```

We started off by creating a `ProductIterator` which implements the standard PHP `\Iterator` interface. We then added the `ProductCollection` which implements the standard PHP `\IteratorAggregate` interface. The client creates an instance of `ProductCollection`, stacking values into it via the `addProduct` method call and loops through the entire collection.

Mediator pattern

The more classes we have in our software, the more complex their communication becomes. The mediator pattern addresses this complexity by encapsulating it into a mediator object. Objects no longer communicate directly, but rather through a mediator object, therefore lowering the overall coupling.

The following is an example of mediator pattern implementation:

```
interface MediatorInterface {
    public function fight();
    public function talk();
    public function registerA(ColleagueA $a);
    public function registerB(ColleagueB $b);
}

class ConcreteMediator implements MediatorInterface {
    protected $talk; // ColleagueA
    protected $fight; // ColleagueB

    public function registerA(ColleagueA $a) {
        $this->talk = $a;
    }

    public function registerB(ColleagueB $b) {
        $this->fight = $b;
    }

    public function fight() {
        echo 'fighting...';
    }
}
```

```php
        public function talk() {
            echo 'talking...';
        }
    }

    abstract class Colleague {
        protected $mediator; // MediatorInterface
        public abstract function doSomething();
    }

    class ColleagueA extends Colleague {

        public function __construct(MediatorInterface $mediator) {
            $this->mediator = $mediator;
            $this->mediator->registerA($this);
        }

    public function doSomething() {
            $this->mediator->talk();
    }
    }

    class ColleagueB extends Colleague {

        public function __construct(MediatorInterface $mediator) {
            $this->mediator = $mediator;
            $this->mediator->registerB($this);
        }

        public function doSomething() {
            $this->mediator->fight();
        }
    }

    // Client
    $mediator = new ConcreteMediator();
    $talkColleague = new ColleagueA($mediator);
    $fightColleague = new ColleagueB($mediator);

    $talkColleague->doSomething();
    $fightColleague->doSomething();
```

We started off by creating a `MediatorInterface` with several methods, implemented by the `ConcreteMediator` class. We then defined the abstract class `Colleague` to force the `doSomething` method implementation on the following `ColleagueA` and `ColleagueB` classes. The client instantiates the `ConcreteMediator` first, and passes its instance to the instances of `ColleagueA` and `ColleagueB`, upon which it calls the `doSomething` method.

Memento pattern

The memento pattern provides the object restore functionality. Implementation is done through three different objects; originator, caretaker, and a memento, where the originator is the one preserving the internal state required for a later restore.

The following is an example of memento pattern implementation:

```
class Memento {
    private $state;

    public function __construct($state) {
        $this->state = $state;
    }

    public function getState() {
        return $this->state;
    }
}

class Originator {
    private $state;

    public function setState($state) {
        return $this->state = $state;
    }

    public function getState() {
        return $this->state;
    }

    public function saveToMemento() {
        return new Memento($this->state);
    }
}
```

```
    public function restoreFromMemento(Memento $memento) {
        $this->state = $memento->getState();
    }
}

// Client - Caretaker
$savedStates = array();

$originator = new Originator();
$originator->setState('new');
$originator->setState('pending');
$savedStates[] = $originator->saveToMemento();
$originator->setState('processing');
$savedStates[] = $originator->saveToMemento();
$originator->setState('complete');
$originator->restoreFromMemento($savedStates[1]);
echo $originator->getState(); // processing
```

We started off by creating a Memento class, which will provide the a current state of the object through the getState method. We then defined the Originator class that pushed the state to Memento. Finally, the client takes the role of caretaker by instantiating Originator, juggling among its few states, saving and restoring them from memento.

Observer pattern

The observer pattern implements a one-too-many dependency between objects. The object that holds the list of dependencies is called **subject**, while the dependents are called **observers**. When the subject object changes state, all of the dependents are notified and updated automatically.

The following is an example of observer pattern implementation:

```
class Customer implements \SplSubject {
    protected $data = array();
    protected $observers = array();

    public function attach(\SplObserver $observer) {
        $this->observers[] = $observer;
    }

    public function detach(\SplObserver $observer) {
        $index = array_search($observer, $this->observers);
```

```
            if ($index !== false) {
                unset($this->observers[$index]);
            }
        }

    public function notify() {
        foreach ($this->observers as $observer) {
            $observer->update($this);
            echo 'observer updated';
        }
    }

    public function __set($name, $value) {
        $this->data[$name] = $value;

        // notify the observers, that user has been updated
        $this->notify();
    }
}

class CustomerObserver implements \SplObserver {
    public function update(\SplSubject $subject) {
        /* Implementation... */
    }
}

// Client
$user = new Customer();
$customerObserver = new CustomerObserver();
$user->attach($customerObserver);

$user->name = 'John Doe';
$user->email = 'john.doe@fake.mail';
```

We started off by creating a Customer class which implements the standard PHP
\SplSubject interface. We then defined the CustomerObserver class which
implements the standard PHP \SplObserver interface. Finally, the client instantiates
the Customer and CustomerObserver objects and attaches the CustomerObserver
objects to Customer. Any changes to name and email properties are then caught by
the observer.

State pattern

The state pattern encapsulates the varying behavior for the same object based on its internal state, making an object appear as if it has changed its class.

The following is an example of state pattern implementation:

```php
interface Statelike {
    public function writeName(StateContext $context, $name);
}

class StateLowerCase implements Statelike {
    public function writeName(StateContext $context, $name) {
        echo strtolower($name);
        $context->setState(new StateMultipleUpperCase());
    }
}

class StateMultipleUpperCase implements Statelike {
    private $count = 0;

    public function writeName(StateContext $context, $name) {
        $this->count++;
        echo strtoupper($name);
        /* Change state after two invocations */
        if ($this->count > 1) {
            $context->setState(new StateLowerCase());
        }
    }
}

class StateContext {
    private $state;

    public function setState(Statelike $state) {
        $this->state = $state;
    }

    public function writeName($name) {
        $this->state->writeName($this, $name);
    }
}
```

```
// Client
$stateContext = new StateContext();
$stateContext->setState(new StateLowerCase());
$stateContext->writeName('Monday');
$stateContext->writeName('Tuesday');
$stateContext->writeName('Wednesday');
$stateContext->writeName('Thursday');
$stateContext->writeName('Friday');
$stateContext->writeName('Saturday');
$stateContext->writeName('Sunday');
```

We started off by creating a `Statelike` interface, followed by `StateLowerCase`
and `StateMultipleUpperCase` which implement that interface. The
`StateMultipleUpperCase` has a bit of counting logic added to its `writeName`, so
it kicks off the new state after two invocations. We then defined the `StateContext`
class, which we will use to switch contexts. Finally, the client instantiates the
`StateContext`, and passes an instance of `StateLowerCase` to it through the
`setState` method, followed by several `writeName` methods.

Strategy pattern

The strategy pattern defines a family of algorithms, each of which is encapsulated
and made interchangeable with other members within that family.

The following is an example of strategy pattern implementation:

```
interface PaymentStrategy {
    public function pay($amount);
}

class StripePayment implements PaymentStrategy {
    public function pay($amount) {
        echo 'StripePayment...';
    }

}

class PayPalPayment implements PaymentStrategy {
    public function pay($amount) {
        echo 'PayPalPayment...';
    }
}
```

```
class Checkout {
    private $amount = 0;

    public function __construct($amount = 0) {
        $this->amount = $amount;
    }

    public function capturePayment() {
        if ($this->amount > 99.99) {
            $payment = new PayPalPayment();
        } else {
            $payment = new StripePayment();
        }

        $payment->pay($this->amount);
    }
}

$checkout = new Checkout(49.99);
$checkout->capturePayment(); // StripePayment...

$checkout = new Checkout(199.99);
$checkout->capturePayment(); // PayPalPayment...
```

We started off by creating a PaymentStrategy interface followed with concrete classes StripePayment and PayPalPayment which implement it. We then defined the Checkout class with a bit of decision making logic within the capturePayment method. Finally, the client instantiates the Checkout, passing a certain amount through its constructor. Based on the amount, the Checkout internally triggers one or another payment when capturePayment is called.

Template pattern

The template design pattern defines the program skeleton of an algorithm in a method. It lets us, via use of class overriding, redefine certain steps of an algorithm without really changing the algorithm's structure.

The following is an example of template pattern implementation:

```
abstract class Game {
    private $playersCount;

    abstract function initializeGame();
    abstract function makePlay($player);
```

```php
    abstract function endOfGame();
    abstract function printWinner();

    public function playOneGame($playersCount)
    {
        $this->playersCount = $playersCount;
        $this->initializeGame();
        $j = 0;
        while (!$this->endOfGame()) {
            $this->makePlay($j);
            $j = ($j + 1) % $playersCount;
        }
        $this->printWinner();
    }
}

class Monopoly extends Game {
    public function initializeGame() {
        // Implementation...
    }

    public function makePlay($player) {
        // Implementation...
    }

    public function endOfGame() {
        // Implementation...
    }

    public function printWinner() {
        // Implementation...
    }
}

class Chess extends Game {
    public function  initializeGame() {
        // Implementation...
    }

    public function  makePlay($player) {
        // Implementation...
    }
```

```
        public function  endOfGame() {
            // Implementation...
        }

        public function  printWinner() {
            // Implementation...
        }
}

$game = new Chess();
$game->playOneGame(2);

$game = new Monopoly();
$game->playOneGame(4);
```

We started off by creating an abstract Game class that provides all of the actual abstract methods encapsulating the game-play. We then defined the Monopoly and Chess classes, both of which extend from the Game class, implementing game specific method game-play for each. The client simply instantiates the Monopoly and Chess objects, calling the playOneGame method on each.

Visitor pattern

The visitor design pattern is a way of separating an algorithm from an object structure on which it operates. As a result, we are able to add new operations to existing object structures without actually modifying those structures.

The following is an example of visitor pattern implementation:

```
    interface RoleVisitorInterface {
        public function visitUser(User $role);
        public function visitGroup(Group $role);
    }

    class RolePrintVisitor implements RoleVisitorInterface {
        public function visitGroup(Group $role) {
            echo 'Role: ' . $role->getName();
        }

        public function visitUser(User $role) {
            echo 'Role: ' . $role->getName();
        }
    }
```

```php
abstract class Role {
    public function accept(RoleVisitorInterface $visitor) {
        $klass = get_called_class();
        preg_match('#([^\\\\]+)$#', $klass, $extract);
        $visitingMethod = 'visit' . $extract[1];

        if (!method_exists(__NAMESPACE__ .
          '\RoleVisitorInterface', $visitingMethod)) {
            throw new \InvalidArgumentException("The visitor you
                provide cannot visit a $klass instance");
        }

        call_user_func(array($visitor, $visitingMethod), $this);
    }
}

class User extends Role {
    protected $name;

    public function __construct($name) {
        $this->name = (string)$name;
    }

    public function getName() {
        return 'User ' . $this->name;
    }
}

class Group extends Role {
    protected $name;

    public function __construct($name) {
        $this->name = (string)$name;
    }

    public function getName() {
        return 'Group: ' . $this->name;
    }
}

$group = new Group('my group');
$user = new User('my user');
```

```
$visitor = new RolePrintVisitor;

$group->accept($visitor);
$user->accept($visitor);
```

We started off by creating a `RoleVisitorInterface`, followed by `RolePrintVisitor` which implements the `RoleVisitorInterface` itself. We then defined the abstract class `Role`, with an accept method taking in the `RoleVisitorInterface` parameter type. We further defined the concrete `User` and `Group` classes, both of which extend from `Role`. The client instantiates `User`, `Group`, and the `RolePrintVisitor`; passing in the `visitor` to the accept method call of `User` and `Group` instances.

Summary

Design patterns are a common, high-level language for developers. They enable a short-hand way of communicating application design among team members. Understanding how to recognize and implement design patterns shifts our focus to business requirement solving, rather than tinkering with how to glue our solution together on a code level.

Coding, like most hand-crafted disciplines, is one of those where you get what you pay for. While implementing a number of design patterns takes a certain amount of time, lack of doing so on a larger project will likely catch up with us in the future, one way or another. Similar to the "use a framework or not" debate, implementing the right design patterns affects *extensibility*, *re-usability*, *adaptability*, and *maintainability* of our code. Therefore, making it more future proof.

Moving forward, in the next chapter, we will look into the SOLID design principles and the role they play in software development processes.

3

SOLID Design Principles

Building modular software requires strong knowledge of the class design. There are numerous guidelines out there, addressing the way we name our classes, number of variables they should have, what the size of methods should be, and so on. The PHP ecosystem managed to pack these into official PSR standard, more precisely **PSR-1: Basic Coding Standard** and **PSR-2: Coding Style Guide**. These are all general programming guidelines that keep our code readable, understandable, and maintainable.

Aside from programming guidelines, there are more specific design principles that we can apply during the class design. Ones that address the notions of low coupling, high cohesion, and strong encapsulation. We call them SOLID design principles, a term coined by Robert Cecil Martin in the early 2000s.

SOLID is an acronym for the following five principles:

- **S**: Single responsibility principle (**SRP**)
- **O**: Open/closed principle (**OCP**)
- **L**: Liskov substitution principle (**LSP**)
- **I**: Interface Segregation Principle (**ISP**)
- **D**: Dependency inversion principle (**DIP**)

Over a decade old, the idea of SOLID principles is far from obsolete, as they are at the heart of good class design. Throughout this chapter, we will look into each of these principles, getting to understand them by observing some of the obvious violations that break them.

In this chapter, we will be covering the following topics:

- Single responsibility principle
- Open/closed principle
- Liskov substitution principle
- Interface Segregation Principle
- Dependency inversion principle

Single responsibility principle

The *single responsibility principle* deals with classes that try to do too much. The responsibility in this context refers to reason to change. As per the Robert C. Martin definition:

> *"A class should have only one reason to change."*

The following is an example of a class that violates the SRP:

```
class Ticket {
    const SEVERITY_LOW = 'low';
    const SEVERITY_HIGH = 'high';
    // ...
    protected $title;
    protected $severity;
    protected $status;
    protected $conn;

    public function __construct(\PDO $conn) {
        $this->conn = $conn;
    }

    public function setTitle($title) {
        $this->title = $title;
    }

    public function setSeverity($severity) {
        $this->severity = $severity;
    }

    public function setStatus($status) {
        $this->status = $status;
    }
```

```
    private function validate() {
        // Implementation...
    }

    public function save() {
        if ($this->validate()) {
            // Implementation...
        }
    }

}


// Client
$conn = new PDO(/* ... */);
$ticket = new Ticket($conn);
$ticket->setTitle('Checkout not working!');
$ticket->setStatus(Ticket::STATUS_OPEN);
$ticket->setSeverity(Ticket::SEVERITY_HIGH);
$ticket->save();
```

The Ticket class deals with validation and saving of the ticket entity to the database. These two responsibilities are its two reasons to change. Whenever the requirements change regarding the ticket validation, or regarding the saving of the ticket, the Ticket class will have to be modified. To address the SRP violation here, we can use the assisting classes and interfaces to split the responsibilities.

The following is an example of refactored implementation, which complies with SRP:

```
interface KeyValuePersistentMembers {
    public function toArray();
}


class Ticket implements KeyValuePersistentMembers {
    const STATUS_OPEN = 'open';
    const SEVERITY_HIGH = 'high';
    //...
    protected $title;
    protected $severity;
    protected $status;

    public function setTitle($title) {
        $this->title = $title;
    }
```

```php
        public function setSeverity($severity) {
            $this->severity = $severity;
        }

        public function setStatus($status) {
            $this->status = $status;
        }

        public function toArray() {
            // Implementation...
        }
    }

    class EntityManager {
        protected $conn;

        public function __construct(\PDO $conn) {
            $this->conn = $conn;
        }

        public function save(KeyValuePersistentMembers $entity)
        {
            // Implementation...
        }
    }

    class Validator {
        public function validate(KeyValuePersistentMembers $entity) {
            // Implementation...
        }
    }

    // Client
    $conn = new PDO(/* ... */);

    $ticket = new Ticket();
    $ticket->setTitle('Payment not working!');
    $ticket->setStatus(Ticket::STATUS_OPEN);
    $ticket->setSeverity(Ticket::SEVERITY_HIGH);

    $validator = new Validator();
```

```
if ($validator->validate($ticket)) {
    $entityManager = new EntityManager($conn);
    $entityManager->save($ticket);
}
```

Here we introduced a simple `KeyValuePersistentMembers` interface with a single `toArray` method, which is then used with both `EntityManager` and `Validator` classes, both of which take on a single responsibility now. The `Ticket` class became a simple data holding model, whereas client now controls *instantiation, validation,* and *save* as three different steps. While this is certainly no universal formula of how to separate responsibilities, it does provide a simple and clear example of how to approach it.

Designing with the single responsibilities principle in mind yields smaller classes with greater readability and easier to test code.

Open/closed principle

The **open/closed principle** states that a class should be open for extension but closed for modification, as per the definition found on Wikipedia:

> *"software entities (classes, modules, functions, etc.) should be open for extension, but closed for modification"*

The open for extension part means that we should design our classes so that new functionality can be added if needed. The closed for modification part means that this new functionality should fit in without modifying the original class. The class should only be modified in case of a bug fix, not for adding new functionality.

The following is an example of a class that violates the open/closed principle:

```
class CsvExporter {
    public function export($data) {
        // Implementation...
    }
}

class XmlExporter {
    public function export($data) {
        // Implementation...
    }
}
```

```
class GenericExporter {
    public function exportToFormat($data, $format) {
        if ('csv' === $format) {
            $exporter = new CsvExporter();
        } elseif ('xml' === $format) {
            $exporter = new XmlExporter();
        } else {
            throw new \Exception('Unknown export format!');
        }
        return $exporter->export($data);
    }
}
```

Here we have two concrete classes, CsvExporter and XmlExporter, each with a single responsibility. Then we have a GenericExporter with its exportToFormat method that actually triggers the export function on a proper instance type. The problem here is that we cannot add a new type of exporter to the mix without modifying the GenericExporter class. To put it in other words, GenericExporter is not open for extension and closed for modification.

The following is an example of refactored implementation, which complies with OCP:

```
interface ExporterFactoryInterface {
    public function buildForFormat($format);
}

interface ExporterInterface {
    public function export($data);
}

class CsvExporter implements ExporterInterface {
    public function export($data) {
        // Implementation...
    }
}

class XmlExporter implements ExporterInterface {
    public function export($data) {
        // Implementation...
    }
}
```

```php
class ExporterFactory implements ExporterFactoryInterface {
    private $factories = array();

    public function addExporterFactory($format, callable $factory)
      {
          $this->factories[$format] = $factory;
    }

    public function buildForFormat($format) {
        $factory = $this->factories[$format];
        $exporter = $factory(); // the factory is a callable

        return $exporter;
    }
}

class GenericExporter {
    private $exporterFactory;

    public function __construct
      (ExporterFactoryInterface $exporterFactory) {
        $this->exporterFactory = $exporterFactory;
    }

    public function exportToFormat($data, $format) {
        $exporter = $this->exporterFactory->
          buildForFormat($format);
        return $exporter->export($data);
    }
}

// Client
$exporterFactory = new ExporterFactory();

$exporterFactory->addExporterFactory(
'xml',
    function () {
        return new XmlExporter();
    }
);

$exporterFactory->addExporterFactory(
'csv',
    function () {
```

```
            return new CsvExporter();
        }
    );


    $data = array(/* ... some export data ... */);
    $genericExporter = new GenericExporter($exporterFactory);
    $csvEncodedData = $genericExporter->exportToFormat($data, 'csv');
```

Here we added two interfaces, `ExporterFactoryInterface` and
`ExporterInterface`. We then modified the `CsvExporter` and `XmlExporter` to
implement that interface. The `ExporterFactory` was added, implementing the
`ExporterFactoryInterface`. Its main role is defined by the `buildForFormat`
method, which returns the exporter as a callback function. Finally, the
`GenericExporter` was rewritten to accept the `ExporterFactoryInterface` via its
constructor, and its `exportToFormat` method now builds the exporter by use of an
exporter factory and calls the `execute` method on it.

The client itself has taken a more robust role now, by first instantiating the
`ExporterFactory` and adding two exporters to it, which it then passed onto
`GenericExporter`. Adding a new export format to `GenericExporter` now, no
longer requires modifying it, therefore making it open for extension and closed for
modification. Again, this is by no means a universal formula, rather a concept of
possible approach towards satisfying the OCP.

Liskov substitution principle

The **Liskov substitution principle** talks about inheritance. It specifies how we
should design our classes so that client dependencies can be replaced by subclasses
without the client seeing the difference, as per the definition found on Wikipedia:

> *"objects in a program should be replaceable with instances of their subtypes
> without altering the correctness of that program"*

While there might be some specific functionality added to the subclass, it has to
conform to the same behavior as its base class. Otherwise the Liskov principle
is violated.

When it comes to PHP and sub-classing, we have to look beyond simple concrete
classes and differentiate: concrete class, abstract class, and interface. Each of the three
can be put in the context of a base class, while everything extending or implementing
it can be looked at as a derived class.

The following is an example of LSP violation, where the derived class does not have an implementation for all methods:

```php
interface User {
    public function getEmail();
    public function getName();
    public function getAge();
}

class Employee implements User {
    public function getEmail() {
        // Implementation...
    }

    public function getAge() {
        // Implementation...
    }
}
```

Here we see an `employee` class which does not implement the `getName` method enforced by the interface. We could have easily used an abstract class instead of the interface and abstract method type for the `getName` method, the effect would have been the same. Luckily, the PHP would throw an error in this case, warning us that we haven't really implemented the interface fully.

The following is an example of Liskov principle violation, where different derived classes return things of different types:

```php
class UsersCollection implements \Iterator {
    // Implementation...
}

interface UserList {
    public function getUsers();
}

class Emloyees implements UserList {
    public function getUsers() {
        $users = new UsersCollection();
        //...
        return $users;
    }
}
```

```
class Directors implements UserList {
    public function getUsers() {
        $users = array();
        //...
        return $users;
    }
}
```

Here we see a simple example of an edge case. Calling getUsers on both derived classes will return a result we can loop through. However, PHP developers tend to use the count method often on array structures, and using it on Employees instances the getUsers result will not work. This is because the Employees class returns UsersCollection which implements Iterator, not the actual array structure. Since UsersCollection does not implement Countable, we cannot use count on it, which leads to potential bugs down the line.

We can further spot LSP violations in cases where the derived class behaves less permissively with regard to method arguments. These can usually be spotted by use of the instance of type operator, as shown in the following example:

```
interface LoggerProcessor {
    public function log(LoggerInterface $logger);
}

class XmlLogger implements LoggerInterface {
    // Implementation...
}

class JsonLogger implements LoggerInterface {
    // Implementation...
}

class FileLogger implements LoggerInterface {
    // Implementation...
}

class Processor implements LoggerProcessor {
    public function log(LoggerInterface $logger) {
        if ($logger instanceof XmlLogger) {
            throw new \Exception('This processor does not work
                with XmlLogger');
        } else {
            // Implementation...
        }
    }
}
```

Here, the derived class `Processor` puts restrictions on method arguments, while it should accept everything conforming to the `LoggerInterface`. By being less permissive, it alters the behavior implied by the base class, in this case `LoggerInterface`.

The outlined examples are merely a fragment of what constitutes a violation of LSP. To satisfy the principle, we need to make sure that derived classes do not, in any way, alter the behavior imposed by the base class.

Interface Segregation Principle

The **Interface Segregation Principle** states that clients should only implement interfaces they actually use. They should not be forced to implement interfaces they do not use. As per the definition found on Wikipedia:

> *"many client-specific interfaces are better than one general-purpose interface"*

What this means is that we should split large and fat interfaces into several small and lighter ones, segregating it so that smaller interfaces are based on groups of methods, each serving one specific functionality.

Let's take a look at the following leaky abstraction that violates the ISP:

```
interface Appliance {
    public function powerOn();
    public function powerOff();
    public function bake();
    public function mix();
    public function wash();

}

class Oven implements Appliance {
    public function powerOn() { /* Implement ... */ }
    public function powerOff() { /* Implement ... */ }
    public function bake() { /* Implement... */ }
    public function mix() { /* Nothing to implement ... */ }
    public function wash() { /* Cannot implement... */ }
}

class Mixer implements Appliance {
    public function powerOn() { /* Implement... */ }
    public function powerOff() { /* Implement... */ }
    public function bake() { /* Cannot implement... */ }
```

```
    public function mix() { /* Implement... */ }
    public function wash() { /* Cannot implement... */ }
}

class WashingMachine implements Appliance {
    public function powerOn() { /* Implement... */ }
    public function powerOff() { /* Implement... */ }
    public function bake() { /* Cannot implement... */ }
    public function mix() { /* Cannot implement... */ }
    public function wash() { /* Implement... */ }
}
```

Here we have an interface setting requirements for several appliance related methods. Then we have several classes implementing that interface. The problem is quite obvious; not all appliances can be squeezed into the same interface. It makes no sense for a washing machine to be forced to implement bake and mix methods. These methods need to be split each into its own interface. That way concrete appliance classes get to implement only the methods that actually make sense.

Dependency inversion principle

The **dependency inversion principle** states that entities should depend on abstractions and not on concretions. That is, a high level module should not depend on a low level module, rather the abstraction. As per the definition found on Wikipedia:

> *"One should depend upon abstractions. Do not depend upon concretions."*

This principle is important as it plays a major role in decoupling our software.

The following is an example of a class that violates the DIP:

```
class Mailer {
    // Implementation...
}

class NotifySubscriber {
    public function notify($emailTo) {
        $mailer = new Mailer();
        $mailer->send('Thank you for...', $emailTo);
    }
}
```

Here we can see a `notify` method within the `NotifySubscriber` class coding in a dependency towards the `Mailer` class. This makes for tightly coupled code, which is what we are trying to avoid. To rectify the problem, we can pass the dependency through the class constructor, or possibly via some other method. Furthermore, we should move away from concrete class dependency towards an abstracted one, as shown in the rectified example shown here:

```
interface MailerInterface {
    // Implementation...
}

class Mailer implements MailerInterface {
    // Implementation...
}

class NotifySubscriber {
    private $mailer;

    public function __construct(MailerInterface $mailer) {
        $this->mailer = $mailer;
    }

    public function notify($emailTo) {
        $this->mailer->send('Thank you for...', $emailTo);
    }
}
```

Here we see a dependency being injected through the constructor. The injection is abstracted by a type hinting interface, and the actual concrete class. This makes our code loosely coupled. The DIP can be used anytime a class needs to call a method of another class, or shall we say send a message to it.

Summary

When it comes to modular development, extensibility is something to constantly think about. Writing a code that locks itself in will likely result in a future failure to integrate it with other projects or libraries. While SOLID design principles might look like an overreach for some of the parts, actively applying these principles is likely to result in components that are easy to maintain and extend over time.

Embracing the SOLID principles for class design prepares our code for future changes. It does so by localizing and minimizing these changes within our classes, so any integration using it does not feel the significant impact of the change.

Moving forward, in the next chapter, we will look into defining our application specification which we will build across all other chapters.

4
Requirement Specification for a Modular Web Shop App

Building a software application from the ground up requires diverse skills, as it involves more than just writing down a code. Writing down functional requirements and sketching out a wireframe are often among the first steps in the process, especially if we are working on a client project. These steps are usually done by someone other than the developer, as they require certain insight into client business case, user behavior, and the like. Being part of a larger development team means that we, as developers, usually get requirements, designs, and wireframes then start coding against them. Delivering projects by oneself, makes it tempting to skip these steps and get our hands started with code alone. More often than not, this is an unproductive approach. Laying down functional requirements and a few wireframes is a skill worth knowing and following, even if one is just a developer.

Later in this chapter, we will go over a high-level application requirement, alongside a rough wireframe.

In this chapter, we will be covering the following topics:

- Defining application requirements
- Wireframing
- Defining technology stack:
    - Symfony framework
    - Foundation framework

Defining application requirements

We need to build a simple, but responsive web shop application. In order to do so, we need to lay out some basic requirements. The types of requirements we are interested in at the moment are those that touch upon interactions between a user and a system. The two most common techniques to specify requirements in regards to user usage are use case and user story. The user stories are a less formal yet descriptive enough way to outline these requirements. Using user stories, we encapsulate the customer and store manager actions as mentioned here.

A customer should be able to do the following:

- Browse through static info pages (about us, customer service)
- Reach out to the store owner via a contact form
- Browse the shop categories
- See product details (price, description)
- See the product image with a large view (zoom)
- See items on sale
- See best sellers
- Add the product to the shopping cart
- Create a customer account
- Update customer account info
- Retrieve a lost password
- Check out
- See the total order cost
- Choose among several payment methods
- Choose among several shipment methods
- Get an email notification after an order has been placed
- Check order status
- Cancel an order
- See order history

A store manager should be able to do the following:

- Create a product (with the minimum following attributes: `title`, `price`, `sku`, `url-key`, `description`, `qty`, `category`, and `image`)
- Upload a picture of the product
- Update and delete a product
- Create a category (with the minimum following attributes: `title`, `url-key`, `description`, and `image`)
- Upload a picture to a category
- Update and delete a category
- Be notified if a new sales order has been created
- Be notified if a new sales order has been canceled
- See existing sales orders by their statuses
- Update the status of the order
- Disable a customer account
- Delete a customer account

User stories are a convenient high-level way of writing down application requirements. Especially useful as an agile mode of development.

Wireframing

With user stories laid out, let's shift our focus to actual wireframing. For reasons we will get into later on, our wireframing efforts will be focused around the customer perspective.

There are numerous wireframing tools out there, both free and commercial. Some commercial tools like `https://ninjamock.com`, which we will use for our examples, still provide a free plan. This can be very handy for personal projects, as it saves us a lot of time.

The starting point of every web application is its home page. The following wireframe illustrates our web shop app's homepage:

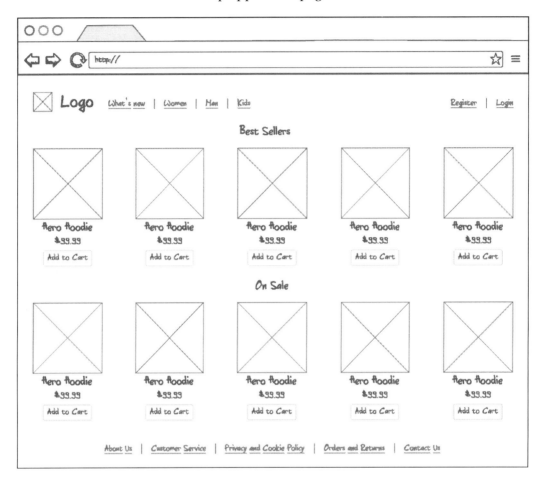

Here we can see a few sections determining the page structure. The header is comprised of a logo, category menu, and user menu. The requirements don't say anything about category structure, and we are building a simple web shop app, so we are going to stick to a flat category structure, without any sub-categories. The user menu will initially show **Register** and **Login** links, until the user is actually logged in, in which case the menu will change as shown in following wireframes. The content area is filled with best sellers and on sale items, each of which have an image, title, price, and **Add to Cart** button defined. The footer area contains links to mostly static content pages, and a **Contact Us** page.

The following wireframe illustrates our web shop app's category page:

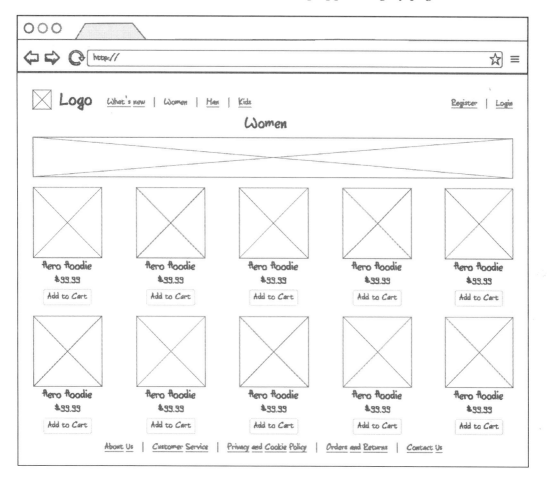

The header and footer areas remain conceptually the same across the entire site. The content area has now changed to list products within any given category. Individual product areas are rendered in the same manner as it is on the home page. Category names and images are rendered above the product list. The width of a category image gives some hints as to what type of images we should be preparing and uploading onto our categories.

The following wireframe illustrates our web shop app's product page:

The content area here now changes to list individual product information. We can see a large image placeholder, title, sku, stock status, price, quantity field, **Add to Cart** button, and product description being rendered. The **IN STOCK** message is to be displayed when an item is available for purchase and **OUT OF STOCK** when an item is no longer available. This is to be related to the product quantity attribute. We also need to keep in mind the "See the product image with a big view (zoom)" requirement, where clicking on an image would zoom into it.

The following wireframe illustrates our web shop app's register page:

The content area here now changes to render a registration form. There are many ways that we can implement the registration system. More often than not, the minimal amount of information is asked on a registration screen, as we want to get the user in as quickly as possible. However, let's proceed as if we are trying to get more complete user information right here on the registration screen. We ask not just for an e-mail and password, but for entire address information as well.

The following wireframe illustrates our web shop app's login page:

The content area here now changes to render a customer login and forgotten password form. We provide the user with **Email** and **Password** fields in case of login, or just an **Email** field in case of a password reset action.

The following wireframe illustrates our web shop app's customer account page:

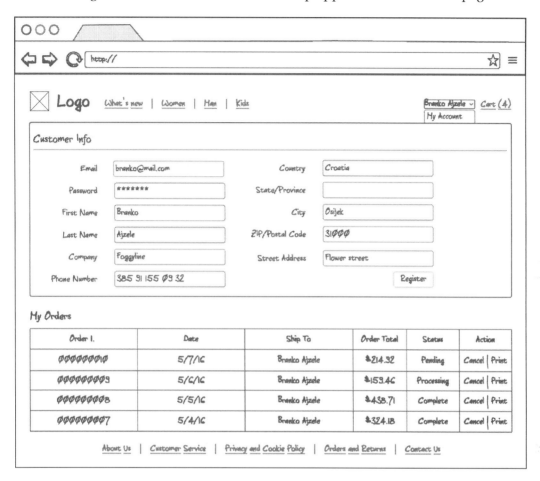

The content area here now changes to render the customer account area, visible only to logged in customers. Here we see a screen with two main pieces of information. The customer information being one, and order history being the other. The customer can change their e-mail, password, and other address information from this screen. Furthermore, the customer can view, cancel, and print all of their previous orders. The **My Orders** table lists orders top to bottom, from newest to oldest. Though not specified by the user stories, the order cancelation should work only on pending orders. This is something that we will touch upon in more detail later on.

This is also the first screen that shows the state of the user menu when the user is logged in. We can see a dropdown showing the user's full name, **My Account**, and **Sign Out** links. Right next to it, we have the **Cart (%s)** link, which is to list exact quantities in a cart.

The following wireframe illustrates our web shop app's checkout cart page:

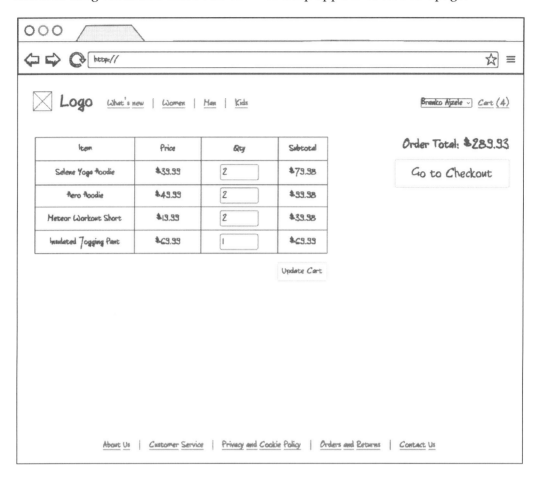

The content area here now changes to render the cart in its current state. If the customer has added any products to the cart, they are to be listed here. Each item should list the product title, individual price, quantity added, and subtotal. The customer should be able to change quantities and press the **Update Cart** button to update the state of the cart. If 0 is provided as the quantity, clicking the **Update Cart** button will remove such an item from the cart. Cart quantities should at all time reflect the state of the header menu **Cart (%s)** link. The right-hand side of a screen shows a quick summary of current order total value, alongside a big, clear **Go to Checkout** button.

The following wireframe illustrates our web shop app's checkout cart shipping page:

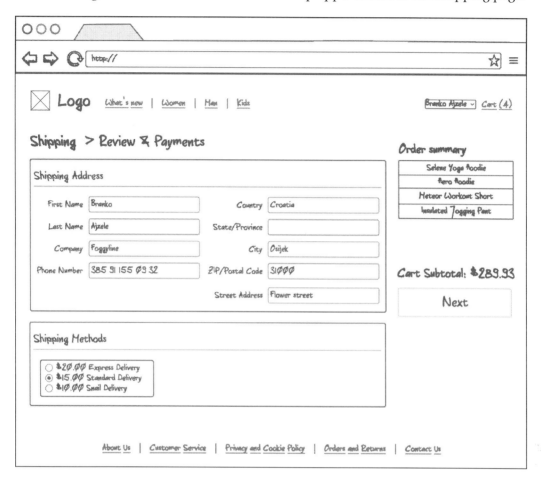

The content area here now changes to render the first step of a checkout process, the shipping information collection. This screen should not be accessible for non-logged in customers. The customer can provide us with their address details here, alongside a shipping method selection. The shipping method area lists several shipping methods. On the right hand side, the collapsible order summary section is shown, listing current items in the cart. Below it, we have the cart subtotal value and a big clear **Next** button. The **Next** button should trigger only when all of the required information is provided, in which case it should take us to payment information on the checkout cart payment page.

The following wireframe illustrates our web shop app's checkout cart payment page:

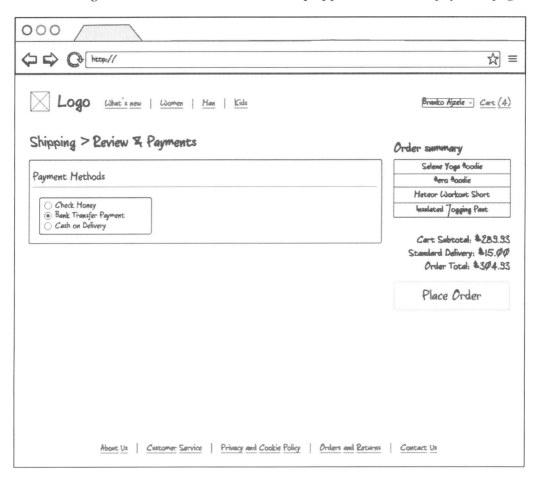

The content area here now changes to render the second step of a checkout process, the payment information collection. This screen should not be accessible for non-logged in customers. The customer is presented with a list of available payment methods. For the simplicity of the application, we will focus only on flat/fixed payments, nothing robust such as PayPal or Stripe. On the right-hand side of the screen, we can see a collapsible **Order summary** section, listing current items in the cart. Below it, we have the order totals section, individually listing **Cart Subtotal**, **Standard Delivery**, **Order Total**, and a big clear **Place Order** button. The **Place Order** button should trigger only when all of the required information is provided, in which case it should take us to the checkout success page.

The following wireframe illustrates our web shop app's checkout success page:

The content area here now changes to output the checkout successful message. Clearly this page is only visible to logged in customers that just finished the checkout process. The order number is clickable and links to the **My Account** area, focusing on the exact order. By reaching this screen, both the customer and store manager should receive a notification email, as per the *Get email notification after order has been placed* and *Be notified if the new sales order has been created* requirements.

With this, we conclude our customer facing wireframes.

In regards to store manager user story requirements, we will simply define a landing administration interface for now, as shown in the following screenshot:

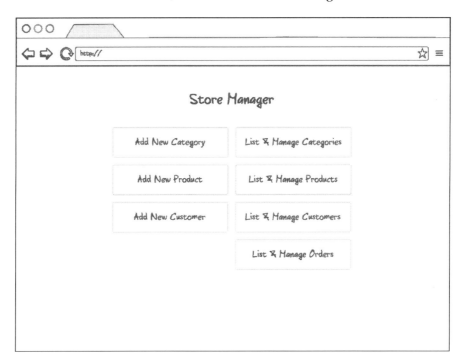

Using the framework later on, we will get a complete auto-generated CRUD interface for the multiple **Add New** and **List & Manage** links. The access to this interface and its links will be controlled by the framework's security component, since this user will not be a customer or any user in the database as such.

Furthermore, throughout the following chapters, we will split our application into several modules. In such a setup, each module will take ownership of individual functionalities, taking care of customer, catalog, checkout, and other requirements.

Defining a technology stack

Once the requirements and wireframes are set, we can focus our attention to the selection of a technology stack. In *Chapter 1*, *Ecosystem Overview* we glossed over several of the most popular PHP frameworks, pointing out their strengths. Choosing the right one in this case, is more of a matter of preference, as application requirements for the most part can be easily met by be met any one of those frameworks. Our choice, however, falls to Symfony. Aside from PHP frameworks, we still need a CSS framework to deliver some structure, styling, and responsiveness within the browser on the client side. Since the focus of this book is on PHP technologies, let's just say we chose the Foundation CSS framework for that task.

The Symfony framework

The Symfony framework makes a nice choice for our application. It is an enterprise level framework that has been around for years, and is extremely well documented and supported. It can be downloaded from the official `http://symfony.com` page as shown here:

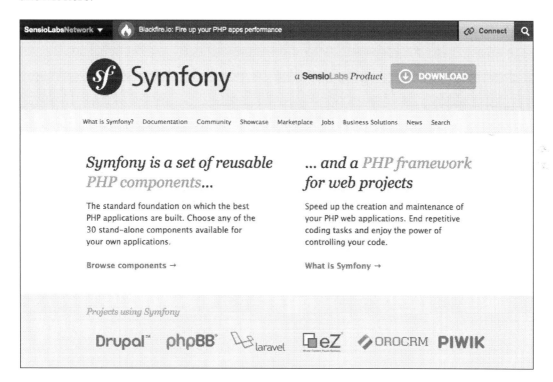

The benefits of using Symfony as part of our technology stack are numerous. The framework provides robust and well documented:

- Controllers
- Routing
- ORM (via Doctrine)
- Forms
- Validation
- Security

These are essential features required by our application. The ORM in particular, plays a major role in rapid application development. Having to worry less about coding, every aspect of CRUD can boost the speed of development by a factor or two. The great thing about Symfony in this regard is that it allows for automatic generation of entities and CRUD actions around them by executing two simple commands such as the following:

```
php bin/console doctrine:generate:entity
php app/console generate:doctrine:crud
```

By doing so, Symfony generates entity models and necessary controllers that empower us to perform the following operations:

- List all records
- Show one given record identified by its primary key
- Create a new record
- Edit an existing record
- Delete an existing record

Basically, we get a minimal store manager interface for free. This alone covers most of the CRUD related requirements set for the store manager role. We can then easily modify the generated templates to further integrate the remaining functionality.

On top of that, security components provide authentication and authorization that we can use to satisfy the customer and store manager logins. So a store manager will be a fixed, pre-created user attached to Symfony's firewall, the only one having access to CRUD controller actions.

Foundation framework

Backed by the company Zurb, the Foundation framework makes a great choice for a modern responsive web application. We might say it is an enterprise level framework, providing a collection of HTML, CSS, and JavaScript that we can build upon. It can be downloaded from the official `http://foundation.zurb.com` page as shown here:

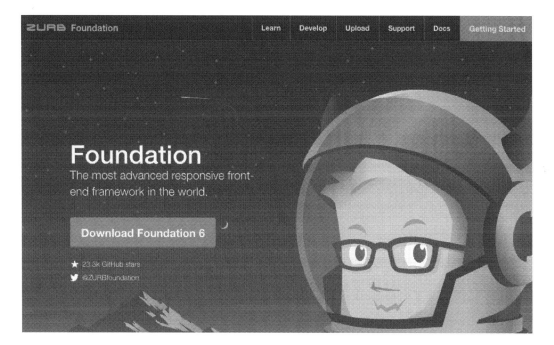

Foundation comes in three flavors:

- Foundation for sites
- Foundation for e-mail
- Foundation for apps

We are interested in the sites version. Aside from general styling, Foundation for sites provides a great deal of controls, navigational elements, containers, media elements, and plugins. These will be particularly useful in our application, for things like header menus, category product listings, responsive cart tables, and so on.

Foundation is built as a mobile-first framework, where we code for small screens first and larger screens then inherit those styles. Its default 12-column grid system enables us to create powerful multi-device layouts quickly and easily.

We will use Foundation simply to provide structure, some basic styling, and responsiveness to our application, without writing a single line of CSS on our own. This alone should make our application visually pleasing enough to work with both on mobile and desktop screens, while still focusing the majority of our coding skills around backend things.

Aside from providing robust functionality, the company behind Foundation also provides premium technical support. Though we will not need it as part of this book, these sorts of things establish confidence when choosing application frameworks.

Summary

Creating web applications can be a tedious and time consuming task, web shops probably being one of the most robust and intensive type of application out there, as they encompass a great deal of features. There are many components involved in delivering the final product; from database, server side (PHP) code to client side (HTML, CSS, and JavaScript) code. In this chapter, we started off by defining some basic user stories which in turn defined high-level application requirements for our small web shop. Adding wireframes to the mix helped us to visualize the customer facing interface, while the store manager interface is to be provided out of the box by the framework.

We further glossed over two of the most popular frameworks that support modular application design. We turned our attention to Symfony as server side technology and Foundation as a client side responsive framework.

Moving forward, in the next chapter, we will take a more in-depth look into Symfony. As well as being a set of reusable components, Symfony is also one of the most robust and popular full-stack PHP frameworks. Therefore, it is an interesting choice for rapid web application development.

5
Symfony at a Glance

Full-stack frameworks like Symfony help ease the process of building modular applications by providing all of the necessary components, from user interface to data store. This enables a much rapid cycle of delivering individual bits and pieces of application as it grows. We will experience this later on by segmenting our application in several smaller modules, or bundles in Symfony terminology.

Moving forward we will install Symfony, create a blank project, and start looking into individual framework features essential for building modular application:

- Controller
- Routing
- Templates
- Forms
- The bundle system
- Databases and Doctrine
- Testing
- Validation

Installing Symfony

Installing Symfony is pretty straightforward. We can use the following command to install Symfony on Linux or Mac OS X:

```
sudo curl -LsS https://symfony.com/installer -o /usr/local/bin/
  symfony

sudo chmod a+x /usr/local/bin/symfony
```

We can use the following command to install Symfony on Windows:

```
c:\> php -r "file_put_contents('symfony', file_get_contents
   ('https://symfony.com/installer'));"
```

Once the command is executed, we can simply move the newly created `symfony` file to our project directory and execute it further as `symfony`, or `php symfony` in Windows.

This should trigger an output shown as follows:

```
Brankos-MacBook-Pro:test-app branko$ symfony

Symfony Installer (1.5.1)
============================

This is the official installer to start new projects based on the
Symfony full-stack framework.

To create a new project called blog in the current directory using
the latest stable version of Symfony, execute the following command:

   symfony new blog

Create a project based on the Symfony Long Term Support version (LTS):

   symfony new blog lts

Create a project based on a specific Symfony branch:

   symfony new blog 2.3

Create a project based on a specific Symfony version:

   symfony new blog 2.5.6

Create a demo application to learn how a Symfony application works:

   symfony demo

Updating the Symfony Installer
-------------------------------

New versions of the Symfony Installer are released regularly. To update your
installer version, execute the following command:

   symfony self-update
```

Preceding response indicates we have successfully setup Symfony and are now ready to start creating new projects.

Creating a blank project

Now that we have a Symfony installer all setup, let's go ahead and create a new blank project. We do so by simply executing a `symfony new test-app` command, as shown in the following command line instance:

```
Brankos-MacBook-Pro:www branko$ symfony new test-app

Downloading Symfony...

   4.98 MB/4.98 MB ████████████████████████████████████████  100%

Preparing project...

✓ Symfony 3.0.6 was successfully installed. Now you can:

   * Change your current directory to /Users/branko/www/test-app

   * Configure your application in app/config/parameters.yml file.

   * Run your application:
       1. Execute the php bin/console server:run command.
       2. Browse to the http://localhost:8000 URL.

   * Read the documentation at http://symfony.com/doc

Brankos-MacBook-Pro:www branko$ ▉
```

Here we are creating a new project, called `test-app`. We can see that the Symfony installer is downloading the latest Symfony framework from the internet, alongside outputting a brief instruction on how to run the built in PHP server via Symfony console application. The whole process might take up to a few minutes.

The structure of newly created `test-app` directory occurs similar to the following one:

There are numerous files and directories created here for us. Our interest, however, is focused on app and src directories. The app directory is where the site wide application configuration resides. Here we can find configuration for database, routing, security, and other services. Also, this is where default layout and template file reside, as shown in the following screenshot:

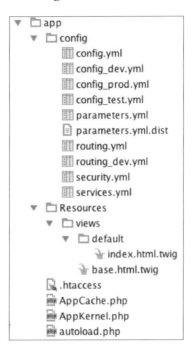

The src directory on the other hand contains already modularized code in form of the base AppBundle module, as in the following screenshot:

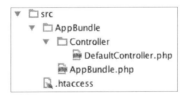

We are going to speak about the role of these files in more details later as we progress. For now, its worth nothing that pointing our browser to this project would make DefaultController.php the one to actually render the output.

Using Symfony console

Symfony framework comes with a built-in console tool that we can trigger by simply executing the following command within our project root directory:

```
php bin/console
```

By doing so, an extensive list of available commands is shown on screen, sectioned into the following groups:

- `assets`
- `cache`
- `config`
- `debug`
- `doctrine`
- `generate`
- `lint`
- `orm`
- `router`
- `security`
- `server`
- `swiftmailer`
- `translation`

These empower us with various functionalities. Our special interest moving forward is going to be around `doctrine` and `generate` commands. The `doctrine` command, more specifically `doctrine:generate:crud`, generates a CRUD based on an existing Doctrine entity. Furthermore, the `doctrine:generate:entity` command generates a new Doctrine entity inside an existing bundle. These can be extremely handy for cases where we want a quick and easy entity creation, alongside the entire CRUD around it. Similarly, `generate:doctrine:entity` and `generate:doctrine:crud` do the same thing.

Before we go ahead and test these commands, we need to make sure we have our database configuration parameters in place so that Symfony can see and talk to our database. To do so, we need to set appropriate values in `app/config/parameters.yml` file.

For the purpose of this section, let's go ahead and create a simple Customer entity within the default `AppBundle` bundle, with entire CRUD around it, assuming the following properties on Customer entity: `firstname`, `lastname`, and `e-mail`. We start by running the `php bin/console generate:doctrine:entity` command from within the project root directory, which results in the following output:

```
Welcome to the Doctrine2 entity generator


This command helps you generate Doctrine2 entities.

First, you need to give the entity name you want to generate.
You must use the shortcut notation like AcmeBlogBundle:Post.

The Entity shortcut name: AppBundle:Customer

Determine the format to use for the mapping information.

Configuration format (yml, xml, php, or annotation) [annotation]:

Instead of starting with a blank entity, you can add some fields now.
Note that the primary key will be added automatically (named id).

Available types: array, simple_array, json_array, object,
boolean, integer, smallint, bigint, string, text, datetime, datetimetz,
date, time, decimal, float, binary, blob, guid.

New field name (press <return> to stop adding fields):
```

Here we first provided `AppBundle:Customer` as entity name and confirmed the use of annotations as configuration format.

Finally, we are asked to start adding the fields to our entity. Typing in the first name and hitting enter moves us through a series of short questions about our field type, length, nullable, and unique states, as shown in the following screenshot:

```
New field name (press <return> to stop adding fields): firstname
Field type [string]: string
Field length [255]:
Is nullable [false]:
Unique [false]:

New field name (press <return> to stop adding fields): lastname
Field type [string]:
Field length [255]:
Is nullable [false]:
Unique [false]:

New field name (press <return> to stop adding fields): email
Field type [string]:
Field length [255]:
Is nullable [false]:
Unique [false]: true

New field name (press <return> to stop adding fields):

 Entity generation


> Generating entity class src/AppBundle/Entity/Customer.php: OK!
> Generating repository class src/AppBundle/Repository/CustomerRepository.php: OK!

 Everything is OK! Now get to work :).
```

We should now have two classes generated for our Customer entity. Via the help of Symfony and Doctrine, these classes are put in context of **Object Relational Mapper (ORM)**, as they link the Customer entity with the proper database table. However, we haven't yet instructed Symfony to actually create the table for our entity. To do so, we execute the following command:

```
php bin/console doctrine:schema:update --force
```

This should produce the output as shown in the following screenshot:

```
[Brankos-MacBook-Pro:test-app branko$ php bin/console doctrine:schema:update --force
Updating database schema...
Database schema updated successfully! "1" query was executed
```

If we now take a look at the database, we should see a customer table with all the proper columns created with SQL create dsyntax as follows:

```
CREATE TABLE `customer` (
  `id` int(11) NOT NULL AUTO_INCREMENT,
  `firstname` varchar(255) COLLATE utf8_unicode_ci NOT NULL,
  `lastname` varchar(255) COLLATE utf8_unicode_ci NOT NULL,
  `email` varchar(255) COLLATE utf8_unicode_ci NOT NULL,
  PRIMARY KEY (`id`),
```

```
     UNIQUE KEY `UNIQ_81398E09E7927C74` (`email`)
) ENGINE=InnoDB DEFAULT CHARSET=utf8 COLLATE=utf8_unicode_ci;
```

At this point, we still do not have an actual CRUD functionality in place. We simply have an ORM empowered Customer entity class and appropriate database table behind it. The following command will generate the actual CRUD controllers and templates for us:

```
php bin/console generate:doctrine:crud
```

This should produce the following interactive output:

By providing the fully classified entity name AppBundle:Customer, generator proceeds with a series of additional inputs, from generating write actions, type of configuration to read, to prefix of route, as shown in the following screenshot:

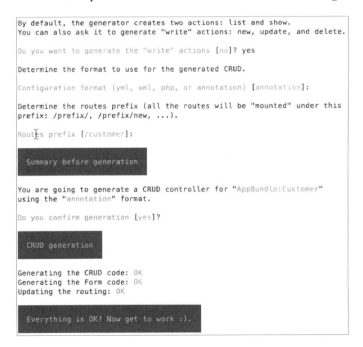

Once done, we should be able to access our Customer CRUD actions by simply opening a URL like `http://test.app/customer/` (assuming `test.app` is the host we set for our example) as shown:

If we click on the **Create a new entry** link, we will be redirected to the `/customer/new/` URL, as shown in the following screenshot:

Here we can enter the actual values for our Customer entity and click **Create** button in order to persist it into the database `customer` table. After adding a few entities, the initial `/customer/` URL is now able to list them all, as shown in the following screenshot:

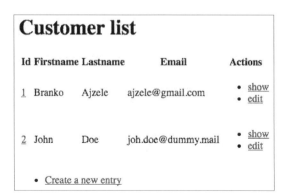

Here we see links to **show** and **edit** actions. The **show** action is what we might consider the customer facing action, whereas the **edit** action is the administrator facing action. Clicking on the **edit** action, takes us to the URL of the form `/customer/1/edit/`, whereas number `1` in this case is the ID of customer entity in database:

Here we can change the property values and click **Edit** to persist them back into the database, or we can click on the **Delete** button to remove the entity from the database.

If we were to create a new entity with an already existing e-mail, which is flagged as a unique field, the system would throw a generic error as such the following one:

Oops! An Error Occurred

The server returned a "500 Internal Server Error".

Something is broken. Please let us know what you were doing when this error occurred. We will fix it as soon as possible. Sorry for any inconvenience caused.

This is merely default system behavior, and as we progress further we will look into making this more user friendly. By now, we have seen how powerful Symfony's console is. With a few simple commands, we were able to create our entity and its entire CRUD actions. There is plenty more the console is capable of. We can even create our own console commands as we can implement any type of logic. However, for the purpose of our needs, current implementation will suffice for a moment.

Controller

Controllers play a major role in web applications by being at the forefront of any application output. They are the endpoints, the code that executes behind each URL. In a more technical manner, we can say the controller is any callable (a function, method on an object, or a closure) that takes the HTTP request and returns an HTTP response. The response is not bound to a single format like HTML, it can be anything from XML, JSON, CSV, image, redirect, error, and so on.

Let's take a look at the previously created (partial) `src/AppBundle/Controller/CustomerController.php` file, more precisely its `newAction` method:

```
/**
 * Creates a new Customer entity.
 *
 * @Route("/new", name="customer_new")
 * @Method({"GET", "POST"})
 */
public function newAction(Request $request)
{
  //...

  return $this->render('customer/new.html.twig', array(
    'customer' => $customer,
    'form' => $form->createView(),
  ));
}
```

If we ignore the actual data retrieval part (//...), there are three important things to note in this little example:

- `@Route`: this is the Symfony's annotation way of specifying HTTP endpoint, the URL we will use to access this. The first `"/new"` parameter states the actual endpoint, the second `name="customer_new"` parameter sets the name for this route that we can then use as an alias in URL generation functions in templates and so on. It is worth noting, that this builds upon the `@Route("/customer")` annotation set on the actual `CustomerController` class where the method is defined, thus making for the full URL to be something like `http://test.app/customer/new`.

- `@Method`: This takes the name of one or more HTTP methods. This means that the `newAction` method will trigger only if the HTTP requests match the previously defined `@Route` and are of one or more HTTP method types defined in `@Method`.

- `$this->render`: This returns the `Response` object. The `$this->render` calls the `render` function of the `Symfony\Bundle\FrameworkBundle\Controller\Controller` class, which instantiates new `Response()`, sets its content, and returns the whole instance of that object.

Now let's take a look at the `editAction` method within our controller, as partially shown in the following code block:

```
/**
 * Displays a form to edit an existing Customer entity.
 *
 * @Route("/{id}/edit", name="customer_edit")
 * @Method({"GET", "POST"})
 */
public function editAction(Request $request, Customer $customer)
{
  //...
}
```

Here we see a route that accepts a singe ID, marked as `{id}` within the first `@Route` annotation parameter. The body of the method (excluded here), does not contain any direct reference to fetching the `id` parameter. We can see that the `editAction` function accepts two parameters, one being `Request`, the other being `Customer`. But how does the method know to accept the `Customer` object? This is where Symfony's `@ParamConverter` annotation comes into play. It calls converters to convert the request parameters to objects.

The great thing about `@ParamConverter` annotation is that we can use it explicitly or implicitly. That is, if we do not add `@ParamConverter` annotation but add type hinting to the method parameter, Symfony is going to try and load the object for us. This is the exact case we have in our example above, as we did not explicitly type the `@ParamConverter` annotation.

Terminology wise, controllers are often exchanged for routing. However, they are not the same thing.

Routing

In the shortest terms, routing is about linking the controllers with URLs entered in browser. Todays modern web applications need nice URLs. This means moving away from URLs like `/index.php?product_id=23` to something like `/catalog/product/t-shirt`. This is where routing comes in to play.

Symfony has a powerful routing mechanism that enables us to do the following:

- Create complex routes which map to controllers
- Generate URLs inside templates
- Generate URLs inside controllers
- Load routing resources from various locations

The way routing works in Symfony is that all of the requests come through `app.php`. Then, the Symfony core asks the router to inspect the request. The router then matches the incoming URL to a specific route and returns information about the route. This information, among other things, includes the controller that should be executed. Finally, the Symfony kernel executes the controller, which returns a response object.

All of the application routes are loaded from a single routing configuration file, usually `app/config/routing.yml` file, as shown by our test app:

```
app:
   resource: "@AppBundle/Controller/"
   type:     annotation
```

The app is simply one of many possible entries. Its resource value points to `AppBundle` controller directory, and type is set to annotation which means that the class annotations will be read to specify exact routes.

We can define a route with several variations. One of them is shown in the following block:

```
// Basic Route Configuration
/**
 * @Route("/")
 */
public function homeAction()
{
  // ...
}

// Routing with Placeholders
/**
 * @Route("/catalog/product/{sku}")
 */
public function showAction($sku)
{
  // ...
}
```

```
// >>Required<< and Optional Placeholders
/**
 * @Route("/catalog/product/{id}")
 */
public function indexAction($id)
{
  // ...
}
// Required and >>Optional<< Placeholders
/**
 * @Route("/catalog/product/{id}", defaults={"id" = 1})
 */
public function indexAction($id)
{
  // ...
}
```

The preceding examples show several ways we can define our route. The interesting one is the case with required and optional parameter. If we think about it, removing ID from the latest example will match the example before it with sku. The Symfony router will always choose the first matching route it finds. We can solve the problem by adding regular expression requirements attributed on @Route annotation as follows:

```
@Route(
    "/catalog/product/{id}",
    defaults={"id": 1},
    requirements={"id": "\d+"}
)
```

There is more to be said about controllers and routing, as we will see once we start building our application.

Templates

Previously we said that controllers accept request and return response. The response, however, can often be any content type. The production of actual content is something controllers delegate to the templating engine. The templating engine then has the capability to turn the response into HTML, JSON, XML, CSV, LaTeX, or any other text-based content type.

In the old days, programmers mixed PHP with HTML into the so called PHP templates (.php and .phtml). Though still used with some platforms, this kind of approach is considered insecure and lacking in many aspects. One of which was cramming business logic into template files.

To address these shortcomings, Symfony packs its own templating language called Twig. Unlike PHP, Twig is meant to strictly express presentation and not to thinker about program logic. We cannot execute any of the PHP code within the Twig. And the Twig code is nothing more than an HTML with a few special syntax types.

Twig defines three types of special syntax:

- `{{ ... }}`: This outputs variable or the result of an expression to the template.
- `{% ... %}`: This tag controls the logic of the template (`if` and `for` loops, and others).
- `{# ... #}`: It is the equivalent of the PHP `/* comment */` syntax. The Comments content isn't included in the rendered page.

Filters are another nice feature of Twig. They act like chained method calls upon a variable value, modifying the content before it is outputted, as follows:

```
<h1>{{ title|upper }}</h1>

{{ filter upper }}
<h1>{{ title }}</h1>
{% endfilter %}

<h1>{{ title|lower|escape }}</h1>

{% filter lower|escape %}
<h1>{{ title }}</h1>
{% endfilter %}
```

It also supports functions listed as follows:

```
{{ random(['phone', 'tablet', 'laptop']) }}
```

The preceding random function call would return one random value from within the array. With all the built-in list of filters and functions, Twig also allows for writing our own if needed.

Similar to PHP class inheritance, Twig also supports template and layout inheritance. Let's take a quick look back at the the `app/Resources/views/customer/index.html.twig` file as follows:

```
{% extends 'base.html.twig' %}

{% block body %}
<h1>Customer list</h1>
...
{% endblock %}
```

Here we see a customer `index.html.twig` template using the `extends` tag to extend a template from another one, in this case `base.html.twig` found in `app/Resources/views/` directory with content as follows:

```
<!DOCTYPE html>
<html>
  <head>
    <meta charset="UTF-8" />
    <title>{% block title %}Welcome!{% endblock %}</title>
    {% block stylesheets%}{% endblock %}
    <link rel="icon" type="image/x-icon"href="{{
      asset('favicon.ico') }}" />
  </head>
  <body>
    {% block body %}{% endblock %}
    {% block javascripts%}{% endblock %}
  </body>
</html>
```

Here we see several block tags: `title`, `stylesheets`, `body`, and `javascripts`. We can declare as many blocks as we want here and name them any way we like. This makes the `extend` tag a key to template inheritance. It tells the Twig to first evaluate the base template, which sets the layout and defines blocks, after which the child template like `customer/index.html.twig` fills in the content of these blocks.

Templates live in two locations:

- `app/Resources/views/`
- `bundle-directory/Resources/views/`

What this means is in order to `render/extend app/Resources/views/base.html.twig` we would use `base.html.twig` within our template file, and to `render/extend app/Resources/views/customer/index.html.twig` we would use the `customer/index.html.twig` path.

When used with templates that reside in bundles, we have to reference them slightly differently. In this case, the `bundle:directory:filename` string syntax is used. Take the `FoggylineCatalogBundle:Product:index.html.twig` path for example. This would be a full path to use one of the bundles template file. Here the `FoggylineCatalogBundle` is a bundle name, `Product` is a name of a directory within that bundle `Resources/views` directory, and `index.html.twig` is the name of the actual template within the `Product` directory.

Each template filename has two extensions that first specify the format and then the engine for that template; such as `*.html.twig`, `*.html.php`, and `*.css.twig`.

We will get into more details regarding these templates once we move onto building our app.

Forms

Sign up, sign in, add to cart, checkout, all of these and more are actions that make use of HTML forms in web shop applications and beyond. Building forms is one of the most common tasks for developers. One that often takes time to do it right.

Symfony has a `form` component through which we can build HTML forms in an OO way. The component itself is also a standalone library that can be used independently of Symfony.

Let's take a look at the content of the `src/AppBundle/Entity/Customer.php` file, our `Customer` entity class that was auto-generated for us when we defined it via console:

```php
class Customer {
  private $id;
  private $firstname;
  private $lastname;
  private $email;

  public function getId() {
    return $this->id;
  }

  public function setFirstname($firstname) {
    $this->firstname = $firstname;
    return $this;
  }

  public function getFirstname() {
    return $this->firstname;
  }

  public function setLastname($lastname) {
    $this->lastname = $lastname;
    return $this;
  }

  public function getLastname() {
```

```
    return $this->lastname;
  }

  public function setEmail($email) {
    $this->email = $email;
    return $this;
  }

  public function getEmail() {
    return $this->email;
  }
}
```

Here we have a plain PHP class, which does not extend anything nor is in any other way linked to Symfony. It represents a single customer entity, for which it sets and gets the data. With the entity class in place, we would like to render a form that will pick up all of the relevant data used by our class. This is where the Form component comes in place.

When we used the CRUD generator via console earlier, it created the Form class for our Customer entity within the src/AppBundle/Form/CustomerType.php file with content as follows:

```
namespace AppBundle\Form;

use Symfony\Component\Form\AbstractType;
use Symfony\Component\Form\FormBuilderInterface;
use Symfony\Component\OptionsResolver\OptionsResolver;

class CustomerType extends AbstractType
{
  public function buildForm(FormBuilderInterface $builder, array
    $options) {
    $builder
    ->add('firstname')
    ->add('lastname')
    ->add('email')
    ;
  }

  public function configureOptions(OptionsResolver $resolver) {
    $resolver->setDefaults(array(
      'data_class' =>'AppBundle\Entity\Customer'
    ));
  }
}
```

We can see the simplicity behind the form component comes down to the following:

- **Extend form type**: We extend from `Symfony\Component\Form\AbstractType` class

- **Implement buildForm method**: This is where we add actual fields we want to show on the form

- **Implement configureOptions**: This specifies at least the `data_class` configuration which points to our Customer entity.

The form builder object is the one doing the heavy lifting here. It does not take much for it to create a form. With the `form` class in place, let's take a look at the `controller` action in charge of feeding the template with the form. In this case, we will focus on `newAction` within the `src/AppBundle/Controller/CustomerController.php` file, with content shown as follows:

```
$customer = new Customer();
$form = $this->createForm('AppBundle\Form\CustomerType',
  $customer);
$form->handleRequest($request);

if ($form->isSubmitted() && $form->isValid()) {
  $em = $this->getDoctrine()->getManager();
  $em->persist($customer);
  $em->flush();

  return $this->redirectToRoute('customer_show', array('id' =>
    $customer->getId()));
}

return $this->render('customer/new.html.twig', array(
  'customer' => $customer,
  'form' => $form->createView(),
));
```

The preceding code first instantiates the `Customer` entity class. The `$this->createForm(...)` is actually calling `$this->container->get('form.factory')->create(...)`, passing it our `form` class name and instance of `customer` object. We then have the `isSubmitted` and `isValid` check, to see if this is a GET or valid POST request. Based on that check, the code either returns to customer listing or sets the `form` and `customer` instance to be used with the template `customer/new.html.twig`. We will speak more about the actual validation later on.

Finally, lets take a look at the actual template found in the `app/Resources/views/customer/new.html.twig` file:

```twig
{% extends 'base.html.twig' %}

{% block body %}
<h1>Customer creation</h1>

{{ form_start(form) }}
{{ form_widget(form) }}
<input type="submit" value="Create" />
{{ form_end(form) }}

<ul>
  <li>
    <a href="{{ path('customer_index') }}">Back to the list</a>
  </li>
</ul>
{% endblock %}
```

Here we see `extends` and `block` tags, alongside some form of related functions. Symfony adds several form rendering function to Twig as follows:

- `form(view, variables)`
- `form_start(view, variables)`
- `form_end(view, variables)`
- `form_label(view, label, variables)`
- `form_errors(view)`
- `form_widget(view, variables)`
- `form_row(view, variables)`
- `form_rest(view, variables)`

Most of our application forms will be auto-generated like this one, so we are able to get a fully functional CRUD without going too deep into the rest of form functionality.

Configuring Symfony

In order to keep up with modern demands, today's frameworks and applications require a flexible configuration system. Symfony fulfils this role nicely through its robust configuration files and environments concept.

The default Symfony configuration file `config.yml` is located under the `app/config/` directory, with (partial) content sectioned as follows:

```
imports:
  - { resource: parameters.yml }
  - { resource: security.yml }
  - { resource: services.yml }

framework:
...


# Twig Configuration
twig:
...


# Doctrine Configuration
doctrine:
...


# Swiftmailer Configuration
swiftmailer:
...
```

The top-level entries like `framework`, `twig`, `doctrine`, and `swiftmailer` define the configuration of an individual bundle.

Optionally, the configuration file can be of XML or PHP format (`config.xml` or `config.php`). While YAML is simple and readable, XML is more powerful, whereas PHP is powerful but less readable.

We can use the console tool to dump the entire configuration as shown here:

`php bin/console config:dump-reference FrameworkBundle`

The preceding example lists the config file for core `FrameworkBundle`. We can use the same command to show possible configurations for any bundle that implements container extension, something we will look into later on.

Symfony has a nice implementation of environment concept. Looking into the `app/config` directory, we can see that default Symfony project actually starts with three different environments:

- `config_dev.yml`
- `config_prod.yml`
- `config_test.yml`

Each application can run in various environments. Each environment shares the same code, but different configuration. Whereas dev environment might make use of extensive logging, a prod environment might make use of extensive caching.

The way these environments get triggered is via the front controller file, as in the following partial examples:

```
# web/app.php
...
$kernel = new AppKernel('prod', false);
...


# web/app_dev.php
...
$kernel = new AppKernel('dev', true);
...
```

The test environment is missing here, as it is used only when running automated tests and cannot be accessed directly via a browser.

The app/AppKernel.php file is the one that actually loads the configuration, whether it is YAML, XML, or PHP as shown in the following code fragment:

```
public function registerContainerConfiguration(LoaderInterface
  $loader)
{
  $loader->load($this->getRootDir().'/config/config_'.
    $this->getEnvironment().'.yml');
}
```

The environments follow the same concept, whereas each environment imports the base configuration file and then modifies its values to suit the needs of the specific environment.

The bundle system

Most of the popular frameworks and platforms support some form of modules, plugins, extensions or bundles. For most of the time, the difference really lies just in the naming, while the concept of extensibility and modularity is the same. With Symfony, these modular blocks are called bundles.

Bundles are a first-class citizen in Symfony, as they support all of the operations available to other components. Everything in Symfony is a bundle, even the core framework. Bundles enable us to build modularized applications, whereas the entire code for a given feature is contained within a single directory.

A single bundle holds all its PHP files, templates, style sheets, JavaScript files, tests, and anything else in one root directory.

When we first setup our test app, it created an `AppBundle` for us, under the `src` directory. As we moved forward with the auto-generated CRUD, we saw our bundle getting all sorts of directories and files.

For a bundle to be noticed by Symfony, it needs to be added to the `app/AppKernel.php` file, with the `registerBundles` method as shown here:

```
public function registerBundles()
{
  $bundles = [
    new Symfony\Bundle\FrameworkBundle\FrameworkBundle(),
    new Symfony\Bundle\SecurityBundle\SecurityBundle(),
    new Symfony\Bundle\TwigBundle\TwigBundle(),
    new Symfony\Bundle\SwiftmailerBundle\SwiftmailerBundle(),
    new Doctrine\Bundle\DoctrineBundle\DoctrineBundle(),
    //…
    new AppBundle\AppBundle(),
  ];

  //…

  return $bundles;
}
```

Creating a new bundle is as simple as creating a single PHP file. Let's go ahead and create an `src/TestBundle/TestBundle.php` file with content that looks like:

```
namespace TestBundle;

use Symfony\Component\HttpKernel\Bundle\Bundle;

class TestBundle extends Bundle
{
  …
}
```

Once the file is in place, all we need to do is to register it via the `registerBundles` method of the `app/AppKernel.php` file as shown here:

```
class AppKernel extends Kernel {
//…
  public function registerBundles() {
```

```
    $bundles = [
      // …
      new TestBundle\TestBundle(),
      // …
    ];
    return $bundles;
  }
  //…
}
```

An even easier way to create a bundle would be to just run a console command as follows:

php bin/console generate:bundle --namespace=Foggyline/TestBundle

This would trigger a series of questions about bundle that in the end results in bundle creation that looks like the following screenshot:

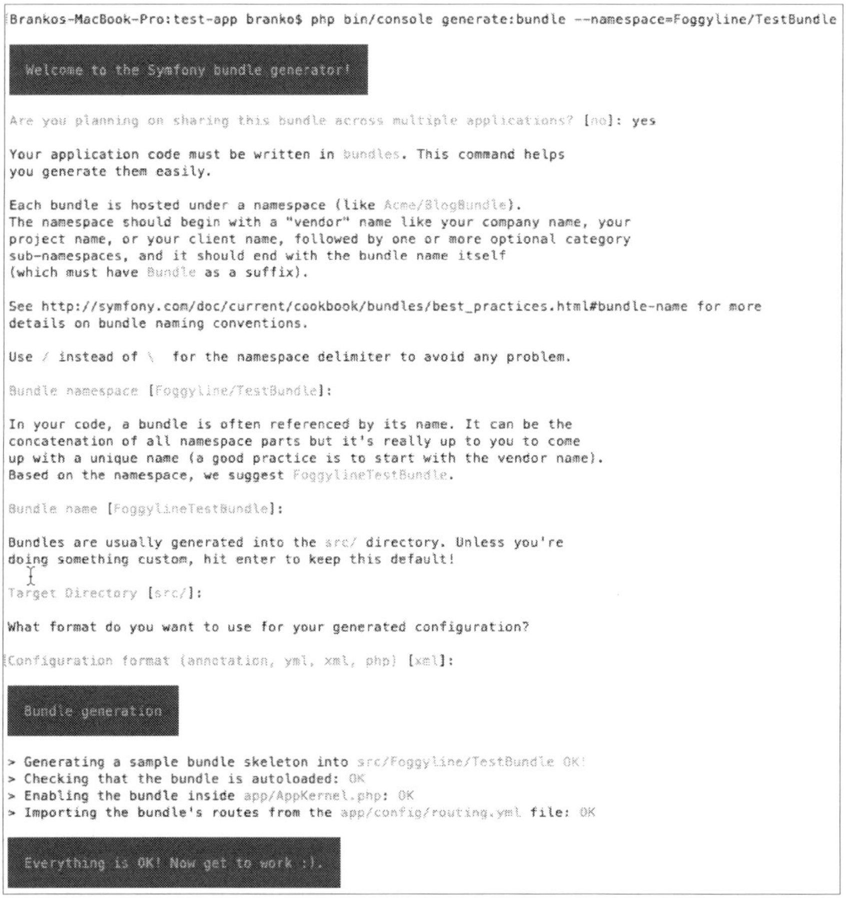

Once the process is complete, a new bundle with several directories and files is created as shown in the following screenshot:

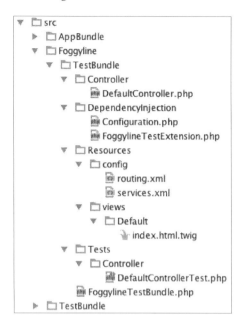

Bundle generator was kind enough to create controller, dependency injection extension extension, routing, prepare services configuration, templates, and even tests. Since we chose to share our bundle, Symfony opted for XML as default configuration format. The dependency extension simply means we can access our bundle configuration by using `foggyline_test` as the root element in Symfony's main `config.yml`. The actual `foggyline_test` element is defined within the `DependencyInjection/Configuration.php` file.

Databases and Doctrine

Databases are the backbone of almost every web application. Every time we need to store or retrieve data, we do so with the help of databases. The challenge in the modern OOP world is to abstract the database so that our PHP code is database agnostic. MySQL is probably the most known database in the PHP world. PHP itself has a great support for working with MySQL, whether it is via the `mysqli_*` extension or via PDO. However, both approaches are MySQL specific, to o close to database. Doctrine solves this problem by introducing a level of abstraction, enabling us to work with PHP objects that represent tables, rows, and their relations in MySQL.

Doctrine is completely decoupled from Symfony, so using it is completely optional. The great thing about it, however, is that the Symfony console provides great auto-generated CRUD based on Doctrine ORM, as we saw in previous examples when creating Customer entity.

As soon as we created the project, Symfony provided us with an auto-generated `app/config/parameters.yml` file. This is the file in which we, among other things, provide database access information as shown in the following example:

```
parameters:
database_host: 127.0.0.1
database_port: null
database_name: symfony
database_user: root
database_password: mysql
```

Once we configure proper parameters, we can use console generation features.

It is worth noting that parameters within this file are merely a convention, as `app/config/config.yml` is pulling them under `doctrine dbal` configuration like the one shown here:

```
doctrine:
dbal:
  driver:    pdo_mysql
  host:      "%database_host%"
  port:      "%database_port%"
  dbname:    "%database_name%"
  user:      "%database_user%"
  password:  "%database_password%"
  charset:   UTF8
```

The Symfony console tool allows us to drop and create a database based on this config, which comes in handy during development, as shown in the following code block:

```
php bin/console doctrine:database:drop --force
php bin/console doctrine:database:create
```

We saw previously how the console tool enables us to create entities and their mapping into database tables. This will suffice for our needs throughout this book. Once we have them created, we need to be able to perform CRUD operations on them. If we gloss over the auto-generated CRUD controller `src/AppBundle/Controller/CustomerController.php` file, we can the CRUD related code as follows:

```
// Fetch all entities
$customers = $em->getRepository('AppBundle:Customer')->findAll();
```

```
// Persist single entity (existing or new)
$em = $this->getDoctrine()->getManager();
$em->persist($customer);
$em->flush();

// Delete single entity
$em = $this->getDoctrine()->getManager();
$em->remove($customer);
$em->flush();
```

There is a lot more to be said about Doctrine, which is far out of the scope of this book. More information can be found at the official page (http://www.doctrine-project.org).

Testing

Nowadays testing has become an integral part of every modern web application. Usually the term testing implies unit and functional testing. Unit testing is about testing our PHP classes. Every single PHP class is considered to be a unit, thus the name unit test. Functional tests on the other hand test various layers of our application, usually concentrated on testing the functionality overall, like the sign in or sign up process.

The PHP ecosystem has a great unit testing framework called **PHPUnit**, available for download at https://phpunit.de. It enables us to write primarily unit, but also functional type tests. The great thing about Symfony is that it comes with built in support for PHPUnit.

Before we can start running Symfony's tests, we need to make sure we have PHPUnit installed and available as console command. When executed, PHPUnit automatically tries to pick up and read testing configuration from phpunit.xml or phpunit.xml.dist within the current working directory, if available. By default Symfony comes with a phpunit.xml.dist file in its root folder, thus making it possible for the phpunit command to pick up its test configuration.

The following is a partial example of a default phpunit.xml.dist file:

```
<phpunit ... >
  <php>
    <ini name="error_reporting" value="-1" />
    <server name="KERNEL_DIR" value="app/" />
  </php>

  <testsuites>
```

```
    <testsuite name="Project Test Suite">
      <directory>tests</directory>
    </testsuite>
  </testsuites>

  <filter>
    <whitelist>
      <directory>src</directory>
      <exclude>
        <directory>src/*Bundle/Resources</directory>
        <directory>src/*/*Bundle/Resources</directory>
        <directory>src/*/Bundle/*Bundle/Resources</directory>
      </exclude>
    </whitelist>
  </filter>
</phpunit>
```

The testsuites element defines the directory tests, in which all of our tests are located. The filter element with its children is used to configure the whitelist for the code coverage reporting. The php element with its children is used to configure PHP settings, constants, and global variables.

Running a phpunit command against a default project like ours would result in output like the following:

```
Brankos-MacBook-Pro:test-app branko$ phpunit
PHPUnit 4.7.6 by Sebastian Bergmann and contributors.

.

Time: 545 ms, Memory: 17.00Mb

OK (1 test, 2 assertions)
```

Note that bundle tests are not automatically picked up. Our src/AppBundle/ Tests/Controller/CustomerControllerTest.php file, which was created for us automatically when we used auto-generated CRUD, was not executed. Not because its content is commented out by default, but because the bundle test directory isn't visible to phpunit. To make it execute, we need to extend the phpunit.xml.dist file by adding to directory testsuite as follows:

```
<testsuites>
  <testsuite name="Project Test Suite">
    <directory>tests</directory>
    <directory>src/AppBundle/Tests</directory>
  </testsuite>
</testsuites>
```

Depending on how we build our application, we might want to add all of our bundles to the `testsuite` list, even if we plan on distributing bundles independently.

There is plenty more to be said about testing. We will do so bit by bit as we progress through further chapters and cover the needs of individual bundles. For the moment, it is suffice to know how to trigger tests and how to add new locations to testing configuration.

Validation

Validation plays an essential role in modern applications. When talking about web applications, we can say we differentiate between two main types of validation; form data and persisted data validation. Taking input from a user via a web form should be validated, the same as any persisting data that goes into a database.

Symfony excels here by providing a Validation component based on JSR 303 Bean Validation drafted and available at `http://beanvalidation.org/1.0/spec/`. If we look back at our `app/config/config.yml`, under the `framework` root element, we can see that the `validation` service is turned on by default:

```
framework:
  validation:{ enable_annotations: true }
```

We can access the validation service from any controller class by simply calling it via the `$this->get('validator')` expression, as shown in the following example:

```
$customer = new Customer();

$validator = $this->get('validator');

$errors = $validator->validate($customer);

if (count($crrors) > 0) {
  // Handle error state
}

// Handle valid state
```

The problem with the example above is that validation would never return any errors. The reason for this is that we do not have any assertions set on our class. The console auto-generated CRUD did not really define any constraints on our `Customer` class. We can confirm that by trying to add a new customer and typing in any text in the e-mail field, as we can see the e-mail wont be validated.

Let's go ahead and edit the `src/AppBundle/Entity/Customer.php` file by adding the `@Assert\Email` function to the `$email` property like the one shown here:

```
//...
use Symfony\Component\Validator\Constraints as Assert;
//...
class Customer
{
    //...
    /**
     * @var string
     *
     * @ORM\Column(name="email", type="string", length=255, unique=true)
     * @Assert\Email(
     *      checkMX = true,
     *      message = "Email '{{ value }}' is invalid.",
     * )
     */
    private $email;
    //...
}
```

The great thing about assertions constraints is that they accept parameters just as functions. We can therefore fine-tune individual constraints to our specific needs. If we now try to skip or add a faulty e-mail address, we would get a message like **Email "'john@gmail.test'" is invalid**.

There are numerous constraints available, for the full list we can consult the `http://symfony.com/doc/current/book/validation.html` page.

Constraints can be applied to a class property or a public getter method. While the property constraints are most common and easy to use, the getter method constraints allow us to specify more complex validation rules.

Let's take look at the `newAction` method of an `src/AppBundle/Controller/CustomerController.php` file as follows:

```
$customer = new Customer();
$form = $this->createForm('AppBundle\Form\CustomerType',
   $customer);
$form->handleRequest($request);

if ($form->isSubmitted() && $form->isValid()) {
// ...
```

Here we see an instance of a `CustomerType` form being bind to the `Customer` instance. The actual GET or POST request data is passed to an instance of a form via the `handleRequest` method. The form is now able to understand entity validation constraints and respond properly via its `isValid` method call. What this means is that we do not have to manually validate by using the validation service ourselves, the forms can do it for us.

We will continue to expand on validation features as we progress through individual bundles.

Summary

Throughout this chapter we touched on some important functionality, which makes Symfony so great. Controllers, templates, Doctrine, ORM, forms, and validation make for a complete solution from data presentation and persistence. We have seen the flexibility and power behind each of the components. The bundle system takes it a step further by wrapping these into individual mini applications, or modules. We are now able to take full control of incoming HTTP requests, manipulate the data store, and present data to the user, all of this within a single bundle.

Moving forward, in the next chapter, we will utilize the insights and knowledge gained throughout the previous chapters to finally start building our modular application according to the requirements.

6
Building the Core Module

Up until now we have familiarized ourselves with the latest changes in PHP 7, design patterns, design principles, and popular PHP frameworks. We also took a more detailed look into Symfony as our framework of choice moving forward. We have now finally reached a point where we can start building our modular application. Building modular applications with Symfony is done via the bundles mechanism. Terminology-wise, from this point on, we will consider bundle and module to be the same thing.

In this chapter we will be covering the following topics with respect to the core module:

- Requirements
- Dependencies
- Implementation
- Unit testing
- Functional testing

Requirements

Looking back in *Chapter 4*, *Requirement Specification for Modular Web Shop App*, and the wireframes presented there, we can outline some of the requirements this module will have. The core module is going to be used to set general, application-wide features, as follows:

- Include Foundation CSS for sites to the project
- Build a home page
- Build other static pages

- Build a Contact Us page
- Setup a basic firewall, where admin users can manage all the auto-generated CRUD from other modules later on

Dependencies

The core module on its own does not have any specific dependencies on other modules that we are going to write as part of this book, or any other third-party module outside of standard Symfony installation.

Implementation

We start by creating an entirely new Symfony project, running the following console command:

```
symfony new shop
```

This creates a new `shop` directory with all of the required files needed to run our application in the browser. Among these files and directories is the `src/AppBundle` directory, which is actually our core module. Before we can run our application in the browser, we need to map the newly created `shop` directory to a hostname, let's say `shop.app`, so we can access it in the browser via `http://shop.app` URL. Once this is done, if we open `http://shop.app`, we should see **Welcome to Symfony 3.1.0** screen as shown here:

Welcome to
Symfony 3.1.0

Your application is now ready. You can start working on it at:
`/Users/branko/www/shop/`

What's next?

Read the documentation to learn
How to create your first page in Symfony

Though we have no need for the database just yet, other modules we will develop later on will assume database connection, so it's worth setting it up right from the start. We do so by configuring `app/config/parameters.yml` with proper database connection parameters.

We then download Foundation for Sites from `http://foundation.zurb.com/` `sites.html`. Once downloaded, we need to unpack it and copy over the `/js` and `/css` directories into the `Symfony` `/web` directory as shown in the following screenshot:

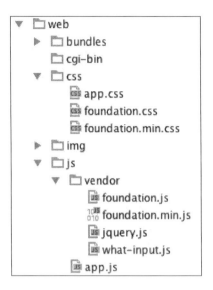

 It is worth noting that this is a simplified setup of Foundation that we are using with our module, where we simply use CSS and JavaScript files without setting up anything relating to Sass.

With Foundation CSS and JavaScript files in place, we edit the `app/Resources/` `views/base.html.twig` file as follows:

```
<!doctype html>
<html class="no-js"lang="en">
  <head>
    <meta charset="utf-8"/>
    <meta http-equiv="x-ua-compatible" content="ie=edge">
    <meta name="viewport" content="width=device-width, initial-
      scale=1.0"/>
    <title>{% block title %}Welcome!{% endblock %}</title>
    <link rel="stylesheet"href="{{ asset('css/foundation.css')
      }}"/>
    {% block stylesheets%}{% endblock %}
  </head>
  <body>
    <!-- START BODY -->
```

```
<!-- TOP-MENU -->
<!-- SYSTEM-WIDE-MESSAGES -->
<!-- PER-PAGE-BODY -->
<!-- FOOTER -->
<!-- START BODY -->
<script src="{{ asset('js/vendor/jquery.js') }}"></script>
<script src="{{ asset('js/vendor/what-input.js')
  }}"></script>
<script src="{{ asset('js/vendor/foundation.js')
  }}"></script>
<script>
  $(document).foundation();
</script>
{% block javascripts%}{% endblock %}
</body>
</html>
```

Here we are setting the entire head and before body end areas, with all the necessary CSS and JavaScript loading. The Twigs `asset` tag helps us with building URL paths, where we simply pass on the URL path itself and it builds a complete URL for us. In regard to the actual body of the page, there are several things to consider here. How are we going to build category, customer, and checkout menus? At this point we do not have any of these modules, and neither do we want to make them mandatory for our core module. So how do we solve the challenge of accounting for something that is not there yet?

What we can do for category, customer, and checkout menus is to define global Twig variables for each of those menu items that will then be used to render the menu. These variables will be filed via proper services. Since the core bundle is not aware of future catalog, customer, and checkout modules, we will initially create a few dummy services and hook them to global Twig variables. Later on, when we develop catalog, customer, and checkout modules, those modules will override the appropriate services, thus providing the right values for into menus.

This approach might not fit ideally with the notion of modular application, but it will suffice for our needs, as we are not hard-coding any dependencies as such.

We start off by adding the following entry into the `app/config/config.yml` file:

```
twig:
# ...
globals:
category_menu: '@category_menu'
customer_menu: '@customer_menu'
checkout_menu: '@checkout_menu'
```

```
products_bestsellers: '@bestsellers'
products_onsale: '@onsale'
```

The `category_menu_items`, `customer_menu_items`, `checkout_menu_items`, `products_bestsellers`, and `products_onsale` variables become global Twig variables that we can use in any Twig template as shown in the following example:

```
<ul>
  {% for category in category_menu.getItems() %}
  <li>{{ category.name }}</li>
  {% endfor %}
</ul>
```

The @ character in the Twig global variable `config` is used to denote a beginning of the service name. This is the service that will provide a value object for our Twig variable. Next, we go ahead and create the actual `category_menu`, `customer_menu`, `checkout_menu`, `bestsellers`, and `onsale` services by modifying `app/config/services.yml` as follows:

```
services:
category_menu:
  class: AppBundle\Service\Menu\Category
customer_menu:
  class: AppBundle\Service\Menu\Customer
checkout_menu:
  class: AppBundle\Service\Menu\Checkout
bestsellers:
  class: AppBundle\Service\Menu\BestSellers
onsale:
  class: AppBundle\Service\Menu\OnSale
```

Furthermore, we create each of the listed service classes under the `src/AppBundle/Service/Menu/` directory. We start with the `src/AppBundle/Service/Menu/Bestsellers.php` file with the following content:

```
namespace AppBundle\Service\Menu;

class BestSellers {
  public function getItems() {
    // Note, this can be arranged as per some "Product"
      interface, so to know what dummy data to return
    return array(
      ay('path' =>'iphone', 'name' =>'iPhone', 'img' =>
        '/img/missing-image.png', 'price' => 49.99,
        'add_to_cart_url' =>'#'),
      array('path' =>'lg', 'name' =>'LG', 'img' =>
```

```
          '/img/missing-image.png', 'price' => 19.99,
          'add_to_cart_url' =>'#'),
        array('path' =>'samsung', 'name' =>'Samsung', 'img'
          =>'/img/missing-image.png', 'price' => 29.99,
          'add_to_cart_url' =>'#'),
        array('path' =>'lumia', 'name' =>'Lumia', 'img' =>
          '/img/missing-image.png', 'price' => 19.99,
          'add_to_cart_url' =>'#'),
        array('path' =>'edge', 'name' =>'Edge', 'img' =>
          '/img/missing-image.png', 'price' => 39.99,
          'add_to_cart_url' =>'#'),
      );
  }
}
```

We then add the `src/AppBundle/Service/Menu/Category.php` file with content as follows:

```
class Category {
  public function getItems() {
    return array(
      array('path' =>'women', 'label' =>'Women'),
      array('path' =>'men', 'label' =>'Men'),
      array('path' =>'sport', 'label' =>'Sport'),
    );
  }
}
```

Following this, we add the `src/AppBundle/Service/Menu/Checkout.php` file with content as shown here:

```
class Checkout
{
  public function getItems()
  {
    // Initial dummy menu
    return array(
      array('path' =>'cart', 'label' =>'Cart (3)'),
      array('path' =>'checkout', 'label' =>'Checkout'),
    );
  }
}
```

Once this is done, we will go on and add the following content to the
src/AppBundle/Service/Menu/Customer.php file:

```
class Customer
{
  public function getItems()
  {
    // Initial dummy menu
    return array(
      array('path' =>'account', 'label' =>'John Doe'),
      array('path' =>'logout', 'label' =>'Logout'),
    );
  }
}
```

We then add the src/AppBundle/Service/Menu/OnSale.php file with
the following content:

```
class OnSale
{
  public function getItems()
  {
    // Note, this can be arranged as per some "Product" interface,
      so to know what dummy data to return
    return array(
      array('path' =>'iphone', 'name' =>'iPhone', 'img' =>
        '/img/missing-image.png', 'price' => 19.99,
        'add_to_cart_url' =>'#'),
      array('path' =>'lg', 'name' =>'LG', 'img' =>
        '/img/missing-image.png', 'price'       => 29.99,
        'add_to_cart_url' =>'#'),
      array('path' =>'samsung', 'name' =>'Samsung', 'img'
        =>'/img/missing-image.png', 'price' => 39.99,
        'add_to_cart_url' =>'#'),
      array('path' ->'lumia', 'name' ->'Lumia', 'img' =>
        '/img/missing-image.png', 'price' => 49.99,
        'add_to_cart_url' =>'#'),
      array('path' =>'edge', 'name' =>'Edge', 'img' =>
        '/img/missing-image.png', 'price' => 69.99,
        'add_to_cart_url' =>'#'),
      ;
  }
}
```

We have now defined five global Twig variables that will be used to build our application menus. Even though variables are now hooked to a dummy service that returns nothing more than a dummy array, we have effectively decoupled menu items into other soon-to-be built modules. When we get to building our category, customer, and checkout modules later on, we will simply write a service override and properly fill the menu items array with real items. This would be the ideal situation.

> Ideally we would want our services to return data as per a certain interface, to make sure whoever overrides it or extends it does so by interface. Since we are trying to keep our application at a minimum, we will proceed with simple arrays.

We can now go back to our `app/Resources/views/base.html.twig` file and replace `<!-- TOP-MENU -->` from the preceding code with the following:

```
<div class="title-bar" data-responsive-toggle="appMenu" data-hide-
  for="medium">
  <button class="menu-icon" type="button" data-toggle></button>
  <div class="title-bar-title">Menu</div>
</div>

<div class="top-bar" id="appMenu">
  <div class="top-bar-left">
    {# category_menu is global twig var filled from service,
      and later overriden by another module service #}
    <ul class="menu">
      <li><a href="{{ path('homepage') }}">HOME</a></li>
        {% block category_menu %}
        {% for link in category_menu.getItems() %}
      <li><a href="{{ link.path }}">{{ link.label }}</li></a>
      {% endfor %}
      {% endblock %}
    </ul>
  </div>
  <div class="top-bar-right">
    <ul class="menu">
      {# customer_menu is global twig var filled from
        service, and later overriden by another module
        service #}
      {% block customer_menu %}
      {% for link in customer_menu.getItems() %}
      <li><a href="{{ link.path }}">{{ link.label }}</li></a>
      {% endfor %}
```

```
    {% endblock %}
    {# checkout_menu is global twig var filled from
      service, and later overriden by another module service #}
    {% block checkout_menu %}
    {% for link in checkout_menu.getItems() %}
    <li><a href="{{ link.path }}">{{ link.label }}</li></a>
    {% endfor %}
    {% endblock %}
  </ul>
 </div>
</div>
```

We can then replace `<!-- SYSTEM-WIDE-MESSAGES -->` with the following:

```
<div class="row column">
  {% for flash_message in app.session.flashBag.get('alert') %}
  <div class="alert callout">
    {{ flash_message }}
  </div>
  {% endfor %}
  {% for flash_message in app.session.flashBag.get('warning') %}
  <div class="warning callout">
    {{ flash_message }}
  </div>
  {% endfor %}
  {% for flash_message in app.session.flashBag.get('success') %}
  <div class="success callout">
    {{ flash_message }}
  </div>
  {% endfor %}
</div>
```

We replace `<!-- PER-PAGE-BODY -->` with the following:

```
<div class="row column">
  {% block body %}{% endblock %}
</div>
```

We replace `<!-- FOOTER -->` with the following:

```
<div class="row column">
  <ul class="menu">
    <li><a href="{{ path('about') }}">About Us</a></li>
    <li><a href="{{ path('customer_service') }}">Customer
      Service</a></li>
    <li><a href="{{ path('privacy_cookie') }}">Privacy and
```

```
      Cookie Policy</a></li>
    <li><a href="{{ path('orders_returns') }}">Orders and
       Returns</a></li>
    <li><a href="{{ path('contact') }}">Contact Us</a></li>
  </ul>
</div>
```

Now we can go ahead and edit the `src/AppBundle/Controller/DefaultController.php` file and add the following code to it:

```php
/**
 * @Route("/", name="homepage")
 */
public function indexAction(Request $request)
{
  return $this->render('AppBundle:default:index.html.twig');
}


/**
 * @Route("/about", name="about")
 */
public function aboutAction()
{
  return $this->render('AppBundle:default:about.html.twig');
}


/**
 * @Route("/customer-service", name="customer_service")
 */
public function customerServiceAction()
{
  return $this->render('AppBundle:default:
customer-service.html.twig');
}


/**
 * @Route("/orders-and-returns", name="orders_returns")
 */
public function ordersAndReturnsAction()
{
  return $this->render('AppBundle:default:orders-
returns.html.twig');
}


/**
```

```
 * @Route("/privacy-and-cookie-policy", name="privacy_cookie")
 */
public function privacyAndCookiePolicyAction()
{
  return $this->render('AppBundle:default:privacy-
    cookie.html.twig');
}
```

All of the used template files (`about.html.twig`, `customer-service.html.twig`, `orders-returns.html.twig`, `privacy-cookie.html.twig`) residing within the `src/AppBundle/Resources/views/default` directory can be similarly defined as follows:

```
{% extends 'base.html.twig' %}

{% block body %}
<div class="row">
  <h1>About Us</h1>
</div>
<div class="row">
  <p>Loremipsum dolor sit amet, consecteturadipiscingelit...</p>
</div>
{% endblock %}
```

Here we are merely wrapping header and content into the `div` elements with the `row` class, just to give it some structure. The result should be pages similar to those shown here:

The **Contact Us** page requires a different approach as it will contain a form. To build a form we use Symfony's `Form` component by adding the following to the `src/AppBundle/Controller/DefaultController.php` file:

```
/**
 * @Route("/contact", name="contact")
 */
public function contactAction(Request $request) {

  // Build a form, with validation rules in place
  $form = $this->createFormBuilder()
```

```
    ->add('name', TextType::class, array(
      'constraints' => new NotBlank()
    ))
    ->add('email', EmailType::class, array(
      'constraints' => new Email()
    ))
    ->add('message', TextareaType::class, array(
      'constraints' => new Length(array('min' => 3))
    ))
     ->add('save', SubmitType::class, array(
      'label' =>'Reach Out!',
      'attr' => array('class' =>'button'),
    ))
    ->getForm();

    // Check if this is a POST type request and if so, handle form
    if ($request->isMethod('POST')) {
      $form->handleRequest($request);

      if ($form->isSubmitted() && $form->isValid()) {
        $this->addFlash(
          'success',
          'Your form has been submitted. Thank you.'
        );

        // todo: Send an email out...

        return $this->redirect($this->generateUrl('contact'));
      }
    }

    // Render "contact us" page
    return $this->render('AppBundle:default:contact.html.twig',
      array(
      'form' => $form->createView()
    ));
  }
```

Here we started off by building a form via form builder. The add methods accept both field definitions and field constraints upon which validation can be based. We then added a check for the HTTP POST method, in case of which we feed the form with request parameters and run validation against it.

With the `contactAction` method in place, we still need a template file to actually render the form. We do so by adding the `src/AppBundle/Resources/views/default/contact.html.twig` file with content that follows:

```twig
{% extends 'base.html.twig' %}

{% block body %}

<div class="row">
  <h1>Contact Us</h1>
</div>

<div class="row">
  {{ form_start(form) }}
  {{ form_widget(form) }}
  {{ form_end(form) }}
</div>
{% endblock %}
```

Based on these few tags, Twig handles the form rendering for us. The resulting browser output is a page as shown in the following:

We are almost there with getting all of our pages ready. One thing is missing, though, the body area of our home page. Unlike other pages with static content, this one is actually dynamic, as it lists bestsellers and products on sale. This data is expected to come from other modules, which are not available yet. Still, this does not mean we cannot prepare dummy placeholders for them. Let's go ahead and edit the `app/Resources/views/default/index.html.twig` file as follows:

```twig
{% extends 'base.html.twig' %}
{% block body %}
<!--products_bestsellers -->
```

```
<!--products_onsale -->
{% endblock %}
```

Now we need to replace `<!-- products_bestsellers -->` with the following:

```
{% if products_bestsellers %}
<h2 class="text-center">Best Sellers</h2>
<div class="row products_bestsellers text-center small-up-1
  medium-up-3 large-up-5" data-equalizer data-equalize-by-
  row="true">
  {% for product in products_bestsellers.getItems() %}
  <div class="column product">
    <img src="{{ asset(product.img) }}" alt="missing image"/>
    <a href="{{ product.path }}">{{ product.name }}</a>
    <div>${{ product.price }}</div>
    <div><a class="small button"href="{{ product.add_to_cart_url
      }}">Add to Cart</a></div>
  </div>
  {% endfor %}
</div>
{% endif %}
```

Now we need to replace `<!-- products_onsale -->`with the following:

```
{% if products_onsale %}
<h2 class="text-center">On Sale</h2>
<div class="row products_onsale text-center small-up-1 medium-up-3
  large-up-5" data-equalizer data-equalize-by-row="true">
  {% for product in products_onsale.getItems() %}
  <div class="column product">
    <img src="{{ asset(product.img) }}" alt="missing image"/>
    <a href="{{ product.path }}">{{ product.name }}</a>
  <div>${{ product.price }}</div>
  <div><a class="small button"
    href="{{ product.add_to_cart_url }}"
    >Add to Cart</a></div>
  </div>
  {% endfor %}
</div>
{% endif %}
```

 The `http://dummyimage.com` enables us to create a placeholder images for our app.

At this point we should be seeing the home page as shown here:

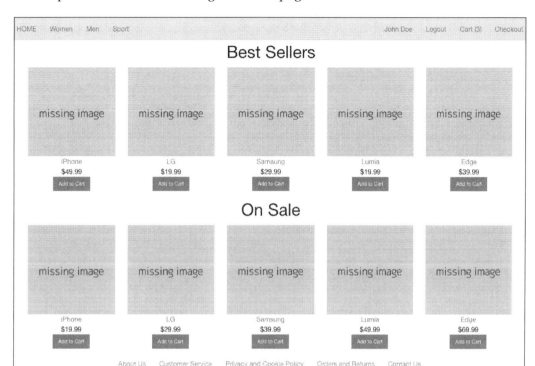

Configuring application-wide security

What we are trying to achieve as part of our applicationwide security is to set some basic protection against future customers or any other user being able to access and use future auto-generated CRUD controllers. We do so by modifying the `app/config/security.yml` file. There are several components to the `security.yml` file we need to address: Firewalls, access control, providers, and encoders. If we observe the auto-generated CRUD from the previous test app, it becomes clear that we need to protect the following from customer access:

- `GET|POST /new`
- `GET|POST /{id}/edit`
- `DELETE /{id}`

In another words, everything that has /new and /edit in the URL, and everything that is of DELETE method, needs to be protected from the customer. With that in mind, we will use Symfony security features to create an in-memory user of role ROLE_ADMIN. We will then create an access control list that allows only ROLE_ADMIN to access the resources we just mentioned, and a firewall that triggers an HTTP basic authentication login form when we try to access these resources.

Using an in-memory provider means hard-coding users in our security.yml file. For purposes of our application, we will do so for the admin type of users. The actual password, however, does not need to be hard-coded. Assuming we will use 1L6lllW9zXg0 for the password, let's jump to the console and type in the following command:

```
php bin/console security:encode-password
```

This will produce an output as follows.

```
Brankos-MacBook-Pro:shop branko$ php bin/console security:encode-password

Symfony Password Encoder Utility

 Type in your password to be encoded:
 >

 ------------------   -----------------------------------------------------------
 Key                  Value
 ------------------   -----------------------------------------------------------
 Encoder used         Symfony\Component\Security\Core\Encoder\BCryptPasswordEncoder
 Encoded password     $2y$12$wvdE1Fjb29hgY6//g/khuedLq3wQOuLbZ/tYqzxI9PfIfBF24fEfa
 ------------------   -----------------------------------------------------------

 ! [NOTE] Bcrypt encoder used: the encoder generated its own built-in salt.

 [OK] Password encoding succeeded
```

We can now edit security.yml by adding an in-memory provider and copy-paste the generated encoded password into it, as shown here:

```
security:
    providers:
        in_memory:
            memory:
                users:
                    john:
                        password:
$2y$12$DFozWehwPkp14sVXr7.IbusW8ugvmZs9dQMExlggtyEa/TxZUStnO
                        roles: 'ROLE_ADMIN'
```

Here we defined a user john of role ROLE_ADMIN with an encoded 1L6lllW9zXg0 password.

Once we have the providers in place, we can go ahead and add encoders to our `security.yml` file. Otherwise Symfony would not know what to make of the current password assigned to `john` user:

```
security:
    encoders:
        Symfony\Component\Security\Core\User\User:
            algorithm: bcrypt
            cost: 12
```

Then we add the firewall as follows:

```
security:
    firewalls:
        guard_new_edit:
            pattern: /(new)|(edit)
            methods: [GET, POST]
            anonymous: ~
            http_basic: ~
        guard_delete:
            pattern: /
            methods: [DELETE]
            anonymous: ~
            http_basic: ~
```

The `guard_new_edit` and `guard_delete` names are freely given names to our two application firewalls. The `guard_new_edit` firewall will be intercepting all GET and POST requests to any route containing the `/new` or `/edit` string in its URL. The `guard_delete` firewall will be intercepting any HTTP DELETE method on any URL. Once these firewalls kick in, they will show an HTTP basic authentication form, and only allow access if the user is logged in.

Then we add the access control list as follows:

```
security:
    access_control:
        # protect any possible auto-generated CRUD actions from
        everyone's access
        - { path: /new, roles: ROLE_ADMIN }
        - { path: /edit, roles: ROLE_ADMIN }
        - { path: /, roles: ROLE_ADMIN, methods: [DELETE] }
```

With these entries in place, an one who tries to access any URL with any of the patterns defined under `access_control` will be presented with the browser login as shown here:

The only user that can login is `john` with the password `1L6l11W9zXg0`. Once authenticated, the user can access all the CRUD links. This should be enough for our simple application.

Unit testing

Our current module has no specific classes other than the controller class and the dummy service class. Therefore, we won't bother ourselves with unit tests here.

Functional testing

Before we start writing our functional tests, we need to edit the `phpunit.xml.dist` file by adding our bundle `Tests` directory to the `testsuite` paths, as follows:

```
<testsuites>
  <testsuite name="Project Test Suite">
    <-- ... other elements ... -->
      <directory>src/AppBundle/Tests</directory>
    <-- ... other elements ... -->
  </testsuite>
</testsuites>
```

Our functional tests will cover only one controller, since we have no other. We start off by creating a `src/AppBundle/Tests/Controller/DefaultControllerTest.php` file with content as follows:

```
namespace AppBundle\Tests\Controller;
```

```
use Symfony\Bundle\FrameworkBundle\Test\WebTestCase;

class DefaultControllerTest extends WebTestCase
{
//...
}
```

The next step is to test each and every one of our controller actions. At the very least we should test if the page content is being outputted properly.

 To get an auto-complete in our IDE we can download the PHPUnit phar file from the official site here https://phpunit.de. Once downloaded, we can simply add it to the root of our project, so that IDE, like **PHPStorm**, picks it up. This makes it easy to follow up on all those $this->assert method calls and their parameters.

The first thing we want to test is our home page. We do so by adding the following to the body of the DefaultControllerTest class.

```
public function testHomepage()
{
  // @var \Symfony\Bundle\FrameworkBundle\Client
  $client = static::createClient();
  /** @var \Symfony\Component\DomCrawler\Crawler */
  $crawler = $client->request('GET', '/');

  // Check if homepage loads OK
  $this->assertEquals(200, $client->getResponse()
    ->getStatusCode());

  // Check if top bar left menu is present
  $this->assertNotEmpty($crawler->filter('.top-bar-left li')
    ->count());

  // Check if top bar right menu is present
  $this->assertNotEmpty($crawler->filter('.top-bar-right li')
    ->count());

  // Check if footer is present
  $this->assertNotEmpty($crawler->filter('.footer li')
    ->children()->count());
}
```

Here we are checking several things at once. We are checking with the page loads OK, with HTTP 200 status. Then we are grabbing the left and right menu and counting their the items to see if they have any. If all of the individual checks pass, the `testHomepage` test is considered to have passed.

We further test all of the static pages by adding the following to the `DefaultControllerTest` class:

```
public function testStaticPages()
{
    // @var \Symfony\Bundle\FrameworkBundle\Client
    $client = static::createClient();
    /** @var \Symfony\Component\DomCrawler\Crawler */

    // Test About Us page
    $crawler = $client->request('GET', '/about');
    $this->assertEquals(200, $client->getResponse()
      ->getStatusCode());
    $this->assertContains('About Us', $crawler->filter('h1')
      ->text());

    // Test Customer Service page
    $crawler = $client->request('GET', '/customer-service');
    $this->assertEquals(200, $client->getResponse()
      ->getStatusCode());
    $this->assertContains('Customer Service', $crawler
      ->filter('h1')->text());

    // Test Privacy and Cookie Policy page
    $crawler = $client->request('GET', '/privacy-and-cookie-
      policy');
    $this->assertEquals(200, $client->getResponse()
      ->getStatusCode());
    $this->assertContains('Privacy and Cookie Policy', $crawler
      ->filter('h1')->text());

    // Test Orders and Returns page
    $crawler = $client->request('GET', '/orders-and-returns');
    $this->assertEquals(200, $client->getResponse()
      ->getStatusCode());
    $this->assertContains('Orders and Returns', $crawler
      ->filter('h1')->text());

    // Test Contact Us page
    $crawler = $client->request('GET', '/contact');
```

```
$this->assertEquals(200, $client->getResponse()
    ->getStatusCode());
$this->assertContains('Contact Us', $crawler->filter('h1')
    ->text());
}
```

Here we are running the same `assertEquals` and `assertContains` functions for all of our pages. We are merely trying to confirm that each page is loaded with HTTP 200, and that the proper value is returned for the page title, that is to say, the `h1` element.

Finally, we address the form submission test which we perform by adding the following into the `DefaultControllerTest` class:

```
public function testContactFormSubmit()
{
    // @var \Symfony\Bundle\FrameworkBundle\Client
    $client = static::createClient();
    /** @var \Symfony\Component\DomCrawler\Crawler */
    $crawler = $client->request('GET', '/contact');

    // Find a button labeled as "Reach Out!"
    $form = $crawler->selectButton('Reach Out!')->form();

    // Note this does not validate form, it merely tests against
    //   submission and response page
    $crawler = $client->submit($form);
    $this->assertEquals(200, $client->getResponse()
        ->getStatusCode());
}
```

Here we are grabbing the form element through its **Reach Out!** submit button. Once the form is fetched, we trigger the `submit` method on the client passing it the instance from element. It is worth noting that the actual form validation is not being tested here. Even so, the submitted form should result in an HTTP 200 status.

These tests are conclusive. We can write them to be much more robust if we wanted to, as there are numerous elements we can test against.

Summary

In this chapter we have built our first module, or bundle in Symfony terminology. The module itself is not really loosely coupled, as it relies on some of the things within the app directory, such as the `app/Resources/views/base.html.twig` layout template. We can get away with this when it comes to core modules, as they are merely a foundation we are setting up for rest of the modules.

Moving forward, in the next chapter, we will build a catalog module. This will be the basis of our web shop application.

Building the Catalog Module

7

The catalog module is an essential part of every web shop application. At the very basic level, it is responsible for the management and display of categories and products. It is a foundation for later modules, such as checkout, that add the actual sales capabilities to our web shop application.

The more robust catalog features might include mass product imports, product exports, multi-warehouse inventory management, private members categories, and so on. These however, are out of the scope of this chapter.

In this chapter, we will be covering following topics:

- Requirements
- Dependencies
- Implementation
- Unit testing
- Functional testing

Requirements

Following the high level application requirements, defined in *Chapter 4, Requirement Specification for Modular Web Shop App*, our module will have several entities and other specific features implemented.

Following is a list of required module entities:

- Category
- Product

The Category entity includes the following properties and their data types:

- `id`: integer, auto-increment
- `title`: string
- `url_key`: string, unique
- `description`: text
- `image`: string

The Product entity includes the following properties:

- `id`: integer, auto-increment
- `category_id`: integer, foreign key that references the category table ID column
- `title`: string
- `price`: decimal
- `sku`: string, unique
- `url_key`: string, unique
- `description`: text
- `qty`: integer
- `image`: string
- `onsale`: boolean

Aside from just adding these entities and their CRUD pages, we also need to override the core module services responsible for building the category menu and on sale items.

Dependencies

The module has no firm dependencies on any other module. The Symfony framework service layer enables us to code modules in such a way that, most of the time, there is no need for a dependency between them. While the module does override a service defined in the core module, the module itself is not dependent on it, as nothing will break if the overriding service is missing.

Implementation

We start off by creating a new module called `Foggyline\CatalogBundle`. We do so with the help of the console, by running the command as follows:

```
php bin/console generate:bundle --namespace=Foggyline/CatalogBundle
```

The command triggers an interactive process that asks us several questions along the way, as shown in the following screenshot:

```
Welcome to the Symfony bundle generator!

Are you planning on sharing this bundle across multiple applications? [no]: yes

Your application code must be written in bundles. This command helps
you generate them easily.

Each bundle is hosted under a namespace (like Acme/BlogBundle).
The namespace should begin with a "vendor" name like your company name, your
project name, or your client name, followed by one or more optional category
sub-namespaces, and it should end with the bundle name itself
(which must have Bundle as a suffix).

See http://symfony.com/doc/current/cookbook/bundles/best_practices.html#bundle-name for more
details on bundle naming conventions.

Use / instead of \  for the namespace delimiter to avoid any problem.

Bundle namespace [Foggyline/CatalogBundle]:

In your code, a bundle is often referenced by its name. It can be the
concatenation of all namespace parts but it's really up to you to come
up with a unique name (a good practice is to start with the vendor name).
Based on the namespace, we suggest FoggylineCatalogBundle.

Bundle name [FoggylineCatalogBundle]:

Bundles are usually generated into the src/ directory. Unless you're
doing something custom, hit enter to keep this default!

Target Directory [src/]:

What format do you want to use for your generated configuration?

Configuration format (annotation, yml, xml, php) [xml]:

Bundle generation

> Generating a sample bundle skeleton into src/Foggyline/CatalogBundle OK!
> Checking that the bundle is autoloaded: OK
> Enabling the bundle inside app/AppKernel.php: OK
> Importing the bundle's routes from the app/config/routing.yml file: OK

Everything is OK! Now get to work :).
```

Once done, the following structure is generated for us:

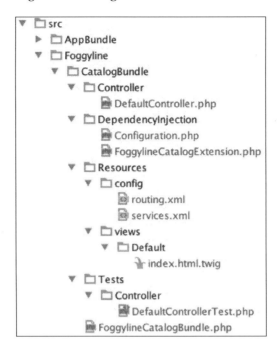

If we now take a look at the app/AppKernel.php file, we would see the following line under the registerBundles method:

```
new Foggyline\CatalogBundle\FoggylineCatalogBundle()
```

Similarly, the app/config/routing.yml has the following route definition added to it:

```
foggyline_catalog:
  resource: "@FoggylineCatalogBundle/
    Resources/config/routing.xml"
  prefix: /
```

Here we need to change prefix: / into prefix: /catalog/, so we don't collide with core module routes. Leaving it as prefix: / would simply overrun our core AppBundle and output Hello World! from the src/Foggyline/CatalogBundle/ Resources/views/Default/index.html.twig template to the browser at this point. We want to keep things nice and separated. What this means is that the module does not define the root route for itself.

Creating entities

Let's go ahead and create a `Category` entity. We do so by using the console, as shown here:

```
php bin/console generate:doctrine:entity
```

```
Brankos-MacBook-Pro:shop branko$ php bin/console generate:doctrine:entity

    Welcome to the Doctrine2 entity generator


This command helps you generate Doctrine2 entities.

First, you need to give the entity name you want to generate.
You must use the shortcut notation like AcmeBlogBundle:Post.

The Entity shortcut name: FoggylineCatalogBundle:Category

Determine the format to use for the mapping information.

Configuration format (yml, xml, php, or annotation) [annotation]:

Instead of starting with a blank entity, you can add some fields now.
Note that the primary key will be added automatically (named id).

Available types: array, simple_array, json_array, object,
boolean, integer, smallint, bigint, string, text, datetime, datetimetz,
date, time, decimal, float, binary, blob, guid.

New field name (press <return> to stop adding fields): title
Field type [string]:
Field length [255]:
Is nullable [false]:
Unique [false]:

New field name (press <return> to stop adding fields): url_key
Field type [string]:
Field length [255]:
Is nullable [false]:
Unique [false]: true

New field name (press <return> to stop adding fields): description
Field type [string]: text
Is nullable [false]: true
Unique [false]:

New field name (press <return> to stop adding fields): image
Field type [string]:
Field length [255]:
Is nullable [false]: true
Unique [false]:

New field name (press <return> to stop adding fields):

    Entity generation


> Generating entity class src/Foggyline/CatalogBundle/Entity/Category.php: OK!
> Generating repository class src/Foggyline/CatalogBundle/Repository/CategoryRepository.php: OK!

    Everything is OK! Now get to work :).
```

This creates the `Entity/Category.php` and `Repository/CategoryRepository.php` files within the `src/Foggyline/CatalogBundle/` directory. After this, we need to update the database, so it pulls in the `Category` entity, as shown in the following command line instance:

```
php bin/console doctrine:schema:update --force
```

This results in a screen that looks similar to the following screenshot:

```
Brankos-MacBook-Pro:shop branko$ php bin/console doctrine:schema:update --force
Updating database schema...
Database schema updated successfully! "1" query was executed
Brankos-MacBook-Pro:shop branko$
```

With entity in place, we are ready to generate its CRUD. We do so by using the following command:

```
php bin/console generate:doctrine:crud
```

This results with interactive output as shown here:

This results in `src/Foggyline/CatalogBundle/Controller/` `CategoryController.php` being created. It also adds an entry to our `app/config/` `routing.yml` file as follows:

```
foggyline_catalog_category:
  resource: "@FoggylineCatalogBundle/Controller/
    CategoryController.php"
  type:     annotation
```

Furthermore, the view files are created under the `app/Resources/views/` `category/` directory, which is not what we might expect. We want them under our module `src/Foggyline/CatalogBundle/Resources/views/Default/category/` directory, so we need to copy them over. Additionally, we need to modify all of the `$this->render` calls within our `CategoryController` by appending the `FoggylineCatalogBundle:default:` string to each of the template paths.

Next, we go ahead and create the `Product` entity by using the interactive generator as discussed earlier:

php bin/console generate:doctrine:entity

We follow the interactive generator, respecting the minimum of the following attributes: `title`, `price`, `sku`, `url_key`, `description`, `qty`, `category`, and `image`. Aside from `price` and `qty`, which are of types decimal and integer, all other attributes are of type string. Furthermore, `sku` and `url_key` are flagged as unique. This creates the `Entity/Product.php` and `Repository/ProductRepository.php` files within the `src/Foggyline/CatalogBundle/` directory.

Similar to what we have done for the `Category view` templates, we need to do for the `Product view` templates. That is, copy them over from the `app/Resources/` `views/product/` directory to `src/Foggyline/CatalogBundle/Resources/` `views/Default/product/` and update all of the `$this->render` calls within our `ProductController` by appending the `FoggylineCatalogBundle:default:` string to each of the template paths.

At this point, we won't rush updating the schema, as we want to add proper relations to our code. Each product should be able to have a relation to a single `Category` entity. To achieve this, we need to edit `Category.php` and `Product.php` from within the `src/Foggyline/CatalogBundle/Entity/` directory, as follows:

```
// src/Foggyline/CatalogBundle/Entity/Category.php

/**
 * @ORM\OneToMany(targetEntity="Product", mappedBy="category")
 */
```

```
private $products;

public function __construct()
{
  $this->products = new \Doctrine\Common\Collections\
ArrayCollection();
}

// src/Foggyline/CatalogBundle/Entity/Product.php

/**
 * @ORM\ManyToOne(targetEntity="Category", inversedBy="products")
 * @ORM\JoinColumn(name="category_id", referencedColumnName="id")
 */
private $category;
```

We further need to edit the `Category.php` file by adding the `__toString` method implementation to it, as follows:

```
public function __toString()
{
    return $this->getTitle();
}
```

The reason we are doing so is that, later on, our Product-editing form would know what labels to list under the Category selection, otherwise the system would throw the following error:

```
Catchable Fatal Error: Object of class
   Foggyline\CatalogBundle\Entity\Category could not be converted
   to string
```

With the above changes in place, we can now run the schema update, as follows:

php bin/console doctrine:schema:update --force

If we now take a look at our database, the CREATE command syntax for our `product` table looks like the following:

```
CREATE TABLE `product` (
  `id` int(11) NOT NULL AUTO_INCREMENT,
  `category_id` int(11) DEFAULT NULL,
  `title` varchar(255) COLLATE utf8_unicode_ci NOT NULL,
  `price` decimal(10,2) NOT NULL,
  `sku` varchar(255) COLLATE utf8_unicode_ci NOT NULL,
  `url_key` varchar(255) COLLATE utf8_unicode_ci NOT NULL,
  `description` longtext COLLATE utf8_unicode_ci,
```

```
`qty` int(11) NOT NULL,
`image` varchar(255) COLLATE utf8_unicode_ci DEFAULT NULL,
PRIMARY KEY (`id`),
UNIQUE KEY `UNIQ_D34A04ADF9038C4` (`sku`),
UNIQUE KEY `UNIQ_D34A04ADDFAB7B3B` (`url_key`),
KEY `IDX_D34A04AD12469DE2` (`category_id`),
CONSTRAINT `FK_D34A04AD12469DE2` FOREIGN KEY (`category_id`)
  REFERENCES `category` (`id`)
) ENGINE=InnoDB DEFAULT CHARSET=utf8 COLLATE=utf8_unicode_ci;
```

We can see two unique keys and one foreign key restraint defined, as per the entries provided to our interactive entity generator. Now we are ready to generate the CRUD for our `Product` entity. To do so, we run the `generate:doctrine:crud` command and follow the interactive generator as shown here:

Managing image uploads

At this point, if we access either /category/new/ or /product/new/ URL, the image field is just a simple input text field, not the actual image upload we would like. To make it into an image upload field, we need to edit the $image property of Category.php and Product.php as follows:

```
//...
use Symfony\Component\Validator\Constraints as Assert;
//...
class [Category|Product]
{
  //...
  /**
   * @var string
   *
   * @ORM\Column(name="image", type="string", length=255,
     nullable=true)
   * @Assert\File(mimeTypes={ "image/png", "image/jpeg" },
     mimeTypesMessage="Please upload the PNG or JPEG image
     file.")
   */
  private $image;
  //...
}
```

As soon as we do so, the input fields turn into the file upload fields, as shown here:

Next, we will go ahead and implement the upload functionality into the forms.

We do so by first defining the service that will handle the actual upload. Service is defined by adding the following entry into the src/Foggyline/CatalogBundle/Resources/config/services.xml file, under the services element:

```
<service id="foggyline_catalog.image_uploader"
  class="Foggyline\CatalogBundle\Service\ImageUploader">
  <argument>%foggyline_catalog_images_directory%</argument>
</service>
```

The %foggyline_catalog_images_directory% argument value is the name of a parameter the we will soon define.

We then create the `src/Foggyline/CatalogBundle/Service/ImageUploader.php` file with content as follows:

```
namespace Foggyline\CatalogBundle\Service;

use Symfony\Component\HttpFoundation\File\UploadedFile;

class ImageUploader
{
  private $targetDir;

  public function __construct($targetDir)
  {
    $this->targetDir = $targetDir;
  }

  public function upload(UploadedFile $file)
  {
    $fileName = md5(uniqid()) . '.' . $file->guessExtension();
    $file->move($this->targetDir, $fileName);
    return $fileName;
  }
}
```

We then create our own `parameters.yml` file within the `src/Foggyline/CatalogBundle/Resources/config` directory with content as follows:

```
parameters:
  foggyline_catalog_images_directory: "%kernel.root_dir%/../
    web/uploads/foggyline_catalog_images"
```

This is the parameter our service expects to find. It can easily be overridden with the same entry under `app/config/parameters.yml` if needed.

In order for our bundle to see the `parameters.yml` file, we still need to edit the `FoggylineCatalogExtension.php` file within the `src/Foggyline/CatalogBundle/DependencyInjection/` directory, by adding the following `loader` to the end of the `load` method:

```
$loader = new Loader\YamlFileLoader($container, new
  FileLocator(__DIR__.'/../Resources/config'));
$loader->load('parameters.yml');
```

At this point, our Symfony module is able to read its `parameters.yml`, thus making it possible for the defined service to pickup the proper value for its argument. All that is left is to adjust the code for our `new` and `edit` forms, attaching the upload functionality to them. Since both forms are the same, the following is a `Category` example that equally applies to the `Product` form as well:

```php
public function newAction(Request $request) {
    // ...

    if ($form->isSubmitted() && $form->isValid()) {
        /* @var $image \Symfony\Component\
          HttpFoundation\File\UploadedFile */
        if ($image = $category->getImage()) {
            $name = $this->get('foggyline_catalog.image_uploader')
              ->upload($image);
            $category->setImage($name);
        }

        $em = $this->getDoctrine()->getManager();
        // ...
    }

    // ...
}

public function editAction(Request $request, Category $category) {
    $existingImage = $category->getImage();
    if ($existingImage) {
        $category->setImage(
          new File($this->getParameter
            ('foggyline_catalog_images_directory') . '/' .
            $existingImage)
        );
    }

    $deleteForm = $this->createDeleteForm($category);
    // ...

    if ($editForm->isSubmitted() && $editForm->isValid()) {
        /* @var $image \Symfony\Component\HttpFoundation\
          File\UploadedFile */
        if ($image = $category->getImage()) {
            $name = $this->get('foggyline_catalog.image_uploader')
              ->upload($image);
            $category->setImage($name);
```

```
    } elseif ($existingImage) {
      $category->setImage($existingImage);
    }

    $em = $this->getDoctrine()->getManager();
    // ...
  }

  // ...
}
```

Both the `new` and `edit` forms should now be able to handle file uploads.

Overriding core module services

Now let's go ahead and address the category menu and the on-sale items. Back when we were building the core module, we defined the global variables under the `twig:global` section of the `app/config/config.yml` file. These variables were pointing to services defined in the `app/config/services.yml` file. In order for us to change the content of the category menu and the on sale items, we need to override those services.

We start off by adding the following two service definitions under the `src/Foggyline/CatalogBundle/Resources/config/services.xml` file:

```
<service id="foggyline_catalog.category_menu"
  class="Foggyline\CatalogBundle\Service\Menu\Category">
  <argument type="service" id="doctrine.orm.entity_manager" />
  <argument type="service" id="router" />
</service>

<service id="foggyline_catalog.onsale"
  class="Foggyline\CatalogBundle\Service\Menu\OnSale">
  <argument type="service" id="doctrine.orm.entity_manager" />
  <argument type="service" id="router" />
</service>
```

Both of the services accept the Doctrine ORM entity manager and router service arguments, as we will need to use those internally.

We then create the actual `Category` and `OnSale` service classes within the `src/Foggyline/CatalogBundle/Service/Menu/` directory as follows:

```
//Category.php

namespace Foggyline\CatalogBundle\Service\Menu;
```

```php
class Category
{
  private $em;
  private $router;

  public function __construct(
    \Doctrine\ORM\EntityManager $entityManager,
    \Symfony\Bundle\FrameworkBundle\Routing\Router $router
  )
  {
    $this->em = $entityManager;
    $this->router = $router;
  }

  public function getItems()
  {
    $categories = array();
    $_categories = $this->em->getRepository
      ('FoggylineCatalogBundle:Category')->findAll();

    foreach ($_categories as $_category) {
      /* @var $_category \Foggyline\CatalogBundle\
        Entity\Category */
      $categories[] = array(
        'path' => $this->router->generate('category_show',
          array('id' => $_category->getId())),
        'label' => $_category->getTitle(),
      );
    }

    return $categories;
  }
}
 //OnSale.php

namespace Foggyline\CatalogBundle\Service\Menu;

class OnSale
{
  private $em;
  private $router;

  public function __construct(\Doctrine\ORM\
    EntityManager $entityManager, $router)
    {
```

```
        $this->em = $entityManager;
        $this->router = $router;
    }

    public function getItems()
    {
        $products = array();
        $_products = $this->em->getRepository
            ('FoggylineCatalogBundle:Product')->findBy(
                array('onsale' => true),
                null,
                5
        );

        foreach ($_products as $_product) {
            /* @var $_product \Foggyline\CatalogBundle\
                Entity\Product */
            $products[] = array(
                'path' => $this->router->generate('product_show',
                    array('id' => $_product->getId())),
                'name' => $_product->getTitle(),
                'image' => $_product->getImage(),
                'price' => $_product->getPrice(),
                'id' => $_product->getId(),
            );
        }

        return $products;
    }
}
```

This alone won't trigger the override of the core module services. Within the src/
Foggyline/CatalogBundle/DependencyInjection/Compiler/ directory we
need to create an OverrideServiceCompilerPass class that implements the
CompilerPassInterface. Within its process method, we can then change the
definition of the service, as follows:

```
namespace Foggyline\CatalogBundle\DependencyInjection\Compiler;

use Symfony\Component\DependencyInjection\Compiler\
    CompilerPassInterface;
use Symfony\Component\DependencyInjection\ContainerBuilder;

class OverrideServiceCompilerPass implements CompilerPassInterface
{
```

```
public function process(ContainerBuilder $container)
{
  // Override the core module 'category_menu' service
  $container->removeDefinition('category_menu');
  $container->setDefinition('category_menu',
    $container->getDefinition
  ('foggyline_catalog.category_menu'));

  // Override the core module 'onsale' service
  $container->removeDefinition('onsale');
  $container->setDefinition('onsale',
    $container->getDefinition('foggyline_catalog.onsale'));
  }
}
```

Finally, we need to edit the `build` method of the `src/Foggyline/CatalogBundle/` `FoggylineCatalogBundle.php` file in order to add this compiler pass as shown here:

```
public function build(ContainerBuilder $container)
{
  parent::build($container);
  $container->addCompilerPass(new \Foggyline\CatalogBundle\
    DependencyInjection\Compiler\OverrideServiceCompilerPass());
}
```

Now our `Category` and `OnSale` services should override the ones defined in the core module, thus providing the right values for the header **Category** menu and **On Sale** section of the homepage.

Setting up a Category page

The auto-generated CRUD made a Category page for us with the layout as follows:

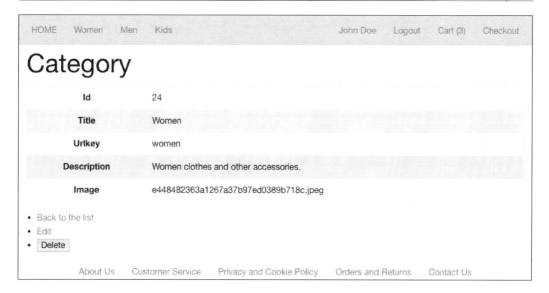

This is significantly different from the Category page defined under *Chapter 4, Requirement Specification for Modular Web Shop App*. We therefore need to make amends to our Category Show page, by modifying the `show.html.twig` file within the `src/Foggyline/CatalogBundle/Resources/views/Default/category/` directory. We do so by replacing the entire content of `body` block with code as follows:

```
<div class="row">
  <div class="small-12 large-12 columns text-center">
    <h1>{{ category.title }}</h1>
    <p>{{ category.description }}</p>
  </div>
</div>

<div class="row">
  <img src="{{ asset('uploads/foggyline_catalog_images/' ~
    category.image) }}"/>
</div>

{% set products = category.getProducts() %}
{% if products %}
<div class="row products_onsale text-center small-up-1
  medium-up-3 large-up-5" data-equalizer
  data-equalize-by-row="true">
{% for product in products %}
<div class="column product">
```

```
    <img src="{{ asset('uploads/
      foggyline_catalog_images/' ~ product.image) }}"
      alt="missing image"/>
    <a href="{{ path('product_show', {'id':
      product.id}) }}">{{ product.title }}</a>

    <div>${{ product.price }}</div>
    <div><a class="small button" href="{{
      path('product_show', {'id': product.id})
      }}">View</a></div>
    </div>
    {% endfor %}
  </div>
  {% else %}
  <div class="row">
    <p>There are no products assigned to this category.</p>
  </div>
  {% endif %}

  {% if is_granted('ROLE_ADMIN') %}
  <ul>
    <li>
      <a href="{{ path('category_edit', { 'id': category.id
        }) }}">Edit</a>
    </li>
    <li>
      {{ form_start(delete_form) }}
      <input type="submit" value="Delete">
      form_end(delete_form) }}
    </li>
  </ul>
  {% endif %}
```

The body is now sectioned into three areas. First, we are addressing the category title and description output. We are then fetching and looping through the list of products assigned to category, rendering each individual product. Finally, we are using the is_granted Twig extension to check if the current user role is ROLE_ADMIN, in which case we show the Edit and Delete links for the category.

Setting up a Product page

The auto-generated CRUD made a Product page for us with the layout as follows:

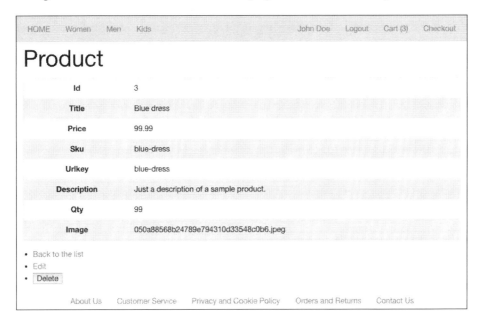

This differs from the Product page defined under *Chapter 4*, *Requirement Specification for Modular Web Shop App*. To rectify the problem, we need to make amends to our Product Show page, by modifying the `show.html.twig` file within the `src/Foggyline/CatalogBundle/Resources/views/Default/product/` directory. We do so by replacing entire content of `body` block with code as follows:

```
<div class="row">
   <div class="small-12 large-6 columns">
      <img class="thumbnail" src="{{ asset('uploads/
         foggyline_catalog_images/' ~ product.image) }}"/>
   </div>
   <div class="small-12 large-6 columns">
      <h1>{{ product.title }}</h1>
      <div>SKU: {{ product.sku }}</div>
      {% if product.qty %}
      <div>IN STOCK</div>
      {% else %}
      <div>OUT OF STOCK</div>
      {% endif %}
      <div>$ {{ product.price }}</div>
      <form action="{{ add_to_cart_url.getAddToCartUrl
```

```
        (product.id) }}" method="get">
        <div class="input-group">
          <span class="input-group-label">Qty</span>
          <input class="input-group-field" type="number">
          <div class="input-group-button">
            <input type="submit" class="button" value=
              "Add to Cart">
          </div>
        </div>
      </form>
    </div>
  </div>

  <div class="row">
    <p>{{ product.description }}</p>
  </div>

  {% if is_granted('ROLE_ADMIN') %}
  <ul>
    <li>
      <a href="{{ path('product_edit', { 'id': product.id })
        }}">Edit</a>
    </li>
    <li>
      {{ form_start(delete_form) }}
      <input type="submit" value="Delete">
      {{ form_end(delete_form) }}
    </li>
  </ul>
  {% endif %}
```

The body is now sectioned into two main areas. First, we are addressing the product image, title, stock status, and add to cart output. The add to cart form uses the `add_to_cart_url` service to provide the right link. This service is defined under the core module and, at this point, only provides a dummy link. Later on, when we get to the checkout module, we will implement an override for this service and inject the right add to cart link. We then output the description section. Finally, we use the `is_granted` Twig extension, like we did on the Category example, to determine if the user can access the `Edit` and `Delete` links for a product.

Unit testing

We now have several class files that are not related to the controllers, meaning we can run unit tests against them. Still, we won't be going after a full code coverage as part of this book, rather focus on some of the little-big things, like using containers within our test classes.

We start of by adding the following line under the `testsuites` element of our `phpunit.xml.dist` file:

```
<directory>src/Foggyline/CatalogBundle/Tests</directory>
```

With that in place, running the `phpunit` command from the root of our shop should pick up any test we have defined under the `src/Foggyline/CatalogBundle/Tests/` directory.

Now let's go ahead and create a test for our Category service menu. We do so by creating an `src/Foggyline/CatalogBundle/Tests/Service/Menu/CategoryTest.php` file with the following content:

```
namespace Foggyline\CatalogBundle\Tests\Service\Menu;

use Symfony\Bundle\FrameworkBundle\Test\KernelTestCase;
use Foggyline\CatalogBundle\Service\Menu\Category;

class CategoryTest extends KernelTestCase
{
  private $container;
  private $em;
  private $router;

  public function setUp()
  {
    static::bootKernel();
    $this->container = static::$kernel->getContainer();
    $this->em = $this->container->get
      ('doctrine.orm.entity_manager');
    $this->router = $this->container->get('router');
  }

  public function testGetItems()
  {
    $service = new Category($this->em, $this->router);
    $this->assertNotEmpty($service->getItems());
  }
```

```
    protected function tearDown()
    {
      $this->em->close();
      unset($this->em, $this->router);
    }
}
```

The preceding example shows the usage of the setUp and tearDown method calls, which are analogous in behavior to the PHP's __construct and __destruct methods. We use the setUp method to set the entity manager and router service that we can use through out the rest of the class. The tearDown method is merely a clean up. Now if we run the phpunit command, we should see our test being picked up and executed alongside other tests.

We can even target this class specifically by executing a phpunit command with the full class path, as shown here:

```
phpunit src/Foggyline/CatalogBundle/Tests/Service/
  Menu/CategoryTest.php
```

Similarly to what we did for CategoryTest, we can go ahead and create OnSaleTest; the only difference between the two being the class name.

Functional testing

The great thing about the auto-generate CRUD tool is that it generates even the functional tests for us. More specifically, in this case, it generated the CategoryControllerTest.php and ProductControllerTest.php files within the src/Foggyline/CatalogBundle/Tests/Controller/ directory.

 Auto-generated functional tests have a commented out methods within class body. This throws an error during the phpunit run. We need to at least define a dummy test method in them to allow phpunit to overlook them.

If we look into these two files, we can see that they both have a single testCompleteScenario method defined, which is entirely commented out. Let's go ahead and change the CategoryControllerTest.php content as follows:

```
// Create a new client to browse the application
$client = static::createClient(
  array(), array(
    'PHP_AUTH_USER' => 'john',
    'PHP_AUTH_PW' => '1L6lllW9zXg0',
```

```
  )
);

// Create a new entry in the database
$crawler = $client->request('GET', '/category/');
$this->assertEquals(200, $client->getResponse()->getStatusCode(),
  "Unexpected HTTP status code for GET /product/");
$crawler = $client->click($crawler->selectLink('Create a new
  entry')->link());

// Fill in the form and submit it
$form = $crawler->selectButton('Create')->form(array(
  'category[title]' => 'Test',
  'category[urlKey]' => 'Test urlKey',
  'category[description]' => 'Test description',
));

$client->submit($form);
$crawler = $client->followRedirect();

// Check data in the show view
$this->assertGreaterThan(0, $crawler
  ->filter('h1:contains("Test")')->count(),
  'Missing element h1:contains("Test")');

// Edit the entity
$crawler = $client->click($crawler->selectLink('Edit')->link());

$form = $crawler->selectButton('Edit')->form(array(
  'category[title]' => 'Foo',
  'category[urlKey]' => 'Foo urlKey',
  'category[description]' => 'Foo description',
));

$client->submit($form);
$crawler = $client->followRedirect();

// Check the element contains an attribute with value equals "Foo"
$this->assertGreaterThan(0, $crawler->filter('[value="Foo"]')
  ->count(), 'Missing element [value="Foo"]');

// Delete the entity
$client->submit($crawler->selectButton('Delete')->form());
$crawler = $client->followRedirect();
```

```
// Check the entity has been delete on the list
$this->assertNotRegExp('/Foo title/', $client->getResponse()
  ->getContent());
```

We started off by setting PHP_AUTH_USER and PHP_AUTH_PW as parameters for the createClient method. This is because our /new and /edit routes are protected by the core module security. These settings allow us to pass the basic HTTP authentication along the request. We then tested if the category listing page can be accessed and if its Create a new entry link can be clicked. Furthermore, both the create and edit forms were tested, along with their results.

All that remains is to repeat the approach we just used for CategoryControllerTest.php with ProductControllerTest.php. We simply need to change a few labels within the ProductControllerTest class file to match the product routes and expected results.

Running the phpunit command now should successfully execute our tests.

Summary

Throughout this chapter we have built a miniature, but functional, catalog module. It allowed us to create, edit, and delete categories and products. By adding a few custom lines of code on top of the auto-generated CRUD, we were able to achieve image upload functionality for both categories and products. We also saw how to override the core module service, by simply removing the existing service definition and providing a new one. In regard to tests, we saw how we can pass the authentication along our requests to test for protected routes.

Moving forward, in the next chapter, we will build a customer module.

8
Building the Customer Module

The customer module provides a basis for further sales functionality of our web shop. At the very basic level, it is responsible for register, login, management and display of relevant customer information. It is a requirement for the later sales module, that adds the actual sales capabilities to our web shop application.

In this chapter we will be covering following topics:

- Requirements
- Dependencies
- Implementation
- Unit testing
- Functional testing

Requirements

Following the high level application requirements, defined under *Chapter 4, Requirement Specification for Modular Web Shop App*, our module will have a single Customer entity defined.

The Customer entity includes the following properties:

- id: integer, auto-increment
- email: string, unique
- username: string, unique, needed for login system
- password: string

- `first_name`: string
- `last_name`: string
- `company`: string
- `phone_number`: string
- `country`: string
- `state`: string
- `city`: string
- `postcode`: string
- `street`: string

Throughout this chapter, aside from just adding the `Customer` entity and its CRUD pages, we also need to address the creation of login, register, forgot your password pages, as well as override a core module service responsible for building a customer menu.

Dependencies

The module has no firm dependencies on any other module. While it does override a service defined in core module, the module itself is not dependent on it. Furthermore, some security config will need to be provided as part of the core application, as we will see later on.

Implementation

We start of by creating a new module called `Foggyline\CustomerBundle`. We do so with the help of console, by running the command as follows:

```
php bin/console generate:bundle --namespace=Foggyline/CustomerBundle
```

The command triggers an interactive process asking us several questions along the way, as shown in the following screenshot:

```
Brankos-MacBook-Pro:shop branko$ php bin/console generate:bundle --namespace=Foggyline/CustomerBundle

  Welcome to the Symfony bundle generator!

Are you planning on sharing this bundle across multiple applications? [no]: yes

Your application code must be written in bundles. This command helps
you generate them easily.

Each bundle is hosted under a namespace (like Acme/BlogBundle).
The namespace should begin with a "vendor" name like your company name, your
project name, or your client name, followed by one or more optional category
sub-namespaces, and it should end with the bundle name itself
(which must have Bundle as a suffix).

See http://symfony.com/doc/current/cookbook/bundles/best_practices.html#bundle-name for more
details on bundle naming conventions.

Use / instead of \  for the namespace delimiter to avoid any problem.

Bundle namespace [Foggyline/CustomerBundle]:

In your code, a bundle is often referenced by its name. It can be the
concatenation of all namespace parts but it's really up to you to come
up with a unique name (a good practice is to start with the vendor name).
Based on the namespace, we suggest FoggylineCustomerBundle.

Bundle name [FoggylineCustomerBundle]:

Bundles are usually generated into the src/ directory. Unless you're
doing something custom, hit enter to keep this default!

Target Directory [src/]:

What format do you want to use for your generated configuration?

Configuration format (annotation, yml, xml, php) [xml]:

  Bundle generation

> Generating a sample bundle skeleton into src/Foggyline/CustomerBundle OK!
> Checking that the bundle is autoloaded: OK
> Enabling the bundle inside app/AppKernel.php: OK
> Importing the bundle's routes from the app/config/routing.yml file: OK

  Everything is OK! Now get to work :).
```

Once done, the following structure is generated for us:

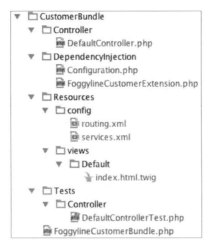

If we now take a look at the `app/AppKernel.php` file, we would see the following line under the `registerBundles` method:

```
new Foggyline\CustomerBundle\FoggylineCustomerBundle()
```

Similarly, the `app/config/routing.yml` directory has the following route definition added to it:

```
foggyline_customer:
  resource: "@FoggylineCustomerBundle/
    Resources/config/routing.xml"
  prefix:   /
```

Here we need to change `prefix: /` into `prefix: /customer/`, so we don't collide with core module routes. Leaving it as `prefix: /` would simply overrun our core AppBundle and output **Hello World!** from the `src/Foggyline/CustomerBundle/Resources/views/Default/index.html.twig` template to the browser at this point. We want to keep things nice and separated. What this means is that the module does not define `root` route for itself.

Creating a customer entity

Let's go ahead and create a `Customer` entity. We do so by using the console, as shown here:

```
php bin/console generate:doctrine:entity
```

This command triggers the interactive generator, where we need to provide entity properties. Once done, the generator creates the `Entity/Customer.php` and `Repository/CustomerRepository.php` files within the `src/Foggyline/CustomerBundle/` directory. After this, we need to update the database, so it pulls in the `Customer` entity, by running the following command:

```
php bin/console doctrine:schema:update --force
```

This results in a screen as shown in the following screenshot:

```
Brankos-MacBook-Pro:shop branko$ php bin/console doctrine:schema:update --force
Updating database schema...
Database schema updated successfully! "1" query was executed
Brankos-MacBook-Pro:shop branko$
```

With entity in place, we are ready to generate its CRUD. We do so by using the following command:

```
php bin/console generate:doctrine:crud
```

This results in an interactive output as shown here:

This results in the `src/Foggyline/CustomerBundle/Controller/` `CustomerController.php` directory being created. It also adds an entry to our `app/config/routing.yml` file as follows:

```
foggyline_customer_customer:
  resource:
    "@FoggylineCustomerBundle/Controller/CustomerController.php"
  type:     annotation
```

Again, the view files were created under the `app/Resources/views/customer/` directory, which is not what we might expect. We want them under our module `src/Foggyline/CustomerBundle/Resources/views/Default/customer/` directory, so we need to copy them over. Additionally, we need to modify all of the `$this->render` calls within our `CustomerController` by appending the `Foggyline CustomerBundle:default:` string to each of the template path.

Modifying the security configuration

Before we proceed further with the actual changes within our module, let's imagine our module requirements mandate a certain security configuration in order to make it work. These requirements state that we need to apply several changes to the `app /config/security.yml` file. We first edit the `providers` element by adding to it the following entry:

```
foggyline_customer:
  entity:
    class: FoggylineCustomerBundle:Customer
  property: username
```

This effectively defines our `Customer` class as a security provider, whereas the `username` element is the property storing user identity.

We then define the encoder type under the `encoders` element, as follows:

```
Foggyline\CustomerBundle\Entity\Customer:
  algorithm: bcrypt
  cost: 12
```

This tells Symfony to use the `bcrypt` algorithm with a value of `12` for algorithmic cost while encrypting our password. This way our passwords won't end up in clear text when saved in the database.

We then go ahead and define a new firewall entry under the firewalls element, as follows:

```
foggyline_customer:
  anonymous: ~
```

```
provider: foggyline_customer
form_login:
  login_path: foggyline_customer_login
  check_path: foggyline_customer_login
  default_target_path: customer_account
logout:
  path:    /customer/logout
  target: /
```

There is quite a lot going on here. Our firewall uses the `anonymous: ~` definition to denote that it does not really need a user to be logged in to see certain pages. By default, all Symfony users are authenticated as anonymous, as shown in the following screenshot, on the **Developer** toolbar:

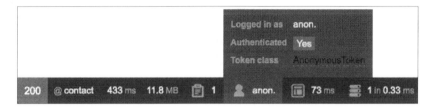

The `form_login` definition takes three properties. The `login_path` and the `check_path` point to our custom route `foggyline_customer_login`. When the security system initiates the authentication process, it will redirect the user to the `foggyline_customer_login` route, where we will soon implement needed controller logic and view templates in order to handle the login form. Once logged in, the `default_target_path` determines where the user will be redirected to.

Finally, we reuse the Symfony anonymous user feature in order to exclude certain pages from being forbidden. We want our non-authenticated customer to be able to access login, register, and forgotten password pages. To make that possible, we add the following entries under the `access_control` element:

```
  { path: customer/login, roles: IS_AUTHENTICATED_ANONYMOUSLY }
- { path: customer/register, roles: IS_AUTHENTICATED_ANONYMOUSLY }
- { path: customer/forgotten_password, roles:
  IS_AUTHENTICATED_ANONYMOUSLY }
- { path: customer/account, roles: ROLE_USER }
- { path: customer/logout, roles: ROLE_USER }
- { path: customer/, roles: ROLE_ADMIN }
```

It is worth noting that this approach to handling security between module and base application is by far the ideal one. This is merely one possible example of how we can achieve what is needed for this module to make it functional.

Extending the customer entity

With the preceding `security.yml` additions in place, we are now ready to actually start implementing the registration process. First we edit the `Customer` entity within the `src/Foggyline/CustomerBundle/Entity/` directory, by making it implement the `Symfony\Component\Security\Core\User\UserInterface`, `\Serializable`. This implies implementation of the following methods:

```php
public function getSalt()
{
   return null;
}

public function getRoles()
{
   return array('ROLE_USER');
}

public function eraseCredentials()
{
}

public function serialize()
{
   return serialize(array(
     $this->id,
     $this->username,
     $this->password
   ));
}

public function unserialize($serialized)
{
   list (
     $this->id,
     $this->username,
     $this->password,
   ) = unserialize($serialized);
}
```

Even though all of the passwords need to be hashed with salt, the `getSalt` function in this case is irrelevant since `bcrypt` does this internally. The `getRoles` function is the important bit. We can return one or more roles that individual customers will have. To make things simple, we will only assign one `ROLE_USER` role to each of our customers. But this can easily be made much more robust, so that the roles are stored in the database as well. The `eraseCredentials` function is merely a cleanup method, which we left blank.

Since the user object is first unserialized, serialized, and saved to a session per each request, we implement the `\Serializable` interface. The actual implementation of serialize and unserialize can include only a fraction of customer properties, as we do not need to store everything in the session.

Before we go ahead and start implementing the register, login, forgot your password, and other bits, let's go ahead and define the needed services we are going to use later on.

Creating the orders service

We will create an `orders` service which will be used to fill in the data available under the **My Account** page. Later on, other modules can override this service and inject real customer orders. To define an `orders` service, we edit the `src/Foggyline/CustomerBundle/Resources/config/services.xml` file by adding the following under the `services` element:

```
<service id="foggyline_customer.customer_orders"
  class="Foggyline\CustomerBundle\Service\CustomerOrders">
</service>
```

Then, we go ahead and create the `src/Foggyline/CustomerBundle/Service/CustomerOrders.php` directory with content as follows:

```
namespace Foggyline\CustomerBundle\Service;

class CustomerOrders
{
  public function getOrders()
  {
    return array(
      array(
        'id' => '0000000001',
        'date' => '23/06/2016 18:45',
        'ship_to' => 'John Doe',
        'order_total' => 49.99,
        'status' => 'Processing',
        'actions' => array(
```

```
        array(
          'label' => 'Cancel',
          'path' => '#'
        ),
        array(
          'label' => 'Print',
          'path' => '#'
        )
      )
    ),
  );
  }
}
```

The `getOrders` method simply returns some dummy data here. We can easily make it return an empty array. Ideally, we would want this to return a collection of certain types of element that conform to some specific interface.

Creating the customer menu service

In the previous module we defined a `customer` service that filled in the Customer menu with some dummy data. Now we will create an overriding service that fills the menu with actual customer data, depending on customer login status. To define a `customer menu` service, we edit the `src/Foggyline/CustomerBundle/Resources/config/services.xml` file by adding the following under the `services` element:

```
<service id="foggyline_customer.customer_menu"
  class="Foggyline\CustomerBundle\Service\Menu\CustomerMenu">
  <argument type="service" id="security.token_storage"/>
  <argument type="service" id="router"/>
</service>
```

Here we are injecting the `token_storage` and `router` objects into our service, as we will need them to construct the menu based on the login state of a customer.

We then go ahead and create the `src/Foggyline/CustomerBundle/Service/Menu/CustomerMenu.php` directory with content as follows:

```
namespace Foggyline\CustomerBundle\Service\Menu;

class CustomerMenu
{
  private $token;
  private $router;

  public function __construct(
```

```php
    $tokenStorage,
    \Symfony\Bundle\FrameworkBundle\Routing\Router $router
)
{
    $this->token = $tokenStorage->getToken();
    $this->router = $router;
}


public function getItems()
{
    $items = array();
    $user = $this->token->getUser();

    if ($user instanceof \Foggyline\CustomerBundle\
      Entity\Customer) {
      // customer authentication
      $items[] = array(
        'path' => $this->router->
          generate('customer_account'),
        'label' => $user->getFirstName() . ' ' . $user->
          getLastName(),
      );
      $items[] = array(
        'path' => $this->router->
          generate('customer_logout'),
        'label' => 'Logout',
      );
    } else {
      $items[] = array(
        'path' => $this->router->
          generate('foggyline_customer_login'),
        'label' => 'Login',
      );
      $items[] = array(
        'path' => $this->router->
          generate('foggyline_customer_register'),
        'label' => 'Register',
      );
    }

    return $items;
  }
}
```

Here we see a menu being constructed based on user login state. This way a customer gets to see the **Logout** link when logged in, or **Login** when not logged in.

We then add the `src/Foggyline/CustomerBundle/DependencyInjection/Compiler/OverrideServiceCompilerPass.php` directory with content as follows:

```php
namespace Foggyline\CustomerBundle\DependencyInjection\Compiler;

use Symfony\Component\DependencyInjection\Compiler\
  CompilerPassInterface;
use Symfony\Component\DependencyInjection\ContainerBuilder;

class OverrideServiceCompilerPass implements CompilerPassInterface
{
  public function process(ContainerBuilder $container)
  {
    // Override the core module 'onsale' service
    $container->removeDefinition('customer_menu');
    $container->setDefinition('customer_menu', $container->
      getDefinition('foggyline_customer.customer_menu'));
  }
}
```

Here we are doing the actual `customer_menu` service override. However, this won't kick in until we edit the `src/Foggyline/CustomerBundle/FoggylineCustomerBundle.php` directory, by adding the `build` method to it as follows:

```php
namespace Foggyline\CustomerBundle;

use Symfony\Component\HttpKernel\Bundle\Bundle;
use Symfony\Component\DependencyInjection\ContainerBuilder;
use Foggyline\CustomerBundle\DependencyInjection\
  Compiler\OverrideServiceCompilerPass;

class FoggylineCustomerBundle extends Bundle
{
  public function build(ContainerBuilder $container)
  {
    parent::build($container);;
    $container->addCompilerPass(new
      OverrideServiceCompilerPass());
  }
}
```

The `addCompilerPass` method call accepts the instance of our `OverrideServiceCompilerPass`, ensuring our service override will kick in.

Implementing the register process

To implement a register page, we first modify the `src/Foggyline/`
`CustomerBundle/Controller/CustomerController.php` file as follows:

```php
/**
 * @Route("/register", name="foggyline_customer_register")
 */
public function registerAction(Request $request)
{
  // 1) build the form
  $user = new Customer();
  $form = $this->createForm(CustomerType::class, $user);

  // 2) handle the submit (will only happen on POST)
  $form->handleRequest($request);
  if ($form->isSubmitted() && $form->isValid()) {

    // 3) Encode the password (you could also do this via Doctrine
listener)
    $password = $this->get('security.password_encoder')
    ->encodePassword($user, $user->getPlainPassword());
    $user->setPassword($password);

    // 4) save the User!
    $em = $this->getDoctrine()->getManager();
    $em->persist($user);
    $em->flush();

    // ... do any other work - like sending them an email, etc
    // maybe set a "flash" success message for the user

    return $this->redirectToRoute('customer_account');
  }

  return $this->render(
    'FoggylineCustomerBundle:default:
      customer/register.html.twig',
    array('form' => $form->createView())
  );
}
```

The register page uses a standard auto-generated Customer CRUD form, simply pointing it to the `src/Foggyline/CustomerBundle/Resources/views/Default/customer/register.html.twig` template file with content as follows:

```
{% extends 'base.html.twig' %}
{% block body %}
  {{ form_start(form) }}
  {{ form_widget(form) }}
  <button type="submit">Register!</button>
  {{ form_end(form) }}
{% endblock %}
```

Once these two files are in place, our register functionality should be working.

Implementing the login process

We will implement the login page on its own /customer/login URL, thus we edit the CustomerController.php file by adding the loginAction function as follows:

```
/**
 * Creates a new Customer entity.
 *
 * @Route("/login", name="foggyline_customer_login")
 */
public function loginAction(Request $request)
{
  $authenticationUtils = $this->
    get('security.authentication_utils');

  // get the login error if there is one
  $error = $authenticationUtils->getLastAuthenticationError();

  // last username entered by the user
  $lastUsername = $authenticationUtils->getLastUsername();

  return $this->render(
    'FoggylineCustomerBundle:default:
      customer/login.html.twig',
    array(
      // last username entered by the user
      'last_username' => $lastUsername,
      'error'         => $error,
    )
  );
}
```

Here we are simply checking if the user already tried to login, and if it did we are passing that info to the template, along with the potential errors. We then edit the `src/Foggyline/CustomerBundle/Resources/views/Default/customer/login.html.twig` file with content as follows:

```
{% extends 'base.html.twig' %}
{% block body %}
{% if error %}
<div>{{ error.messageKey|trans(error.messageData,
  'security') }}</div>
{% endif %}

<form action="{{ path('foggyline_customer_login') }}"
  method="post">
  <label for="username">Username:</label>
  <input type="text" id="username" name="_username"
    value="{{ last_username }}"/>
  <label for="password">Password:</label>
  <input type="password" id="password" name="_password"/>
  <button type="submit">login</button>
</form>

<div class="row">
  <a href="{{ path('customer_forgotten_password') }}">Forgot
    your password?</a>
</div>
{% endblock %}
```

Once logged in, the user will be redirected to the `/customer/account` page. We create this page by adding the `accountAction` method to the `CustomerController.php` file as follows:

```
/**
 * Finds and displays a Customer entity.
 *
 * @Route("/account", name="customer_account")
 * @Method({"GET", "POST"})
 */
public function accountAction(Request $request)
{
  if (!$this->get('security.authorization_checker')->
    isGranted('ROLE_USER')) {
    throw $this->createAccessDeniedException();
  }
```

```
if ($customer = $this->getUser()) {

    $editForm = $this->createForm('Foggyline\CustomerBundle\
      Form\CustomerType', $customer, array
      ( 'action' => $this->generateUrl('customer_account')));
    $editForm->handleRequest($request);

    if ($editForm->isSubmitted() && $editForm->isValid()) {
        $em = $this->getDoctrine()->getManager();
        $em->persist($customer);
        $em->flush();

        $this->addFlash('success', 'Account updated.');
        return $this->redirectToRoute('customer_account');
    }

    return $this->render('FoggylineCustomerBundle:default:
      customer/account.html.twig', array(
      'customer' => $customer,
      'form' => $editForm->createView(),
      'customer_orders' => $this->
        get('foggyline_customer.customer_orders')->
        getOrders()
    ));
} else {
    $this->addFlash('notice', 'Only logged in customers can
      access account page.');
    return $this->redirectToRoute('foggyline_customer_login');
}
}
```

Using `$this->getUser()` we are checking if logged in user is set, and if so, passing its info to the template. We then edit the `src/Foggyline/CustomerBundle/Resources/views/Default/customer/account.html.twig` file with content as follows:

```
{% extends 'base.html.twig' %}
{% block body %}
<h1>My Account</h1>
{{ form_start(form) }}
<div class="row">
  <div class="medium-6 columns">
    {{ form_row(form.email) }}
    {{ form_row(form.username) }}
    {{ form_row(form.plainPassword.first) }}
```

```
        {{ form_row(form.plainPassword.second) }}
        {{ form_row(form.firstName) }}
        {{ form_row(form.lastName) }}
        {{ form_row(form.company) }}
        {{ form_row(form.phoneNumber) }}
    </div>
    <div class="medium-6 columns">
        {{ form_row(form.country) }}
        {{ form_row(form.state) }}
        {{ form_row(form.city) }}
        {{ form_row(form.postcode) }}
        {{ form_row(form.street) }}
        <button type="submit">Save</button>
    </div>
</div>
{{ form_end(form) }}
<!-- customer_orders -->
{% endblock %}
```

With this we address the actual customer information section of the **My Account** page. In its current state, this page should render an Edit form as shown in the following screenshot, enabling us to edit all of our customer information:

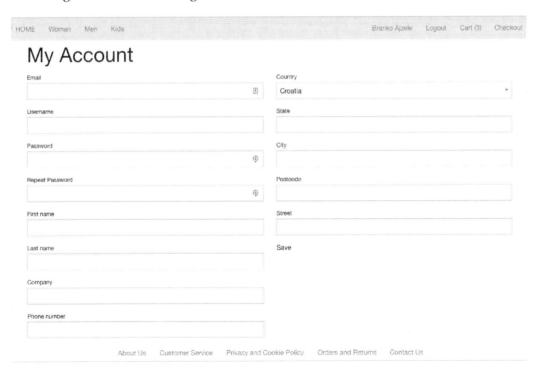

We then address the `<!-- customer_orders -->`, by replacing it with the following bits:

```
{% block customer_orders %}
<h2>My Orders</h2>
<div class="row">
  <table>
    <thead>
      <tr>
        <th width="200">Order Id</th>
        <th>Date</th>
        <th width="150">Ship To</th>
        <th width="150">Order Total</th>
        <th width="150">Status</th>
        <th width="150">Actions</th>
      </tr>
    </thead>
    <tbody>
      {% for order in customer_orders %}
      <tr>
        <td>{{ order.id }}</td>
        <td>{{ order.date }}</td>
        <td>{{ order.ship_to }}</td>
        <td>{{ order.order_total }}</td>
        <td>{{ order.status }}</td>
        <td>
          <div class="small button-group">
            {% for action in order.actions %}
            <a class="button" href="{{
              action.path }}">{{ action.label
              }}</a>
            {% endfor %}
          </div>
        </td>
      </tr>
      {% endfor %}
    /tbody>
  </table>
</div>
{% endblock %}
```

This should now render the **My Orders** section of the **My Account** page as shown here:

My Orders

Order Id	Date	Ship To	Order Total	Status	Actions
0000000001	23/06/2016 18:45	John Doe	49.99	Processing	Cancel Print

This is just dummy data coming from service defined in a `src/Foggyline/CustomerBundle/Resources/config/services.xml`. In a later chapter, when we get to the sales module, we will make sure it overrides the `foggyline_customer.customer_orders` service in order to insert real customer data here.

Implementing the logout process

One of the changes we did to `security.yml` when defining our firewall, was configuring the logout path, which we pointed to `/customer/logout`. The implementation of that path is done within the `CustomerController.php` file as follows:

```
/**
 * @Route("/logout", name="customer_logout")
 */
public function logoutAction()
{

}
```

Note, the `logoutAction` method is actually empty. There is no implementation as such. Implementation is not needed, as Symfony intercepts the request and processes the logout for us. We did, however, need to define this route as we referenced it from our `system.xml` file.

Managing forgotten passwords

The forgotten password feature is going to be implemented as a separate page. We edit the `CustomerController.php` file by adding the `forgottenPasswordAction` function to it as follows:

```
/**
 * @Route("/forgotten_password", name="customer_forgotten_password")
 * @Method({"GET", "POST"})
 */
```

```
public function forgottenPasswordAction(Request $request)
{

  // Build a form, with validation rules in place
  $form = $this->createFormBuilder()
  ->add('email', EmailType::class, array(
    'constraints' => new Email()
  ))
  ->add('save', SubmitType::class, array(
    'label' => 'Reset!',
    'attr' => array('class' => 'button'),
  ))
  ->getForm();

  // Check if this is a POST type request and if so, handle form
  if ($request->isMethod('POST')) {
    $form->handleRequest($request);

    if ($form->isSubmitted() && $form->isValid()) {
      $this->addFlash('success', 'Please check your email
        for reset password.');

      // todo: Send an email out to website admin or
        something...

      return $this->redirect($this->
        generateUrl('foggyline_customer_login'));
    }
  }

  // Render "contact us" page
  return $this->
    render('FoggylineCustomerBundle:default:customer/
    forgotten_password.html.twig', array(
      'form' => $form->createView()
    ));
}
```

Here we merely check if the HTTP request is GET or POST, then either send an e-mail or load the template. For the sake of simplicity, we haven't really implemented the actual e-mail sending. This is something that needs to be tackled outside of this book. The rendered template is pointing to the `src/Foggyline/CustomerBundle/Resources/views/Default/customer/ forgotten_password. html.twig` file with content as follows:

```
{% extends 'base.html.twig' %}
{% block body %}
```

```
<div class="row">
  <h1>Forgotten Password</h1>
</div>

<div class="row">
  {{ form_start(form) }}
  {{ form_widget(form) }}
  {{ form_end(form) }}
</div>
{% endblock %}
```

Unit testing

Aside from the auto-generated `Customer` entity and its CRUD controller, there are only two custom service classes that we created as part of this module. Since we are not going after full code coverage, we will merely cover `CustomerOrders` and `CustomerMenu` service classes as part of the unit testing.

We start off by adding the following line under the `testsuites` element of our `phpunit.xml.dist` file:

```
<directory>src/Foggyline/CustomerBundle/Tests</directory>
```

With that in place, running the `phpunit` command from the root of our shop should pick up any test we have defined under the `src/Foggyline/CustomerBundle/Tests/` directory.

Now let's go ahead and create a test for our `CustomerOrders` service. We do so by creating a `src/Foggyline/CustomerBundle/Tests/Service/CustomerOrders.php` file with content as follows:

```
namespace Foggyline\CustomerBundle\Tests\Service;

use Symfony\Bundle\FrameworkBundle\Test\KernelTestCase;

class CustomerOrders extends KernelTestCase
{
  private $container;

  public function setUp()
  {
    static::bootKernel();
    $this->container = static::$kernel->getContainer();
```

```
    }

    public function testGetItemsViaService()
    {
      $orders = $this->container->
        get('foggyline_customer.customer_orders');
      $this->assertNotEmpty($orders->getOrders());
    }

    public function testGetItemsViaClass()
    {
      $orders = new \Foggyline\CustomerBundle\
        Service\CustomerOrders();
      $this->assertNotEmpty($orders->getOrders());
    }
  }
}
```

Here we have two tests in total, one instantiating the class through the service and the other directly. We are using the setUp method merely to set the container property which we then reuse in the testGetItemsViaService method.

Next, we create the CustomerMenu test within the directory as follows:

```
namespace Foggyline\CustomerBundle\Tests\Service\Menu;
use Symfony\Bundle\FrameworkBundle\Test\KernelTestCase;

class CustomerMenu extends KernelTestCase
{
  private $container;
  private $tokenStorage;
  private $router;

  public function setUp()
  {
    static::bootKernel();
    $this->container = static::$kernel->getContainer();
    $this->tokenStorage = $this->container->
      get('security.token_storage');
    $this->router = $this->container->get('router');
  }

  public function testGetItemsViaService()
  {
    $menu = $this->container->
      get('foggyline_customer.customer_menu');
```

```
        $this->assertNotEmpty($menu->getItems());
    }

    public function testGetItemsViaClass()
    {
        $menu = new \Foggyline\CustomerBundle\
            Service\Menu\CustomerMenu(
            $this->tokenStorage,
            $this->router
        );

        $this->assertNotEmpty($menu->getItems());
    }
}
```

Now, if we run the `phpunit` command, we should see our test being picked up and executed alongside other tests. We can even target these two tests specifically by executing a `phpunit` command with full class path, as shown here:

phpunit src/Foggyline/CustomerBundle/Tests/Service/CustomerOrders.php

**phpunit src/Foggyline/CustomerBundle/Tests/Service/Menu/
  CustomerMenu.php**

Functional testing

The auto-generate CRUD tool generated the `CustomerControllerTest.php` file for us within the `src/Foggyline/CustomerBundle/Tests/Controller/` directory. In the previous chapter we showed how to pass an authentication parameter to `static::createClient` in order to make it simulate user logging. However, that is not the same login as our customers will be using. We are no longer using a basic HTTP authentication, rather a full blown login form.

In order to address the login form testing, let's go ahead and edit the `src/Foggyline/CustomerBundle/Tests/Controller/CustomerControllerTest.php` file as follows:

```
namespace Foggyline\CustomerBundle\Tests\Controller;

use Symfony\Bundle\FrameworkBundle\Test\WebTestCase;
use Symfony\Component\BrowserKit\Cookie;
use Symfony\Component\Security\Core\Authentication\Token
  \UsernamePasswordToken;

class CustomerControllerTest extends WebTestCase
{
```

```
    private $client = null;

    public function setUp()
    {
      $this->client = static::createClient();
    }

    public function testMyAccountAccess()
    {
      $this->logIn();
      $crawler = $this->client->request('GET', '/customer/
        account');

      $this->assertTrue($this->client->getResponse()->
        isSuccessful());
      $this->assertGreaterThan(0, $crawler->
        filter('html:contains("My Account")')->count());
    }

    private function logIn()
    {
      $session = $this->client->getContainer()->get('session');
      $firewall = 'foggyline_customer'; // firewall name
      $em = $this->client->getContainer()->get('doctrine')->
        getManager();
      $user = $em->getRepository('FoggylineCustomerBundle:
        Customer')->findOneByUsername('john@test.loc');
      $token = new UsernamePasswordToken($user, null, $firewall,
        array('ROLE_USER'));
      $session->set('_security_' . $firewall, serialize
        ($token));
      $session->save();
      $cookie = new Cookie($session->getName(), $session->
        getId());
      $this->client->getCookieJar()->set($cookie);
    }
}
```

Here we first created the logIn method, whose purpose is to simulate the login, by
setting up the proper token value into the session, and passing on that session ID to
the client via a cookie. We then created the testMyAccountAccess method, which
first calls the logIn method and then checks if the crawler was able to access the **My
Account** page. The great thing about this approach is that we did not have to code in
the user password, only its username.

Now, let's go ahead and address the customer registration form, by adding the following to the `CustomerControllerTest`:

```
public function testRegisterForm()
{
    $crawler = $this->client->request('GET', '/customer/
        register');
    $uniqid = uniqid();
    $form = $crawler->selectButton('Register!')->form(array(
        'customer[email]' => 'john_' . $uniqid . '@test.loc',
        'customer[username]' => 'john_' . $uniqid,
        'customer[plainPassword][first]' => 'pass123',
        'customer[plainPassword][second]' => 'pass123',
        'customer[firstName]' => 'John',
        'customer[lastName]' => 'Doe',
        'customer[company]' => 'Foggyline',
        'customer[phoneNumber]' => '00 385 111 222 333',
        'customer[country]' => 'HR',
        'customer[state]' => 'Osijek',
        'customer[city]' => 'Osijek',
        'customer[postcode]' => '31000',
        'customer[street]' => 'The Yellow Street',
    ));

    $this->client->submit($form);
    $crawler = $this->client->followRedirect();
    //var_dump($this->client->getResponse()->getContent());
    $this->assertGreaterThan(0, $crawler->
        filter('html:contains("customer/login")')->count());
}
```

We have already seen a test similar to this one in the previous chapter. Here we are merely opening a customer/register page, then finding a button with **Register!** label, so we can fetch the entire form through it. We then set all of the required form data, and simulate the form submit. If successful, we observe for the redirect body and assert against value expected in it.

Running the `phpunit` command now should successfully execute our tests.

Summary

Throughout this chapter we built a miniature but functional customer module. The module assumed a certain level of setup done on our `security.yml` file, which can be covered as part of module documentation if we were to redistribute it. These changes included defining our own custom firewall, with a custom security provider. The security provider pointed to our `customer` class, which in turn was built in a way that complies to the Symfony `UserInterface`. We then built a register, login, and forgot your password form. Though each comes with a minimal set of functionalities, we saw how simple it is to build a fully custom register and login system.

Furthermore, we applied some forward thinking, by using the specially defined service to set up the **My Orders** section under the **My Account** page. This is by far the ideal way of doing it, and it serves a purpose, as we will later override this service cleanly from the `sales` module.

Moving forward, in the next chapter, we will build a `payment` module.

Building the Payment Module

9

The payment module provides a basis for further sales functionality in our web shop. It will enable us to actually choose a payment method when we reach the checkout process of the upcoming sales module. The payment methods can generally be of various types. Some can be static, like Check Money and Cash on Delivery, while others can be regular credit cards like Visa, MasterCard, American Express, Discover, and Switch/Solo. Throughout this chapter we will address both types.

In this chapter, we will be looking into the following topics:

- Requirements
- Dependencies
- Implementation
- Unit testing
- Functional testing

Requirements

Our application requirements, defined under *Chapter 4, Requirement Specification for Modular Web Shop App*, do not really say anything about the type of payment method we need to implement. Thus, for the purpose of this chapter, we will develop two payment methods: a card payment and a check money payment. In regards to the credit card payment, we will not be connecting to a real payment processor, but everything else will be done as if we are working with a credit card.

Ideally, we want this done by an interface, similar to the following:

```
namespace Foggyline\SalesBundle\Interface;

interface Payment
{
```

```
    function authorize();
    function capture();
    function cancel();
}
```

This would then impose the requirement of having the `SalesBundle` module, which we still haven't developed. We will therefore proceed with our payment methods using a simple Symfony `controller` class that provides its own way to address the following features:

- function `authorize();`
- function `capture();`
- function `cancel();`

The `authorize` method is used for cases where we merely want to authorize the transaction, without actually executing it. The result is a transaction ID that our future `SalesBundle` module can store and reuse for further `capture` and `cancel` actions. The `capture` method takes us a step further by first executing the authorize action and then capturing the funds. The `cancel` method performs the cancelation based on a previously stored authorization token.

We will expose our payment methods through tagged Symfony services. The tagging of a service is a nice feature which enables us to view the container and all of the services tagged with the same tag, which is something we can use to fetch all of the `paymentmethod` services. The tag naming has to follow a certain pattern, which we impose on ourselves as application creators. With that in mind, we will tag each payment service with a `name,payment_method`.

Later on, the `SalesBundle` module will fetch and use all of the services tagged with `payment_method` and then use them internally to generate a list of available payment methods that you can work with.

Dependencies

The module has no firm dependencies on any other module. However, it might have been more convenient to build the `SalesBundle` module first and then expose a few interfaces that the `payment` module might use.

Implementation

We start off by creating a new module called `Foggyline\PaymentBundle`. We do so with the help of the console by running the following command:

```
php bin/console generate:bundle --namespace=Foggyline/PaymentBundle
```

The command triggers an interactive process which asks us several questions along the way, shown as follows:

```
Brankos-MacBook-Pro:shop branko$ php bin/console generate:bundle --namespace=Foggyline/PaymentBundle

  Welcome to the Symfony bundle generator!

Are you planning on sharing this bundle across multiple applications? [no]: yes

Your application code must be written in bundles. This command helps
you generate them easily.

Each bundle is hosted under a namespace (like Acme/BlogBundle).
The namespace should begin with a "vendor" name like your company name, your
project name, or your client name, followed by one or more optional category
sub-namespaces, and it should end with the bundle name itself
(which must have Bundle as a suffix).

See http://symfony.com/doc/current/cookbook/bundles/best_practices.html#bundle-name for more
details on bundle naming conventions.

Use / instead of \ for the namespace delimiter to avoid any problem.

Bundle namespace [Foggyline/PaymentBundle]:

In your code, a bundle is often referenced by its name. It can be the
concatenation of all namespace parts but it's really up to you to come
up with a unique name (a good practice is to start with the vendor name).
Based on the namespace, we suggest FoggylinePaymentBundle.

Bundle name [FoggylinePaymentBundle]:

Bundles are usually generated into the src/ directory. Unless you're
doing something custom, hit enter to keep this default!

Target Directory [src/]:

What format do you want to use for your generated configuration?

Configuration format (annotation, yml, xml, php) [xml]:

  Bundle generation

> Generating a sample bundle skeleton into src/Foggyline/PaymentBundle OK!
> Checking that the bundle is autoloaded: OK
> Enabling the bundle inside app/AppKernel.php: OK
> Importing the bundle's routes from the app/config/routing.yml file: OK

  Everything is OK! Now get to work :).
```

Once done, files `app/AppKernel.php` and `app/config/routing.yml` are modified automatically. The `registerBundles` method of an `AppKernel` class has been added to the following line under the `$bundles` array:

```
new Foggyline\PaymentBundle\FoggylinePaymentBundle(),
```

The `routing.yml` has been updated with the following entry:

```
foggyline_payment:
  resource:
    "@FoggylinePaymentBundle/Resources/config/routing.xml"
  prefix:    /
```

In order to avoid colliding with the core application code, we need to change the `prefix: /` to `prefix: /payment/`.

Creating a card entity

Even though we won't be storing any credit cards in our database as part of this chapter, we want to reuse the Symfony auto-generate CRUD feature in order for it to provide us with a credit card model and form. Let's go ahead and create a `Card` entity. We will do so by using the console, shown as follows:

```
php bin/console generate:doctrine:entity
```

The command triggers the interactive generator, providing it with `FoggylinePaymentBundle:Card` for an entity shortcut, where we also need to provide entity properties. We want to model our `Card` entity with the following fields:

- `card_type`: string
- `card_number`: string
- `expiry_date`: date
- `security_code`: string

Once done, the generator creates `Entity/Card.php` and `Repository/CardRepository.php` within the `src/Foggyline/PaymentBundle/` directory. We can now update the database so it pulls in the `Card` entity, shown as follows:

```
php bin/console doctrine:schema:update --force
```

With the entity in place, we are ready to generate its CRUD. We will do so by using the following command:

```
php bin/console generate:doctrine:crud
```

This results in a `src/Foggyline/PaymentBundle/Controller/CardController.php` file being created. It also adds an entry to our `app/config/routing.yml file`, as follows:

```
foggyline_payment_card:
  resource:
    "@FoggylinePaymentBundle/Controller/CardController.php"
  type:    annotation
```

Again, the view files were created under the `app/Resources/views/card/` directory. Since we won't actually be doing any CRUD related actions around cards as such, we can go ahead and delete all of the generated view files, as well as the entire body of the `CardController` class. At this point, we should have our `Card` entity, `CardType` form, and empty `CardController` class.

Creating a card payment service

The card payment service is going to provide the relevant information our future sales module will need for its checkout process. Its role is to provide the payment method label, code, and processing URLs of an order, such as `authorize`, `capture`, and `cancel`.

We will start by defining the following service under the services element of the `src/Foggyline/PaymentBundle/Resources/config/services.xml` file:

```
<service id="foggyline_payment.card_payment"
  class="Foggyline\PaymentBundle\Service\CardPayment">
  <argument type="service" id="form.factory"/>
  <argument type="service" id="router"/>
  <tag name="payment_method"/>
</service>
```

This service accepts two arguments: one being `form.factory` and the other being `router`. `form.factory` that will be used within service to create a form view for the `CardType` form. The tag is a crucial element here, as our `SalesBundle` module will be looking for payment methods based on the `payment_method` tag assigned to the service.

We now need to create the actual service class within the `src/Foggyline/PaymentBundle/Service/CardPayment.php` file as follows:

```
namespace Foggyline\PaymentBundle\Service;

use Foggyline\PaymentBundle\Entity\Card;

class CardPayment
```

```
{
  private $formFactory;
  private $router;

  public function __construct(
    $formFactory,
    \Symfony\Bundle\FrameworkBundle\Routing\Router $router
  )
  {
    $this->formFactory = $formFactory;
    $this->router = $router;
  }

  public function getInfo()
  {
    $card = new Card();
    $form = $this->formFactory->create('Foggyline\
      PaymentBundle\Form\CardType', $card);

    return array(
      'payment' => array(
      'title' =>'Foggyline Card Payment',
      'code' =>'card_payment',
      'url_authorize' => $this->router->generate
        ('foggyline_payment_card_authorize'),
      'url_capture' => $this->router->generate
        ('foggyline_payment_card_capture'),
      'url_cancel' => $this->router->generate
        ('foggyline_payment_card_cancel'),
      'form' => $form->createView()
      )
    );
  }
}
```

The getInfo method is what's going to provide the necessary information to our future SalesBundle module in order for it to construct the payment step of the checkout process. We are passing on three different types of URLs here: authorize, capture, and cancel. These routes do not exist just yet, as we will create them soon. The idea is that we will shift the payment actions and process to the actual payment method. Our future SalesBundle module will merely be doing an **AJAX POST** to these payment URLs, and will expect either a success or error JSON response. A success response should yield some sort of transaction ID and an error response should yield a label message to show to the user.

Creating a card payment controller and routes

We will edit the `src/Foggyline/PaymentBundle/Resources/config/routing.xml` file by adding the following route definitions to it:

```xml
<route id="foggyline_payment_card_authorize" path="/card/
  authorize">
  <default key="_controller">FoggylinePaymentBundle:
    Card:authorize</default>
</route>

<route id="foggyline_payment_card_capture" path="/card/capture">
  <default key="_controller">FoggylinePaymentBundle
    :Card:capture</default>
</route>

<route id="foggyline_payment_card_cancel" path="/card/cancel">
  <default key="_controller">FoggylinePaymentBundle
    :Card:cancel</default>
</route>
```

We will then edit the body of the `CardController` class by adding the following to it:

```php
public function authorizeAction(Request $request)
{
  $transaction = md5(time() . uniqid()); // Just a dummy string,
    simulating some transaction id, if any

  if ($transaction) {
    return new JsonResponse(array(
      'success' => $transaction
    ));
  }

  return new JsonResponse(array(
    'error' =>'Error occurred while processing Card payment.'
  ));
}

public function captureAction(Request $request)
{
  $transaction = md5(time() . uniqid()); // Just a dummy string,
simulating some transaction id, if any

  if ($transaction) {
```

```
      return new JsonResponse(array(
        'success' => $transaction
      ));
    }
  }

  return new JsonResponse(array(
    'error' =>'Error occurred while processing Card payment.'
  ));
}

public function cancelAction(Request $request)
{
  $transaction = md5(time() . uniqid()); // Just a dummy string,
    simulating some transaction id, if any

  if ($transaction) {
    return new JsonResponse(array(
      'success' => $transaction
    ));
  }

  return new JsonResponse(array(
    'error' =>'Error occurred while processing Card payment.'
  ));
}
```

We should now be able to access URLs like /app_dev.php/payment/card/
authorize and see the output of authorizeAction. Implementations given here are
dummy ones. For the purpose of this chapter ,we are not going to connect to a real
payment processing API. What is important for us to know is that the sales module
will, during its checkout process, render any possible form view pushed through
the ['payment']['form'] key of the getInfo method of a payment_method tagged
service. Meaning, the checkout process should show a credit card form under card
payment. The behavior of checking out will be coded such that if payment with
a form is selected and the **Place Order** button is clicked, that payment form will
prevent the checkout process from proceeding until the payment form is submitted
to either authorize or capture the URL defined in the payment itself. We will touch
upon this some more when we get to the SalesBundle module.

Creating a check money payment service

Aside from the credit card payment method, let's go ahead and define one more
static payment, called **Check Money**.

We will start by defining the following service under the services element of the `src/Foggyline/PaymentBundle/Resources/config/services.xml` file:

```xml
<service id="foggyline_payment.check_money"
    class="Foggyline\PaymentBundle\Service\CheckMoneyPayment">
    <argument type="service" id="router"/>
    <tag name="payment_method"/>
</service>
```

The `service` defined here accepts only one `router` argument. The `tag name` is the same as with the card payment service.

We will then create the `src/Foggyline/PaymentBundle/Service/CheckMoneyPayment.php` file, with content as follows:

```php
namespace Foggyline\PaymentBundle\Service;

class CheckMoneyPayment
{
    private $router;

    public function __construct(
        \Symfony\Bundle\FrameworkBundle\Routing\Router $router
    )
    {
        $this->router = $router;
    }

    public function getInfo()
    {
        return array(
            'payment' => array(
                'title' =>'Foggyline Check Money Payment',
                'code' =>'check_money',
                'url_authorize' => $this->router->generate
                    ('foggyline_payment_check_money_authorize'),
                'url_capture' => $this->router->generate
                    ('foggyline_payment_check_money_capture'),
                'url_cancel' => $this->router->generate
                    ('foggyline_payment_check_money_cancel'),
                //'form' =>''
            )
        );
    }
}
```

Unlike a card payment, the check money payment has no form key defined under the `getInfo` method. This is because there are no credit card entries for it to define. It is just going to be a static payment method. However, we still need to define the `authorize`, `capture`, and `cancel` URLs, even though their implementation might be nothing more than just a simple JSON response with success or error keys.

Creating a check money payment controller and routes

Once the check money payment service is in place, we can go ahead and create the necessary routes for it. We will start by adding the following route definitions to the `src/Foggyline/PaymentBundle/Resources/config/routing.xml` file:

```xml
<route id="foggyline_payment_check_money_authorize"
  path="/check_money/authorize">
  <default key="_controller">
    FoggylinePaymentBundle:CheckMoney:authorize</default>
</route>

<route id="foggyline_payment_check_money_capture"
  path="/check_money/capture">
  <default key="_controller">
    FoggylinePaymentBundle:CheckMoney:capture</default>
</route>

<route id="foggyline_payment_check_money_cancel"
  path="/check_money/cancel">
  <default key="_controller">
    FoggylinePaymentBundle:CheckMoney:cancel</default>
</route>
```

We will then create the `src/Foggyline/PaymentBundle/Controller/CheckMoneyController.php` file, with content as follows:

```php
namespace Foggyline\PaymentBundle\Controller;

use Symfony\Component\HttpFoundation\JsonResponse;
use Symfony\Component\HttpFoundation\Request;
use Symfony\Bundle\FrameworkBundle\Controller\Controller;

class CheckMoneyController extends Controller
{
  public function authorizeAction(Request $request)
  {
```

```
    $transaction = md5(time() . uniqid());
    return new JsonResponse(array(
      'success' => $transaction
    ));
  }

  public function captureAction(Request $request)
  {
    $transaction = md5(time() . uniqid());
    return new JsonResponse(array(
      'success' => $transaction
    ));
  }

  public function cancelAction(Request $request)
  {
    $transaction = md5(time() . uniqid());
    return new JsonResponse(array(
      'success' => $transaction
    ));
  }
}
```

Similar to a card payment, here we added a simple dummy implementation of the `authorize`, `capture`, and `cancel` methods. The method responses will feed into the `SalesBundle` module later on. We can easily implement more robust functionality from within these methods, but that is out of the scope of this chapter.

Unit testing

Our `FoggylinePaymentBundle` module is really simple. It provides only two payment methods: card and check money. It does so via two simple `service` classes. Since we are not going after full code coverage tests, we will only cover the `CardPayment` and `CheckMoneyPayment` service classes as part of unit testing.

We will start off by adding the following line under the `testsuites` element of our `phpunit.xml.dist` file:

```
<directory>src/Foggyline/PaymentBundle/Tests</directory>
```

With that in place, running the `phpunit` command from the root of our shop should pick up any test we have defined under the `src/Foggyline/PaymentBundle/Tests/` directory.

Now, let's go ahead and create a test for our `CardPayment` service. We will do so by creating a `src/Foggyline/PaymentBundle/Tests/Service/CardPaymentTest.php` file, with content as follows:

```
namespace Foggyline\PaymentBundle\Tests\Service;

use Symfony\Bundle\FrameworkBundle\Test\KernelTestCase;

class CardPaymentTest extends KernelTestCase
{
  private $container;
  private $formFactory;
  private $router;

  public function setUp()
  {
    static::bootKernel();
    $this->container = static::$kernel->getContainer();
    $this->formFactory = $this->container->get
      ('form.factory');
    $this->router = $this->container->get('router');
  }

  public function testGetInfoViaService()
  {
    $payment = $this->container->get
      ('foggyline_payment.card_payment');
    $info = $payment->getInfo();
    $this->assertNotEmpty($info);
    $this->assertNotEmpty($info['payment']['form']);
  }

  public function testGetInfoViaClass()
  {
    $payment = new \Foggyline\PaymentBundle\
      Service\CardPayment(
        $this->formFactory,
        $this->router
    );

    $info = $payment->getInfo();
    $this->assertNotEmpty($info);
    $this->assertNotEmpty($info['payment']['form']);
  }
}
```

Here, we are running two simple tests to see if we can instantiate a service, either via a container or directly, and simply call its `getInfo` method. The method is expected to return a response that contains the `['payment']['form']` key.

Now, let's go ahead and create a test for our `CheckMoneyPayment` service. We will do so by creating a `src/Foggyline/PaymentBundle/Tests/Service/CheckMoneyPaymentTest.php` file, with content as follows:

```
namespace Foggyline\PaymentBundle\Tests\Service;

use Symfony\Bundle\FrameworkBundle\Test\KernelTestCase;

class CheckMoneyPaymentTest extends KernelTestCase
{
  private $container;
  private $router;

  public function setUp()
  {
    static::bootKernel();
    $this->container = static::$kernel->getContainer();
    $this->router = $this->container->get('router');
  }

  public function testGetInfoViaService()
  {
    $payment = $this->container->get
      ('foggyline_payment.check_money');
    $info = $payment->getInfo();
    $this->assertNotEmpty($info);
  }

  public function testGetInfoViaClass()
  {
    $payment = new \Foggyline\PaymentBundle\
      Service\CheckMoneyPayment(
        $this->router
      );

    $info = $payment->getInfo();
    $this->assertNotEmpty($info);
  }
}
```

Similarly, here we also have two simple tests: one fetching the `payment` method via a container, and the other directly via a class. The difference being that we are not checking for the presence of a form key under the `getInfo` method response.

Functional testing

Our module has two controller classes that we want to test for responses. We want to make sure that the `authorize`, `capture`, and `cancel` methods of the `CardController` and `CheckMoneyController` classes are working.

We first create a `src/Foggyline/PaymentBundle/Tests/Controller/CardControllerTest.php` file, with content as follows:

```
namespace Foggyline\PaymentBundle\Tests\Controller;

use Symfony\Bundle\FrameworkBundle\Test\WebTestCase;


class CardControllerTest extends WebTestCase
{
  private $client;
  private $router;

  public function setUp()
  {
    $this->client = static::createClient();
    $this->router = $this->client->getContainer()->get
      ('router');
  }

  public function testAuthorizeAction()
  {
    $this->client->request('GET', $this->router->generate
      ('foggyline_payment_card_authorize'));
    $this->assertTests();
  }

  public function testCaptureAction()
  {
    $this->client->request('GET', $this->router->generate
      ('foggyline_payment_card_capture'));
    $this->assertTests();
  }
```

```php
public function testCancelAction()
{
  $this->client->request('GET', $this->router->generate
    ('foggyline_payment_card_cancel'));
  $this->assertTests();
}


private function assertTests()
{
  $this->assertSame(200, $this->client->getResponse()->
    getStatusCode());
  $this->assertSame('application/json', $this->client->
    getResponse()->headers->get('Content-Type'));
  $this->assertContains('success', $this->client->
    getResponse()->getContent());
  $this->assertNotEmpty($this->client->getResponse()->
    getContent());
}
}
```

We then create `src/Foggyline/PaymentBundle/Tests/Controller/`
`CheckMoneyControllerTest.php`, with content as follows:

```php
namespace Foggyline\PaymentBundle\Tests\Controller;

use Symfony\Bundle\FrameworkBundle\Test\WebTestCase;

class CheckMoneyControllerTest extends WebTestCase
{
  private $client;
  private $router;

  public function setUp()
  {
    $this->client = static::createClient();
    $this->router = $this->client->getContainer()->
      get('router');
  }

  public function testAuthorizeAction()
  {
    $this->client->request('GET', $this->router->
      generate('foggyline_payment_check_money_authorize'));
    $this->assertTests();
  }
```

```php
public function testCaptureAction()
{
  $this->client->request('GET', $this->router->
    generate('foggyline_payment_check_money_capture'));
  $this->assertTests();
}

public function testCancelAction()
{
  $this->client->request('GET', $this->router->
    generate('foggyline_payment_check_money_cancel'));
  $this->assertTests();
}

private function assertTests()
{
  $this->assertSame(200, $this->client->getResponse()->
    getStatusCode());
  $this->assertSame('application/json', $this->client->
    getResponse()->headers->get('Content-Type'));
  $this->assertContains('success', $this->client->
    getResponse()->getContent());
  $this->assertNotEmpty($this->client->getResponse()->
    getContent());
}
}
```

Both tests are nearly identical. They contain a test for each of the `authorize`, `capture`, and `cancel` methods. Since our methods are implemented with a fixed success JSON response, there are no surprises here. However, we can easily play around with it by extending our payment methods into something more robust.

Summary

Throughout this chapter we have built a payment module with two payment methods. The card payment method is made so that it is simulating payment with the credit cards involved. For that reason, it includes a form as part of its `getInfo` method. The check money payment, on the other hand, is simulating a static payment method - one that does not include any form of credit card. Both methods are implemented as dummy methods, meaning they are not actually communicating to any external payment processor.

The idea was to create a minimal structure that showcases how one can develop a simple payment module for further customization. We did so by exposing each payment method via a tagged service. Using the `payment_method` tag was a matter of consensus, since we are the ones building the full application so we get to choose how we will implement this in the `sales` module.By using the same tag name for each payment method, we effectively created conditions for the future `sales` module to pick all of the payments methods and render them under its checkout process.

Moving forward, in the next chapter we will build a **shipment** module.

10
Building the Shipment Module

The shipment module, alongside the `payment` module, provides a basis for further sales functionality in our web shop. It will enable us to choose the shipment method when we reach the checkout process of the upcoming `sales` module. Similar to `payment`, `shipment` can be sort of static and dynamic. Whereas static might imply a fixed pricing value, or even a calculated one by some simple conditions, dynamic usually implies a connection to external API services.

Throughout this chapter, we will touch base with both types and see how we can set up a basic structure for implementing the `shipment` module.

In this chapter, we will be covering the following topics of the `shipment` module:

- Requirements
- Dependencies
- Implementation
- Unit testing
- Functional testing

Requirements

Application requirements, defined under *Chapter 4*, *Requirement Specification for Modular Web Shop App*, do not give us any specifics as to what type of shipment we need to implement. Thus, for the purpose of this chapter, we will develop two shipment methods: dynamic rate shipment and flat rate shipment. Dynamic rate shipment is used as a way of connecting the shipment method to a real shipment processor, such as UPS, FedEx, and so on. It will not, however, actually connect to any of the external APIs.

Ideally, we want this done by an interface similar to the following:

```
namespace Foggyline\SalesBundle\Interface;

interface Shipment
{
  function getInfo($street, $city, $country, $postcode, $amount,
    $qty);
  function process($street, $city, $country, $postcode, $amount,
    $qty);
}
```

The getInfo method can then be used to fetch the available delivery options for the given order information, while the process method would then process the selected delivery option. For example, we might have an API return "same day delivery ($9.99)",= and "standard delivery ($4.99)" as delivery options under the dynamic rate shipment method.

Having such a shipment interface would then impose the requirement of having the SalesBundle module, which we still haven't developed. We will therefore proceed with our shipment methods, using a Symfony controller for handling the process method and a service for handling the getInfo method.

Similarly, as we did with the payment method in the previous chapter, we will expose our getInfo method through tagged Symfony services. The tag we will be using for shipment methods is shipment_method. Later on, during the checkout process, the SalesBundle module will fetch all of the services tagged with shipment_method and use them internally for a list of available shipment methods to work with.

Dependencies

We are building the module the other way round. That is, we are building it before we know anything about the SalesBundle module, which is the only module that will be using it. With that in mind, the shipment module has no firm dependencies on any other module. However, it might have been more convenient to build the SalesBundle module first and then expose a few interfaces that the shipment module might use.

Implementation

We will start off by creating a new module called `Foggyline\ShipmentBundle`. We will do so with the help of the console by running the following command:

```
php bin/console generate:bundle --namespace=Foggyline/ShipmentBundle
```

The command triggers an interactive process, which asks us several questions along the way, shown as follows:

Once done, files `app/AppKernel.php` and `app/config/routing.yml` are modified automatically. The `registerBundles` method of an `AppKernel` class has been added to the following line under the `$bundles` array:

```
new Foggyline\PaymentBundle\FoggylineShipmentBundle(),
```

The `routing.yml` file has been updated with the following entry:

```
foggyline_payment:
  resource: "@FoggylineShipmentBundle/Resources/
    config/routing.xml"
  prefix:   /
```

In order to avoid colliding with the core application code, we need to change `prefix: /` into `prefix: /shipment/`.

Creating a flat rate shipment service

The flat rate shipment service is going to provide the fixed shipment method that our `sales` module is going to use for its checkout process. Its role is to provide the shipment method labels, code, delivery options, and processing URLs.

We will start by defining the following service under the services element of the `src/Foggyline/ShipmentBundle/Resources/config/services.xml` file:

```
<service id="foggyline_shipment.dynamicrate_shipment"
  class="Foggyline\ShipmentBundle\Service\DynamicRateShipment">
  <argument type="service" id="router"/>
  <tag name="shipment_method"/>
</service>
```

This `service` accepts only one argument: the `router`. The `tagname` value is set to `shipment_method`, as our `SalesBundle` module will be looking for shipment methods based on the `shipment_method` tag assigned to the service.

We will now create the actual `service` class, within the `src/Foggyline/ShipmentBundle/Service/FlatRateShipment.php` file as follows:

```
namespace Foggyline\ShipmentBundle\Service;
class FlatRateShipment
{
  private $router;

  public function __construct(
    \Symfony\Bundle\FrameworkBundle\Routing\Router $router
  )
  {
    $this->router = $router;
  }
```

```
public function getInfo($street, $city, $country, $postcode,
    $amount, $qty)
{
    return array(
        'shipment' => array(
            'title' =>'Foggyline FlatRate Shipment',
            'code' =>'flat_rate',
            'delivery_options' => array(
            'title' =>'Fixed',
            'code' =>'fixed',
            'price' => 9.99
        ),
        'url_process' => $this->router->
            generate('foggyline_shipment_flat_rate_process'),
    )
    ;
    }
}
```

The `getInfo` method is what's going to provide the necessary information to our future `SalesBundle` module in order for it to construct the `shipment` step of the checkout process. It accepts a series of arguments:`$street`, `$city`, `$country`, `$postcode`, `$amount`, and `$qty`. We can consider these to be part of some unified shipment interface. `delivery_options` in this case returns a single, fixed value. `url_process` is the URL to which we will be inserting our selected shipment method. Our future `SalesBundle` module will then merely be doing an AJAX POST to this URL, expecting either a success or error JSON response, which is quite similar to what we imagined doing with payment methods.

Creating a flat rate shipment controller and routes

We edit the `src/Foggyline/ShipmentBundle/Resources/config/routing.xml` file by adding the following route definitions to it:

```
<route id="foggyline_shipment_flat_rate_process"
    path="/flat_rate/process">
    <default key="_controller">
        FoggylineShipmentBundle:FlatRate:process
    </default>
</route>
```

We then create a `src/Foggyline/ShipmentBundle/Controller/FlatRateController.php.` file with content as follows:

```
namespace Foggyline\ShipmentBundle\Controller;

use Symfony\Component\HttpFoundation\JsonResponse;
use Symfony\Component\HttpFoundation\Request;
use Symfony\Bundle\FrameworkBundle\Controller\Controller;

class FlatRateController extends Controller
{
  public function processAction(Request $request)
  {
    // Simulating some transaction id, if any
    $transaction = md5(time() . uniqid());

    return new JsonResponse(array(
      'success' => $transaction
    ));
  }
}
```

We should now be able to access a URL, like `/app_dev.php/shipment/flat_rate/process`, and see the output of `processAction`. Implementations given here are dummy ones. What is important for us to know is that the `sales` module will, during its checkout process, render any possible `delivery_options` pushed through the `getInfo` method of a `shipment_method` tagged service. Meaning, the checkout process should show flat rate shipment as an option. The behavior of checking out will be coded such that if a `shipment` method is not selected, it will prevent the checkout process from going any further. We will touch upon this some more when we get to the `SalesBundle` module.

Creating a dynamic rate payment service

Aside from the flat rate shipment method, let's go ahead and define one more dynamic shipment, called Dynamic Rate.

We will start by defining the following service under the `services` element of the `src/Foggyline/ShipmentBundle/Resources/config/services.xml` file:

```
<service id="foggyline_shipment.dynamicrate_shipment"
  class="Foggyline\ShipmentBundle\Service\DynamicRateShipment">
  <argument type="service" id="router"/>
  <tag name="shipment_method"/>
</service>
```

The `service` defined here accepts only one `router` argument. The `tag name` property is the same as with the flat rate shipment service.

We will then create the `src/Foggyline/ShipmentBundle/Service/DynamicRateShipment.php` file, with content as follows:

```php
namespace Foggyline\ShipmentBundle\Service;

class DynamicRateShipment
{
  private $router;

  public function __construct(
    \Symfony\Bundle\FrameworkBundle\Routing\Router $router
  )
  {
    $this->router = $router;
  }

  public function getInfo($street, $city, $country, $postcode,
    $amount, $qty)
  {
    return array(
      'shipment' => array(
        'title' =>'Foggyline DynamicRate Shipment',
        'code' =>'dynamic_rate_shipment',
        'delivery_options' => $this->getDeliveryOptions
          ($street, $city, $country, $postcode, $amount, $qty),
        'url_process' => $this->router->
          generate('foggyline_shipment_dynamic_rate_process'),
      )
    );
  }

  public function getDeliveryOptions($street, $city, $country,
    $postcode, $amount, $qty)
  {
    // Imagine we are hitting the API with: $street, $city,
$country, $postcode, $amount, $qty
    return array(
      array(
        'title' =>'Same day delivery',
        'code' =>'dynamic_rate_sdd',
        'price' => 9.99
      ),
```

```
      array(
        'title' =>'Standard delivery',
        'code' =>'dynamic_rate_sd',
        'price' => 4.99
      ),
    );
  }
}
```

Unlike the flat rate shipment, here the `delivery_options` key of the `getInfo` method is constructed with the response of the `getDeliveryOptions` method. The method is internal to the service and is not imagined as exposed or to be looked at as part of an interface. We can easily imagine doing some API calls within it, in order to fetch calculated rates for our dynamic shipment method.

Creating a dynamic rate shipment controller and routes

Once the dynamic rates shipment service is in place, we can go ahead and create the necessary route for it. We will start by adding the following route definition to the `src/Foggyline/ShipmentBundle/Resources/config/routing.xml` file:

```
<route id="foggyline_shipment_dynamic_rate_process" path=
  "/dynamic_rate/process">
  <default key="_controller">FoggylineShipmentBundle:
DynamicRate:process
  </default>
</route>
```

We will then create the `src/Foggyline/ShipmentBundle/Controller/DynamicRateController.php` file, with content as follows:

```
namespace Foggyline\ShipmentBundle\Controller;

use Foggyline\ShipmentBundle\Entity\DynamicRate;
use Symfony\Component\HttpFoundation\JsonResponse;
use Symfony\Component\HttpFoundation\Request;
use Symfony\Bundle\FrameworkBundle\Controller\Controller;
use Symfony\Component\Form\Extension\Core\Type\ChoiceType;

class DynamicRateController extends Controller
{
  public function processAction(Request $request)
  {
```

```
    // Just a dummy string, simulating some transaction id
    $transaction = md5(time() . uniqid());

    if ($transaction) {
      return new JsonResponse(array(
'success' => $transaction
      ));
    }

    return new JsonResponse(array(
      'error' =>'Error occurred while processing
        DynamicRate shipment.'
    ));
  }
}
```

Similar to the flat rate shipment, here we have added a simple dummy implementation of the process and method. The incoming $request should contain the same info as the service getInfo method, meaning, it should have the following arguments available: $street, $city, $country, $postcode, $amount, and $qty. The method responses will feed into the SalesBundle module later on. We can easily implement more robust functionality from within these methods, but that is out of the scope of this chapter.

Unit testing

The FoggylineShipmentBundle module is quite simple. By providing only two simple services and two simple controllers, it's easy to test.

We will start off by adding the following line under the testsuites element of our phpunit.xml.dist file:

```
<directory>src/Foggyline/ShipmentBundle/Tests</directory>
```

With that in place, running the phpunit command from root of our shop should pick up any test we have defined under the src/Foggyline/ShipmentBundle/Tests/ directory.

Now, let's go ahead and create a test for our FlatRateShipment service. We will do so by creating a src/Foggyline/ShipmentBundle/Tests/Service/FlatRateShipmentTest.php file, with content as follows:

```
namespace Foggyline\ShipmentBundle\Tests\Service;

use Symfony\Bundle\FrameworkBundle\Test\KernelTestCase;
```

```php
class FlatRateShipmentTest extends KernelTestCase
{
  private $container;
  private $router;

  private $street = 'Masonic Hill Road';
  private $city = 'Little Rock';
  private $country = 'US';
  private $postcode = 'AR 72201';
  private $amount = 199.99;
  private $qty = 7;

  public function setUp()
  {
    static::bootKernel();
    $this->container = static::$kernel->getContainer();
    $this->router = $this->container->get('router');
  }

  public function testGetInfoViaService()
  {
    $shipment = $this->container->get
      ('foggyline_shipment.flat_rate');

    $info = $shipment->getInfo(
      $this->street, $this->city, $this->country, $this->
        postcode, $this->amount, $this->qty
    );

    $this->validateGetInfoResponse($info);
  }

  public function testGetInfoViaClass()
  {
    $shipment = new \Foggyline\ShipmentBundle\Service\
      FlatRateShipment($this->router);

    $info = $shipment->getInfo(
      $this->street, $this->city, $this->country, $this->
        postcode, $this->amount, $this->qty
    );

    $this->validateGetInfoResponse($info);
  }
```

```
   public function validateGetInfoResponse($info)
   {
     $this->assertNotEmpty($info);
     $this->assertNotEmpty($info['shipment']['title']);
     $this->assertNotEmpty($info['shipment']['code']);
     $this->assertNotEmpty
       ($info['shipment']['delivery_options']);
     $this->assertNotEmpty($info['shipment']['url_process']);
   }
 }
```

Two simple tests are being run here. One checks if we can instantiate a service via a container, and the other checks if we can do so directly. Once instantiated, we simply call the getInfo method of a service, passing it a dummy address and order information. Although we are not actually using this data within the getInfo method, we need to pass something along otherwise the test will fail. The method is expected to return a response that contains several keys under the shipment key, most notably title, code, delivery_options, and url_process.

Now, let's go ahead and create a test for our DynamicRateShipment service. We will do so by creating a src/Foggyline/ShipmentBundle/Tests/Service/DynamicRateShipmentTest.php file, with content as follows:

```
namespace Foggyline\ShipmentBundle\Tests\Service;

use Symfony\Bundle\FrameworkBundle\Test\KernelTestCase;
class DynamicRateShipmentTest extends KernelTestCase
{
  private $container;
  private $router;

  private $street = 'Masonic Hill Road';
  private $city = 'Little Rock';
  private $country = 'US';
  private $postcode = 'AR 72201';
  private $amount = 199.99;
  private $qty = 7;

  public function setUp()
  {
    static::bootKernel();
    $this->container = static::$kernel->getContainer();
    $this->router = $this->container->get('router');
  }
```

```
public function testGetInfoViaService()
{
  $shipment = $this->container->
    get('foggyline_shipment.dynamicrate_shipment');
  $info = $shipment->getInfo(
    $this->street, $this->city, $this->country, $this->
      postcode, $this->amount, $this->qty
  );
  $this->validateGetInfoResponse($info);
}


public function testGetInfoViaClass()
{
  $shipment = new \Foggyline\ShipmentBundle\Service\
    DynamicRateShipment($this->router);
  $info = $shipment->getInfo(
    $this->street, $this->city, $this->country, $this->
      postcode, $this->amount, $this->qty
  );

  $this->validateGetInfoResponse($info);
}


public function validateGetInfoResponse($info)
{
  $this->assertNotEmpty($info);
  $this->assertNotEmpty($info['shipment']['title']);
  $this->assertNotEmpty($info['shipment']['code']);

  // Could happen that dynamic rate has none?!
  //$this->assertNotEmpty($info['shipment']
    ['delivery_options']);

  $this->assertNotEmpty($info['shipment']['url_process']);
}
}
```

This test is nearly identical to that of the `FlatRateShipment` service. Here, we also have two simple tests: one fetching the payment method via a container, and the other directly via a class. The difference being that we are no longer asserting the presence of `delivery_options` not being empty. This is because a real API request might not return any options for delivery, depending on the given address and order information.

Functional testing

Our entire module has only two controller classes that we want to test for responses. We want to make sure that the process method of the `FlatRateController` and `DynamicRateController` classes are accessible and working.

We will first create an `src/Foggyline/ShipmentBundle/Tests/Controller/FlatRateControllerTest.php` file, with content as follows:

```
namespace Foggyline\ShipmentBundle\Tests\Controller;

use Symfony\Bundle\FrameworkBundle\Test\WebTestCase;
class FlatRateControllerTest extends WebTestCase
{
  private $client;
  private $router;

  public function setUp()
  {
    $this->client = static::createClient();
    $this->router = $this->client->getContainer()->
      get('router');
  }

  public function testProcessAction()
  {
    $this->client->request('GET', $this->router->
      generate('foggyline_shipment_flat_rate_process'));
    $this->assertSame(200, $this->client->getResponse()->
      getStatusCode());
    $this->assertSame('application/json', $this->client->
      getResponse()->headers->get('Content-Type'));
    $this->assertContains('success', $this->client->
      getResponse()->getContent());
    $this->assertNotEmpty($this->client->getResponse()->
      getContent());
  }
}
```

We will then create a `src/Foggyline/ShipmentBundle/Tests/Controller/DynamicRateControllerTest.php` file, with content as follows:

```
namespace Foggyline\ShipmentBundle\Tests\Controller;

use Symfony\Bundle\FrameworkBundle\Test\WebTestCase;
```

```
class DynamicRateControllerTest extends WebTestCase
{
  private $client;
  private $router;

  public function setUp()
  {
    $this->client = static::createClient();
    $this->router = $this->client->getContainer()->get('router');
  }

  public function testProcessAction()
  {
    $this->client->request('GET', $this->router->generate
      ('foggyline_shipment_dynamic_rate_process'));
    $this->assertSame(200,
      $this->client->getResponse()->getStatusCode());
    $this->assertSame('application/json',
      $this->client->getResponse()->headers->get('Content-Type'));
    $this->assertContains('success',
      $this->client->getResponse()->getContent());
    $this->assertNotEmpty(
      $this->client->getResponse()->getContent());
  }
}
```

Both tests are nearly identical. They contain a test for a single process action method. As it is coded now, the controller process action simply returns a fixed success JSON response. We can easily extend it to return more than just a fixed response and can accompany that change with a more robust functional test.

Summary

Throughout this chapter we have built a `shipment` module with two shipment methods. Each shipment method provided the available delivery options. The flat rate shipment method has only one fixed value under its delivery options, whereas the dynamic rate method gets its values from the `getDeliveryOptions` method. We can easily embed a real shipping API as part of `getDeliveryOptions` in order to provide truly dynamic shipping options.

Obviously, we lack the official interfaces here, as we did with payment methods. However, this is something we can always come back to and refactor in our application as we finalize the `final` module.

Similar to the payment methods, the idea here was to create a minimal structure that showcases how one can develop a simple shipment module for further customization. Using the `shipment_methodservice` tag, we effectively exposed the shipment methods for the future `sales` module.

Moving forward, in the next chapter, we will build a `sales` module, which will finally make use of our `payment` and `shipment` modules.

11
Building the Sales Module

The Sales module is the final one in the series of modules we will build in order to deliver a simple yet functional web shop application. We will do so by adding the cart and the checkout features on top of the catalog. The checkout itself will finally make use of the shipping and payment services defined throughout the previous chapters. The overall focus here will be on absolute basics, since the real shopping cart application would take a far more robust approach. However, understanding how to tie it all together in a simple way is the first step toward opening up a door for more robust web shop application implementations later on.

In this chapter, we will be covering the following topics of the Sales module:

* Requirements
* Dependencies
* Implementation
* Unit testing
* Functional testing

Requirements

Application requirements, defined in *Chapter 4*, *Requirement Specification for Modular Web Shop App*, give us some wireframes relating to the cart and checkout. Based on these wireframes, we can speculate about what type of entities we need to create in order to deliver on functionality.

The following is a list of required module entities:

* Cart
* Cart Item

- Order
- Order Item

The `Cart` entity includes the following properties and their data types:

- `id`: integer, auto-increment
- `customer_id`: string
- `created_at`: datetime
- `modified_at`: datetime

The `Cart Item` entity includes the following properties:

- `id`: integer, auto-increment
- `cart_id`: integer, foreign key that references the category `table id` column
- `product_id`: integer, foreign key that references product `table id` column
- `qty`: string
- `unit_price`: decimal
- `created_at`: datetime
- `modified_at`: datetime

The `Order` entity includes the following properties:

- `id`: integer, auto-increment
- `customer_id`: integer, foreign key that references the customer `table id` column
- `items_price`: decimal
- `shipment_price`: decimal
- `total_price`: decimal
- `status`: string
- `customer_email`: string
- `customer_first_name`: string
- `customer_last_name`: string
- `address_first_name`: string
- `address_last_name`: string
- `address_country`: string
- `address_state`: string
- `address_city`: string

- address_postcode: string
- address_street: string
- address_telephone: string
- payment_method: string
- shipment_method: string
- created_at: datetime
- modified_at: datetime

The Order Item entity includes the following properties:

- id: integer, auto-increment
- sales_order_id: integer, foreign key that references the order table id column
- product_id: integer, foreign key that references product table id column
- title: string
- qty: int
- unit_price: decimal
- total_price: decimal
- created_at: datetime
- modified_at: datetime

Aside from just adding these entities and their CRUD pages, we also need to override a core module service responsible for building the category menu and on-sale items.

Dependencies

The Sales module will have several dependencies across the code. These dependencies are directed toward customer and catalog modules.

Implementation

We start by creating a new module called Foggyline\SalesBundle. We do so with the help of the console, by running the command as follows:

```
php bin/console generate:bundle --namespace=Foggyline/SalesBundle
```

The command triggers an interactive process, asking us several questions along the way, as shown here:

```
Brankos-MacBook-Pro:shop branko$ php bin/console generate:bundle --namespace=Foggyline/SalesBundle

  Welcome to the Symfony bundle generator!

Are you planning on sharing this bundle across multiple applications? [no]: yes

Your application code must be written in bundles. This command helps
you generate them easily.

Each bundle is hosted under a namespace (like Acme/BlogBundle).
The namespace should begin with a "vendor" name like your company name, your
project name, or your client name, followed by one or more optional category
sub-namespaces, and it should end with the bundle name itself
(which must have Bundle as a suffix).

See http://symfony.com/doc/current/cookbook/bundles/best_practices.html#bundle-name for more
details on bundle naming conventions.

Use / instead of \ for the namespace delimiter to avoid any problem.

Bundle namespace [Foggyline/SalesBundle]:

In your code, a bundle is often referenced by its name. It can be the
concatenation of all namespace parts but it's really up to you to come
up with a unique name (a good practice is to start with the vendor name).
Based on the namespace, we suggest FoggylineSalesBundle.

Bundle name [FoggylineSalesBundle]:

Bundles are usually generated into the src/ directory. Unless you're
doing something custom, hit enter to keep this default!

Target Directory [src/]:

What format do you want to use for your generated configuration?

Configuration format (annotation, yml, xml, php) [xml]:

  Bundle generation

> Generating a sample bundle skeleton into src/Foggyline/SalesBundle OK!
> Checking that the bundle is autoloaded: OK
> Enabling the bundle inside app/AppKernel.php: OK
> Importing the bundle's routes from the app/config/routing.yml file: OK

  Everything is OK! Now get to work :).
```

Once done, the `app/AppKernel.php` and `app/config/routing.yml` files get modified automatically. The `registerBundles` method of an `AppKernel` class has been added to the following line under the `$bundles` array:

```
new Foggyline\PaymentBundle\FoggylineSalesBundle(),
```

The `routing.yml` file has been updated with the following entry:

```
foggyline_payment:
  resource: "@FoggylineSalesBundle/Resources/config/routing.xml"
  prefix:    /
```

In order to avoid collision with the core application code, we need to change `prefix: /` into `prefix: /sales/`.

Creating a Cart entity

Let's go ahead and create a `Cart` entity. We do so by using the console, as shown here:

```
php bin/console generate:doctrine:entity
```

This triggers the interactive generator as shown in the following sreenshot:

```
You have new mail in /var/mail/branko
Brankos-MacBook-Pro:shop branko$ php bin/console generate:doctrine:entity

   Welcome to the Doctrine2 entity generator


This command helps you generate Doctrine2 entities.

First, you need to give the entity name you want to generate.
You must use the shortcut notation like AcmeBlogBundle:Post.

The Entity shortcut name: FoggylineSalesBundle:Cart

Determine the format to use for the mapping information.

Configuration format (yml, xml, php, or annotation) [annotation]:

Instead of starting with a blank entity, you can add some fields now.
Note that the primary key will be added automatically (named id).

Available types: array, simple_array, json_array, object,
boolean, integer, smallint, bigint, string, text, datetime, datetimetz,
date, time, decimal, float, binary, blob, guid.

New field name (press <return> to stop adding fields): customer
Field type [string]: integer
Is nullable [false]:
Unique [false]:

New field name (press <return> to stop adding fields): created_at
Field type [datetime]:
Is nullable [false]:
Unique [false]:

New field name (press <return> to stop adding fields): modified_at
Field type [datetime]:
Is nullable [false]:
Unique [false]:

New field name (press <return> to stop adding fields):

   Entity generation


 > Generating entity class src/Foggyline/SalesBundle/Entity/Cart.php: OK!
 > Generating repository class src/Foggyline/SalesBundle/Repository/CartRepository.php: OK!

   Everything is OK! Now get to work :).
```

This creates the `Entity/Cart.php` and `Repository/CartRepository.php` files within the `src/Foggyline/SalesBundle/` directory. After this, we need to update the database, so it pulls in the `Cart` entity, by running the following command:

```
php bin/console doctrine:schema:update --force
```

With the `Cart` entity in place, we can go ahead and generate the `CartItem` entity.

Creating the cart item entity

Let's go ahead and create a `CartItem` entity. We do so by using the now well-known `console` command:

php bin/console generate:doctrine:entity

This triggers the interactive generator as shown in the following screenshot:

```
brankos-mbp:shop branko$ php bin/console generate:doctrine:entity


   Welcome to the Doctrine2 entity generator


This command helps you generate Doctrine2 entities.

First, you need to give the entity name you want to generate.
You must use the shortcut notation like AcmeBlogBundle:Post.

The Entity shortcut name: FoggylineSalesBundle:CartItem

Determine the format to use for the mapping information.

Configuration format (yml, xml, php, or annotation) [annotation]:

Instead of starting with a blank entity, you can add some fields now.
Note that the primary key will be added automatically (named id).

Available types: array, simple_array, json_array, object,
boolean, integer, smallint, bigint, string, text, datetime, datetimetz,
date, time, decimal, float, binary, blob, guid.

New field name (press <return> to stop adding fields): cart
Field type [string]: integer
Is nullable [false]:
Unique [false]:

New field name (press <return> to stop adding fields): qty
Field type [string]: integer
Is nullable [false]:
Unique [false]:

New field name (press <return> to stop adding fields): unit_price
Field type [string]: decimal
Precision [10]:
Scale: 4
Is nullable [false]:
Unique [false]:

New field name (press <return> to stop adding fields): created_at
Field type [datetime]:
Is nullable [false]:
Unique [false]:

New field name (press <return> to stop adding fields): modified_at
Field type [datetime]:
Is nullable [false]:
Unique [false]:

New field name (press <return> to stop adding fields):


   Entity generation


 > Generating entity class src/Foggyline/SalesBundle/Entity/CartItem.php: OK!
 > Generating repository class src/Foggyline/SalesBundle/Repository/CartItemRepository.php: OK!


   Everything is OK! Now get to work :).
```

This creates `Entity/CartItem.php` and `Repository/CartItemRepository.php` within the `src/Foggyline/SalesBundle/` directory. Once the auto generate has done its work, we need to go back and edit the `CartItem` entity to update the `cart` field relation as follows:

```
/**
 * @ORM\ManyToOne(targetEntity="Cart", inversedBy="items")
 * @ORM\JoinColumn(name="cart_id", referencedColumnName="id")
 */
private $cart;
```

Here, we have defined the so-called *bidirectional one-to-many* association. The foreign key in a one-to-many association is being defined on the many side, which in this case is the `CartItem` entity. The bidirectional mapping requires the `mappedBy` attribute on the `OneToMany` association and the `inversedBy` attribute on the `ManyToOne` association. The `OneToMany` side in this case is the `Cart` entity, so we go back to the `src/Foggyline/SalesBundle/Entity/Cart.php` file and add the following to it:

```
/**
 * @ORM\OneToMany(targetEntity="CartItem", mappedBy="cart")
 */
private $items;

public function __construct() {
  $this->items = new \Doctrine\Common\Collections\ArrayCollection();
}
```

We then need to update the database, so it pulls in the `CartItem` entity, by running the following command:

php bin/console doctrine:schema:update --force

With the `CartItem` entity in place, we can go ahead and generate the `Order` entity.

Creating an Order entity

Let's go ahead and create an `Order` entity. We do so by using the console, as shown here:

```
php bin/console generate:doctrine:entity
```

If we tried to provide `FoggylineSalesBundle:Order` as an entity shortcut name, the generated output would throw an error as shown in the following screenshot:

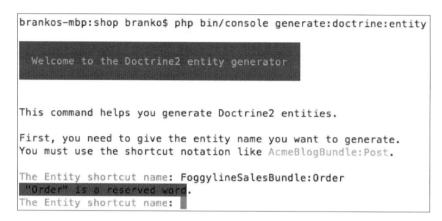

Instead, we will use `SensioGeneratorBundle:SalesOrder` for the entity shortcut name, and follow the generator through as shown here:

```
The Entity shortcut name: SensioGeneratorBundle:SalesOrder

Determine the format to use for the mapping information.

Configuration format (yml, xml, php, or annotation) [annotation]:

Instead of starting with a blank entity, you can add some fields now.
Note that the primary key will be added automatically (named id).

Available types: array, simple_array, json_array, object,
boolean, integer, smallint, bigint, string, text, datetime, datetimetz,
date, time, decimal, float, binary, blob, guid.

New field name (press <return> to stop adding fields): customer
Field type [string]: integer
Is nullable [false]:
Unique [false]:

New field name (press <return> to stop adding fields): items_price
Field type [string]: decimal
Precision [10]:
Scale: 4
Is nullable [false]:
Unique [false]:

New field name (press <return> to stop adding fields): shipment_price
Field type [string]: decimal
Precision [10]:
Scale: 4
Is nullable [false]:
Unique [false]:

New field name (press <return> to stop adding fields): total_price
Field type [string]: decimal
Precision [10]:
Scale: 4
Is nullable [false]:
Unique [false]:

New field name (press <return> to stop adding fields): status
Field type [string]:
Field length [255]:
Is nullable [false]:
Unique [false]:

New field name (press <return> to stop adding fields): payment_method
Field type [string]:
Field length [255]:
Is nullable [false]:
Unique [false]:

New field name (press <return> to stop adding fields): shipment_method
Field type [string]:
Field length [255]:
Is nullable [false]:
Unique [false]:

New field name (press <return> to stop adding fields): created_at
Field type [datetime]:
Is nullable [false]:
Unique [false]:

New field name (press <return> to stop adding fields): modified_at
Field type [datetime]:
Is nullable [false]:
Unique [false]:

New field name (press <return> to stop adding fields):
```

This is followed by the rest of the customer-information-related fields. To get a better idea, look at the following screenshot:

```
New field name (press <return> to stop adding fields): customer_email
Field type [string]:
Field length [255]:
Is nullable [false]:
Unique [false]:

New field name (press <return> to stop adding fields): customer_first_name
Field type [string]:
Field length [255]:
Is nullable [false]:
Unique [false]:

New field name (press <return> to stop adding fields): customer_last_name
Field type [string]:
Field length [255]:
Is nullable [false]:
Unique [false]:
```

This is followed by the rest of the order-address-related fields as shown here:

```
New field name (press <return> to stop adding fields): address_first_name
Field type [string]:
Field length [255]:
Is nullable [false]:
Unique [false]:

New field name (press <return> to stop adding fields): address_last_name
Field type [string]:
Field length [255]:
Is nullable [false]:
Unique [false]:

New field name (press <return> to stop adding fields): address_country
Field type [string]:
Field length [255]:
Is nullable [false]:
Unique [false]:

New field name (press <return> to stop adding fields): address_state
Field type [string]:
Field length [255]:
Is nullable [false]:
Unique [false]:

New field name (press <return> to stop adding fields): address_city
Field type [string]:
Field length [255]:
Is nullable [false]:
Unique [false]:

New field name (press <return> to stop adding fields): address_postcode
Field type [string]:
Field length [255]:
Is nullable [false]:
Unique [false]:

New field name (press <return> to stop adding fields): address_street
Field type [string]:
Field length [255]:
Is nullable [false]:
Unique [false]:

New field name (press <return> to stop adding fields): address_telephone
Field type [string]:
Field length [255]:
Is nullable [false]:
Unique [false]:

New field name (press <return> to stop adding fields):

Entity generation

> Generating entity class vendor/sensio/generator-bundle/Entity/SalesOrder.php: OK!
> Generating repository class Sensio/Bundle/GeneratorBundle/Repository/SalesOrderRepository.php: OK!

Everything is OK! Now get to work :).
```

It is worth noting that normally we would like to extract the address information in its own table, that is make it its own entity. However, to keep things simple, we will proceed by keeping it as part of the `SalesOrder` entity.

Once done, this creates `Entity/SalesOrder.php` and `Repository/SalesOrderRepository.php` files within the `src/Foggyline/SalesBundle/` directory. After this, we need to update the database, so it pulls in the `SalesOrder` entity, by running the following command:

```
php bin/console doctrine:schema:update --force
```

With the `SalesOrder` entity in place, we can go ahead and generate the `SalesOrderItem` entity.

Creating a SalesOrderItem entity

Let's go ahead and create a `SalesOrderItem` entity. We start the code generator by using the following `console` command:

```
php bin/console generate:doctrine:entity
```

When asked for the entity shortcut name, we provide `FoggylineSalesBundle:SalesOrderItem`, and then follow the generator field definitions as shown in the following screenshot:

```
New field name (press <return> to stop adding fields): sales_order
Field type [string]: integer
Is nullable [false]:
Unique [false]:

New field name (press <return> to stop adding fields): product
Field type [string]: integer
Is nullable [false]:
Unique [false]:

New field name (press <return> to stop adding fields): title
Field type [string]:
Field length [255]:
Is nullable [false]:
Unique [false]:

New field name (press <return> to stop adding fields): qty
Field type [string]: integer
Is nullable [false]:
Unique [false]:

New field name (press <return> to stop adding fields): unit_price
Field type [string]: decimal
Precision [10]:
Scale: 4
Is nullable [false]:
Unique [false]:

New field name (press <return> to stop adding fields): total_price
Field type [string]: decimal
Precision [10]:
Scale: 4
Is nullable [false]:
Unique [false]:

New field name (press <return> to stop adding fields): created_at
Field type [datetime]:
Is nullable [false]:
Unique [false]:

New field name (press <return> to stop adding fields): modified_at
Field type [datetime]:
Is nullable [false]:
Unique [false]:

New field name (press <return> to stop adding fields):


  Entity generation


> Generating entity class src/Foggyline/SalesBundle/Entity/SalesOrderItem.php: OK!
> Generating repository class src/Foggyline/SalesBundle/Repository/SalesOrderItemRepository.php: OK!


  Everything is OK! Now get to work :).
```

This creates `Entity/SalesOrderItem.php` and `Repository/SalesOrderItemRepository.php` files within the `src/Foggyline/SalesBundle/` directory. Once the auto-generate has done its work, we need to go back and edit the `SalesOrderItem` entity to update the `SalesOrder` field relation as follows:

```
/**
 * @ORM\ManyToOne(targetEntity="SalesOrder", inversedBy="items")
 * @ORM\JoinColumn(name="sales_order_id",
     referencedColumnName="id")
 */
private $salesOrder;

/**
 * @ORM\OneToOne(targetEntity="Foggyline\CatalogBundle\Entity\
Product")
 * @ORM\JoinColumn(name="product_id", referencedColumnName="id")
 */
private $product;
```

Here, we have defined two types of relations. The first one, relating to `$salesOrder`, is the bidirectional one-to-many association, which we saw in the `Cart` and `CartItem` entities. The second one, relating to `$product`, is the unidirectional one-to-one association. The reference is said to be unidirectional because `CartItem` references `Product`, while `Product` won't be referencing `CartItem`, as we do not want to change something that is part of another module.

We still need to go back to the `src/Foggyline/SalesBundle/Entity/SalesOrder.php` file and add the following to it:

```
/**
 * @ORM\OneToMany(targetEntity="SalesOrderItem",
mappedBy="salesOrder")
 */
private $items;

public function __construct() {
    $this->items = new \Doctrine\Common\Collections\ArrayCollection();
}
```

We then need to update the database, so it pulls in the `SalesOrderItem` entity, by running the following command:

```
php bin/console doctrine:schema:update --force
```

With the `SalesOrderItem` entity in place, we can go ahead and start building the cart and checkout pages.

Overriding the add_to_cart_url service

The add_to_cart_url service was originally declared in FoggylineCustomerBundle with dummy data. This is because we needed a way to build Add to Cart URLs on products before sales functionality was available. While certainly not ideal, it is one possible way of doing it.

Now we are going to override that service with the one declared in our Sales module in order to provide correct Add to Cart URLs. We start off by defining the service within src/Foggyline/SalesBundle/Resources/config/services.xml, by adding the following service element under the services as follows:

```
<service id="foggyline_sales.add_to_cart_url"
  class="Foggyline\SalesBundle\Service\AddToCartUrl">
  <argument type="service" id="doctrine.orm.entity_manager"/>
  <argument type="service" id="router"/>
</service>
```

We then create src/Foggyline/SalesBundle/Service/AddToCartUrl.php with content as follows:

```
namespace Foggyline\SalesBundle\Service;

class AddToCartUrl
{
  private $em;
  private $router;

  public function __construct(
    \Doctrine\ORM\EntityManager $entityManager,
    \Symfony\Bundle\FrameworkBundle\Routing\Router $router
  )
  {
    $this->em = $entityManager;
    $this->router = $router;
  }

  public function getAddToCartUrl($productId)
  {
    return $this->router->generate('foggyline_sales_cart_add',
      array('id' => $productId));
  }
}
```

The `router` service here expects the route named `foggyline_sales_cart_add`, which still does not exist. We create the route by adding the following entry under the `routes` element of the `src/Foggyline/SalesBundle/Resources/config/routing.xml` file as follows:

```
<route id="foggyline_sales_cart_add" path="/cart/add/{id}">
  <default key="_controller">FoggylineSalesBundle:Cart:add</default>
</route>
```

Route definition expects to find the `addAction` function within the cart controller in the `src/Foggyline/SalesBundle/Controller/CartController.php` file, which we define as follows:

```php
namespace Foggyline\SalesBundle\Controller;

use Symfony\Component\HttpFoundation\Request;
use Symfony\Bundle\FrameworkBundle\Controller\Controller;


class CartController extends Controller
{
  public function addAction($id)
  {
    if ($customer = $this->getUser()) {
      $em = $this->getDoctrine()->getManager();
      $now = new \DateTime();

      $product = $em->getRepository
        ('FoggylineCatalogBundle:Product')->find($id);

      // Grab the cart for current user
      $cart = $em->getRepository
        ('FoggylineSalesBundle:Cart')->findOneBy
        (array('customer' => $customer));

      // If there is no cart, create one
      if (!$cart) {
        $cart = new \Foggyline\SalesBundle\Entity\Cart();
        $cart->setCustomer($customer);
        $cart->setCreatedAt($now);
        $cart->setModifiedAt($now);
      } else {
        $cart->setModifiedAt($now);
      }
```

```
$em->persist($cart);
$em->flush();

// Grab the possibly existing cart item
// But, lets find it directly
$cartItem = $em->getRepository
  ('FoggylineSalesBundle:CartItem')->findOneBy
  (array('cart' => $cart, 'product' => $product));

if ($cartItem) {
  // Cart item exists, update it
  $cartItem->setQty($cartItem->getQty() + 1);
  $cartItem->setModifiedAt($now);
} else {
  // Cart item does not exist, add new one
  $cartItem = new
    \Foggyline\SalesBundle\Entity\CartItem();
  $cartItem->setCart($cart);
  $cartItem->setProduct($product);
  $cartItem->setQty(1);
  $cartItem->setUnitPrice($product->getPrice());
  $cartItem->setCreatedAt($now);
  $cartItem->setModifiedAt($now);
}

$em->persist($cartItem);
$em->flush();

$this->addFlash('success', sprintf('%s successfully
  added to cart', $product->getTitle()));

return $this->redirectToRoute('foggyline_sales_cart');
} else {
$this->addFlash('warning', 'Only logged in users can
  add to cart.');
return $this->redirect('/');
}
}
}
}
```

There is quite a bit of logic going on here in the addAction method. We are first checking whether the current user already has a cart entry in the database; if not, we create a new one. We then add or update the existing cart item.

In order for our new `add_to_cart` service to actually override the one from the `Customer`module, we still need to add a compiler. We do so by defining the `src/Foggyline/SalesBundle/DependencyInjection/Compiler/OverrideServiceCompilerPass.php`file with content as follows:

```
namespace Foggyline\SalesBundle\DependencyInjection\Compiler;

use Symfony\Component\DependencyInjection\Compiler\
  CompilerPassInterface;
use Symfony\Component\DependencyInjection\ContainerBuilder;
use Symfony\Component\DependencyInjection\Definition;

class OverrideServiceCompilerPass implements CompilerPassInterface
{
    public function process(ContainerBuilder $container)
    {
        // Override 'add_to_cart_url' service
        $container->removeDefinition('add_to_cart_url');
        $container->setDefinition('add_to_cart_url', $container->
      getDefinition('foggyline_sales.add_to_cart_url'));

        // Override 'checkout_menu' service
        // Override 'foggyline_customer.customer_orders' service
        // Override 'bestsellers' service
        // Pickup/parse 'shipment_method' services
        // Pickup/parse 'payment_method' services
    }
}
```

Later on, we will add the rest of the overrides to this file. In order to tie things up for the moment, and make the `add_to_cart` service override kick in, we need to register the *compiler pass* within the `build` method of our `src/Foggyline/SalesBundle/FoggylineSalesBundle.php` file as follows:

```
public function build(ContainerBuilder $container)
{
    parent::build($container);;
    $container->addCompilerPass(new
OverrideServiceCompilerPass());
}
```

The override should now be in effect, and our `Sales` module should now be providing valid Add to Cart links.

Overriding the checkout_menu service

The checkout menu service defined in the `Customer` module has a simple purpose which is to provide a link to the cart and the first step of the checkout process. Since the Sales module was unknown at the time, the `Customer` module provided a dummy link, which we will now override.

We start by adding the following service entry under the `services` element of the `src/Foggyline/SalesBundle/Resources/config/services.xml` file as follows:

```xml
<service id="foggyline_sales.checkout_menu" class="Foggyline\SalesBundle\Service\CheckoutMenu">
<argument type="service" id="doctrine.orm.entity_manager"/>
<argument type="service" id="security.token_storage"/>
<argument type="service" id="router"/>
</service>
```

We then add the `src/Foggyline/SalesBundle/Service/CheckoutMenu.php` file with content as follows:

```php
namespace Foggyline\SalesBundle\Service;

class CheckoutMenu
{
  private $em;
  private $token;
  private $router;

  public function __construct(
    \Doctrine\ORM\EntityManager $entityManager,
    $tokenStorage,
    \Symfony\Bundle\FrameworkBundle\Routing\Router $router
  )
  {
    $this->em = $entityManager;
    $this->token = $tokenStorage->getToken();
    $this->router = $router;
  }

  public function getItems()
  {
    if ($this->token
      && $this->token->getUser() instanceof
      \Foggyline\CustomerBundle\Entity\Customer
    ) {
      $customer = $this->token->getUser();
```

```
$cart = $this->em->getRepository
   ('FoggylineSalesBundle:Cart')->findOneBy
   (array('customer' => $customer));

if ($cart) {
  return array(
    array('path' => $this->router->generate
    ('foggyline_sales_cart'), 'label' =>
    sprintf('Cart (%s)', count($cart->
    getItems()))),
    array('path' => $this->router->
      generate('foggyline_sales_checkout'),
      'label' =>'Checkout'),
  );
}
}


return array();
}
}
```

The service expects two routes, foggyline_sales_cart and foggyline_sales_ checkout, so we need to amend the src/Foggyline/SalesBundle/Resources/ config/routing.xml by file adding the following route definitions to it:

```
<route id="foggyline_sales_cart" path="/cart/">
  <default key="_controller">
    FoggylineSalesBundle:Cart:index</default>
</route>

<route id="foggyline_sales_checkout" path="/checkout/">
  <default key="_controller">FoggylineSalesBundle:Checkout:index</
default>
</route>
```

The newly added routes expect the cart and checkout controller. The cart controller is already in place, so we just need to add the indexAction to it. At this point, let's just add an empty one as follows:

```
public function indexAction(Request $request)
{

}
```

Similarly, let's create a `src/Foggyline/SalesBundle/Controller/CheckoutController.php` file with content as follows:

```
namespace Foggyline\SalesBundle\Controller;

use Symfony\Component\HttpFoundation\Request;
use Symfony\Bundle\FrameworkBundle\Controller\Controller;
use Symfony\Component\Form\Extension\Core\Type\TextType;
use Symfony\Component\Form\Extension\Core\Type\CountryType;

class CheckoutController extends Controller
{
  public function indexAction()
  {
  }
}
```

Later on, we will revert back to these two `indexAction` methods and add proper method body implementations.

To conclude the service override, we now amend the previously created `src/Foggyline/SalesBundle/DependencyInjection/Compiler/OverrideServiceCompilerPass.php` file, by replacing the `// Override 'checkout_menu'` service comment with the following:

```
$container->removeDefinition('checkout_menu');
$container->setDefinition('checkout_menu', $container->
  getDefinition('foggyline_sales.checkout_menu'));
```

Our newly defined service should now override the one defined in the `Customer` module, thus providing the right checkout and cart (with items in the cart count) URL.

Overriding the customer orders service

The `foggyline_customer.customer_orders` service was to provide a collection of previously created orders for currently logged-in customers. The `Customer` module defined a dummy service for this purpose, just so we can move forward with building up the **My Orders** section under **My Account** page. We now need to override this service, making it return proper orders.

We start by adding the following `service` element under the services of the `src/Foggyline/SalesBundle/Resources/config/services.xml` file as follows:

```xml
<service id="foggyline_sales.customer_orders"
  class="Foggyline\SalesBundle\Service\CustomerOrders">
  <argument type="service" id="doctrine.orm.entity_manager"/>
  <argument type="service" id="security.token_storage"/>
  <argument type="service" id="router"/>
</service>
```

We then add the `src/Foggyline/SalesBundle/Service/CustomerOrders.php` file with content as follows:

```php
namespace Foggyline\SalesBundle\Service;

class CustomerOrders
{
  private $em;
  private $token;
  private $router;

  public function __construct(
    \Doctrine\ORM\EntityManager $entityManager,
    $tokenStorage,
    \Symfony\Bundle\FrameworkBundle\Routing\Router $router
  )
  {
    $this->em = $entityManager;
    $this->token = $tokenStorage->getToken();
    $this->router = $router;
  }

  public function getOrders()
  {
    $orders - array();

    if ($this->token
    && $this->token->getUser() instanceof
      \Foggyline\CustomerBundle\Entity\Customer
    ) {
      $salesOrders = $this->em->
      getRepository('FoggylineSalesBundle:SalesOrder')
      ->findBy(array('customer' => $this->token->
        getUser()));
```

```php
      foreach ($salesOrders as $salesOrder) {
        $orders[] = array(
          'id' => $salesOrder->getId(),
          'date' => $salesOrder->getCreatedAt()->
            format('d/m/Y H:i:s'),
          'ship_to' => $salesOrder->
            getAddressFirstName() . '' . $salesOrder->
            getAddressLastName(),
          'order_total' => $salesOrder->getTotalPrice(),
          'status' => $salesOrder->getStatus(),
          'actions' => array(
            array(
              'label' =>'Cancel',
              'path' => $this->router->generate
                ('foggyline_sales_order_cancel',
                  array('id' => $salesOrder->getId()))
            ),
            array(
              'label' =>'Print',
              'path' => $this->router->generate
                ('foggyline_sales_order_print',
                  array('id' => $salesOrder->getId()))
            )
          )
        );
      }
    }
    return $orders;
  }
}
```

The `route generate` method expects to find two routes, `foggyline_sales_order_cancel` and `foggyline_sales_order_print`, which are not yet created.

Let's go ahead and create them by adding the following under the `route` element of the `src/Foggyline/SalesBundle/Resources/config/routing.xml` file:

```xml
<route id="foggyline_sales_order_cancel"
  path="/order/cancel/{id}">
  <default key="_controller">FoggylineSalesBundle:SalesOrder:
    cancel</default>
</route>

<route id="foggyline_sales_order_print" path="/order/print/{id}">
  <default key="_controller">FoggylineSalesBundle:SalesOrder:
    print</default>
</route>
```

The routes definition, in turn, expects `SalesOrderController` to be defined. Since our application will require an admin user to be able to list and edit the orders, we will use the following Symfony command to auto-generate the CRUD for our `Sales Order` entity:

```
php bin/console generate:doctrine:crud
```

When asked for the entity shortcut name, we simply provide `FoggylineSalesBundle:SalesOrder` and proceed, allowing for creation of write actions. At this point, several files have been created for us, as well as a few entries outside of the `Sales` bundle. One of these entries is the route definition within the `app/config/routing.yml` file, as follows:

```
foggyline_sales_sales_order:
  resource: "@FoggylineSalesBundle/Controller/SalesOrderController.
php"
  type:       annotation
```

We should already have a `foggyline_sales` entry in there as well. The difference being that `foggyline_sales` points to our `router.xml` file and the newly created `foggyline_sales_sales_order` points to the exact newly created `SalesOrderController`. For the sake of simplicity, we can keep them both.

The auto-generator also created a `salesorder` directory under the `app/Resources/views/` directory, which we need to move over into our bundle as the `src/Foggyline/SalesBundle/Resources/views/Default/salesorder/` directory.

We can now address our print and cancel actions by adding the following into the `src/Foggyline/SalesBundle/Controller/SalesOrderController.php` file as follows:

```
public function cancelAction($id)
{
  if ($customer = $this->getUser()) {
    $em = $this->getDoctrine()->getManager();
    $salesOrder = $em->getRepository
      ('FoggylineSalesBundle:SalesOrder')
    ->findOneBy(array('customer' => $customer,
      'id' => $id));

    if ($salesOrder->getStatus() != \Foggyline\SalesBundle
      \Entity\SalesOrder::STATUS_COMPLETE) {
      $salesOrder->setStatus(\Foggyline\SalesBundle\
        Entity\SalesOrder::STATUS_CANCELED);
      $em->persist($salesOrder);
      $em->flush();
```

```
      }
    }

    return $this->redirectToRoute('customer_account');
  }

  public function printAction($id)
  {
    if ($customer = $this->getUser()) {
      $em = $this->getDoctrine()->getManager();
      $salesOrder = $em->getRepository
        ('FoggylineSalesBundle:SalesOrder')
      ->findOneBy(array('customer' => $customer, 'id' =>
        $id));

      return $this->render('FoggylineSalesBundle:default:
        salesorder/print.html.twig', array(
        'salesOrder' => $salesOrder,
        'customer' => $customer
      ));
    }

    return $this->redirectToRoute('customer_account');
  }
}
```

The `cancelAction` method merely checks whether the order in question belongs to the currently logged-in customer; if so, a change of order status is allowed. The `printAction` method merely loads the order if it belongs to the currently logged-in customer, and passes it on to a `print.html.twig` template.

We then create the `src/Foggyline/SalesBundle/Resources/views/Default/salesorder/print.html.twig` template with content as follows:

```
{% block body %}
<h1>Printing Order #{{ salesOrder.id }}</h1>
  {#<p>Just a dummy Twig dump of entire variable</p>#}
  {{ dump(salesOrder) }}
{% endblock %}
```

Obviously, this is just a simplified output, which we can further customize to our needs. The important bit is that we have passed along the `order` object to our template, and can now extract any piece of information needed from it.

Finally, we replace the `// Override 'foggyline_customer.customer_orders'` service comment within the `src/Foggyline/SalesBundle/DependencyInjection/Compiler/OverrideServiceCompilerPass.php` file with code as follows:

```
$container->removeDefinition
  ('foggyline_customer.customer_orders');
$container->setDefinition('foggyline_customer.customer_orders',
  $container->getDefinition('foggyline_sales.customer_orders'));
```

This will make the service override kick in, and pull in all of the changes we just made.

Overriding the bestsellers service

The `bestsellers` service defined in the `Customer` module was supposed to provide dummy data for the bestsellers feature shown on the homepage. The idea is to showcase five of the bestselling products in the store. The `Sales` module now needs to override this service in order to provide the right implementation, where actual sold product quantities will affect the content of the bestsellers shown.

We start off by adding the following definition under the `service` element of the `src/Foggyline/SalesBundle/Resources/config/services.xml` file:

```
<service id="foggyline_sales.bestsellers"
  class="Foggyline\SalesBundle\Service\BestSellers">
  <argument type="service" id="doctrine.orm.entity_manager"/>
  <argument type="service" id="router"/>
</service>
```

We then define the `src/Foggyline/SalesBundle/Service/BestSellers.php` file with content as follows:

```
namespace Foggyline\SalesBundle\Service;

class BestSellers
{
  private $em;
  private $router;

  public function __construct(
    \Doctrine\ORM\EntityManager $entityManager,
    \Symfony\Bundle\FrameworkBundle\Routing\Router $router
  )
  {
    $this->em = $entityManager;
```

```
    $this->router = $router;
  }

  public function getItems()
  {
    $products = array();
    $salesOrderItem = $this->em->getRepository
      ('FoggylineSalesBundle:SalesOrderItem');
    $_products = $salesOrderItem->getBestsellers();

    foreach ($_products as $_product) {
      $products[] = array(
        'path' => $this->router->generate('product_show',
          array('id' => $_product->getId())),
        'name' => $_product->getTitle(),
        'img' => $_product->getImage(),
        'price' => $_product->getPrice(),
        'id' => $_product->getId(),
      );
    }
    return $products;
  }
}
```

Here, we are fetching the instance of the `SalesOrderItemRepository` class and calling the `getBestsellers` method on it. This method still has not been defined. We do so by adding it to file `src/Foggyline/SalesBundle/Repository/SalesOrderItemRepository.php` file as follows:

```
public function getBestsellers()
{

  $products = array();

  $query = $this->_em->createQuery('SELECT IDENTITY(t.product),
    SUM(t.qty) AS HIDDEN q
  FROM Foggyline\SalesBundle\Entity
    \SalesOrderItem t
  GROUP BY t.product ORDER BY q DESC')
  ->setMaxResults(5);

  $_products = $query->getResult();

  foreach ($_products as $_product) {
```

```
    $products[] = $this->_em->getRepository
      ('FoggylineCatalogBundle:Product')
    ->find(current($_product));
  }

  return $products;
}
```

Here, we are using **Doctrine Query Language (DQL)** in order to build a list of the five bestselling products. Finally, we need to replace the `// Override 'bestsellers'` service comment from within the `src/Foggyline/SalesBundle/DependencyInjection/Compiler/OverrideServiceCompilerPass.php` file with code as follows:

```
$container->removeDefinition('bestsellers');
$container->setDefinition('bestsellers', $container->
  getDefinition('foggyline_sales.bestsellers'));
```

By overriding the `bestsellers` service, we are exposing the actual sales-based list of bestselling products for other modules to fetch.

Creating the Cart page

The cart page is where the customer gets to see a list of products added to the cart via **Add to Cart** buttons, from either the homepage, a category page, or a product page. We previously created `CartController` and an empty `indexAction` function. Now let's go ahead and edit the `indexAction` function as follows:

```
public function indexAction()
{
  if ($customer = $this->getUser()) {
    $em = $this->getDoctrine()->getManager();

    $cart = $em->getRepository('FoggylineSalesBundle:Cart')->
      findOneBy(array('customer' => $customer));
    $items = $cart->getItems();
    $total = null;

    foreach ($items as $item) {
      $total += floatval($item->getQty() * $item->
        getUnitPrice());
    }

    return $this->render('FoggylineSalesBundle:default:
      cart/index.html.twig', array(
```

```
            'customer' => $customer,
            'items' => $items,
            'total' => $total,
        ));
    } else {
        $this->addFlash('warning', 'Only logged in customers can
            access cart page.');
        return $this->redirectToRoute('foggyline_customer_login');
    }
}
```

Here, we are checking whether the user is logged in; if they are, we are showing them the cart with all their items. The non-logged-in user is redirected to a customer login URL. The `indexAction` function is expecting the `src/Foggyline/SalesBundle/Resources/views/Default/cart/index.html.twig` file, whose content we define as follows:

```twig
{% extends 'base.html.twig' %}
{% block body %}
<h1>Shopping Cart</h1>
<div class="row">
  <div class="large-8 columns">
    <form action="{{ path('foggyline_sales_cart_update') }}"
      method="post">
    <table>
      <thead>
        <tr>
          <th>Item</th>
          <th>Price</th>
          <th>Qty</th>
          <th>Subtotal</th>
        </tr>
      </thead>
      <tbody>
        {% for item in items %}
        <tr>
          <td>{{ item.product.title }}</td>
          <td>{{ item.unitPrice }}</td>
          <td><input name="item[{{ item.id }}]" value="{{ item.qty
            }}"/></td>
          <td>{{ item.qty * item.unitPrice }}</td>
        </tr>
        {% endfor %}
      </tbody>
```

```
      </table>
      <button type="submit" class="button">Update Cart</button>
    </form>
  </div>
  <div class="large-4 columns">
    <div>Order Total: {{ total }}</div>
    <div><a href="{{ path('foggyline_sales_checkout') }}"
      class="button">Go to Checkout</a></div>
    </div>
  </div>
  {% endblock %}
```

When rendered, the template will show quantity input elements under each added product, alongside the **Update Cart** button. The **Update Cart** button submits the form, whose action is pointing to the foggyline_sales_cart_update route.

Let's go ahead and create foggyline_sales_cart_update, by adding the following entry under the route element of the src/Foggyline/SalesBundle/Resources/config/routing.xml file as follows:

```
<route id="foggyline_sales_cart_update" path="/cart/update">
  <default key="_controller">FoggylineSalesBundle:Cart:update
    </default>
</route>
```

The newly defined route expects to find an updateAction function under the src/Foggyline/SalesBundle/Controller/CartController.php file, which we add as follows:

```
public function updateAction(Request $request)
{
  $items = $request->get('item');

  $em = $this->getDoctrine()->getManager();
  foreach ($items as $_id => $_qty) {
    $cartItem = $em->getRepository
      ('FoggylineSalesBundle:CartItem')->find($_id);
    if (intval($_qty) > 0) {
      $cartItem->setQty($_qty);
      $em->persist($cartItem);
    } else {
      $em->remove($cartItem);
    }
  }
  // Persist to database
```

```
    $em->flush();

    $this->addFlash('success', 'Cart updated.');

    return $this->redirectToRoute('foggyline_sales_cart');
}
```

To remove a product from the cart, we simply insert 0 as the quantity value and click the **Update Cart** button. This completes our simple cart page.

Creating the Payment service

In order to move from cart to checkout, we need to sort out payment and shipment services. The previous Payment and Shipment modules exposed some of their Payment and Shipment services, which we now need to aggregate into a single Payment and Shipment service that our checkout process will use.

We start by replacing the previously added // Pickup/parse 'payment_method' services comment under the src/Foggyline/SalesBundle/DependencyInjection/ Compiler/OverrideServiceCompilerPass.php file with code as follows:

```
$container->getDefinition('foggyline_sales.payment')
  ->addArgument(
  array_keys($container->findTaggedServiceIds
    ('payment_method'))
);
```

The findTaggedServiceIds method returns a key-value list of all the services tagged with payment_method, which we then pass on as argument to our foggyline_sales.payment service. This is the only way to fetch the list of services in Symfony during the compilation time.

We then edit the src/Foggyline/SalesBundle/Resources/config/services.xml file by adding the following under the service element:

```
<service id="foggyline_sales.payment"
  class="Foggyline\SalesBundle\Service\Payment">
  <argument type="service" id="service_container"/>
</service>
```

Finally, we create the Payment class under the src/Foggyline/SalesBundle/ Service/Payment.php file as follows:

```
namespace Foggyline\SalesBundle\Service;

class Payment
```

```
{
  private $container;
  private $methods;

  public function __construct($container, $methods)
  {
    $this->container = $container;
    $this->methods = $methods;
  }

  public function getAvailableMethods()
  {
    $methods = array();

    foreach ($this->methods as $_method) {
      $methods[] = $this->container->get($_method);
    }

    return $methods;
  }
}
```

In compliance with the service definition in the `services.xml` file, our service accepts two parameters, one being `$container` and the second one being `$methods`. The `$methods` argument is passed during compilation time, where we are able to fetch a list of all the `payment_method` tagged services. This effectively means our `getAvailableMethods` is now capable of returning all `payment_method` tagged services, from any module.

Creating the Shipment service

The `Shipment` service is implemented much like the `Payment` service. The overall idea is similar, with merely a few differences along the way. We start by replacing the previously added `// Pickup/parse shipment_method'` services comment under the `src/Foggyline/SalesBundle/DependencyInjection/Compiler/OverrideServiceCompilerPass.php` file with code as follows:

```
$container->getDefinition('foggyline_sales.shipment')
  ->addArgument(
  array_keys($container->findTaggedServiceIds
    ('shipment_method'))
);
```

We then edit the `src/Foggyline/SalesBundle/Resources/config/services.xml` file by adding the following under the `service` element:

```
<service id="foggyline_sales.shipment"
  class="Foggyline\SalesBundle\Service\Payment">
  <argument type="service" id="service_container"/>
</service>
```

Finally, we create the `Shipment` class under the `src/Foggyline/SalesBundle/Service/Shipment.php` file as follows:

```
namespace Foggyline\SalesBundle\Service;

class Shipment
{
  private $container;
  private $methods;

  public function __construct($container, $methods)
  {
    $this->container = $container;
    $this->methods = $methods;
  }

  public function getAvailableMethods()
  {
    $methods = array();
    foreach ($this->methods as $_method) {
      $methods[] = $this->container->get($_method);
    }

    return $methods;
  }
}
```

We are now able to fetch all the `Payment` and `Shipment` services via our unified `Payment` and `Shipment` service, thus making the checkout process easy.

Creating the Checkout page

The checkout page will be constructed out of two checkout steps, the first one being shipment information gathering, and the second one being payment information gathering.

We start off with a shipment step, by changing our src/Foggyline/SalesBundle/ Controller/CheckoutController.php file and its indexAction as follows:

```php
public function indexAction()
{
  if ($customer = $this->getUser()) {

    $form = $this->getAddressForm();

    $em = $this->getDoctrine()->getManager();
    $cart = $em->getRepository('FoggylineSalesBundle:Cart')
      ->findOneBy(array('customer' => $customer));
    $items = $cart->getItems();
    $total = null;

    foreach ($items as $item) {
      $total += floatval($item->getQty() * $item->getUnitPrice());
    }

    return $this->render
      ('FoggylineSalesBundle:default:checkout/index.html.twig',
      array(
      'customer' => $customer,
      'items' => $items,
      'cart_subtotal' => $total,
      'shipping_address_form' => $form->createView(),
      'shipping_methods' => $this->get
        ('foggyline_sales.shipment')->getAvailableMethods()
    ));
  } else {
    $this->addFlash('warning', 'Only logged in customers can
      access checkout page.');
    return $this->redirectToRoute('foggyline_customer_login');
  }
}
private function getAddressForm()
{
  return $this->createFormBuilder()
  ->add('address_first_name', TextType::class)
  ->add('address_last_name', TextType::class)
  ->add('company', TextType::class)
  ->add('address_telephone', TextType::class)
  ->add('address_country', CountryType::class)
  ->add('address_state', TextType::class)
  ->add('address_city', TextType::class)
```

```
    ->add('address_postcode', TextType::class)
    ->add('address_street', TextType::class)
    ->getForm();
}
```

Here, we are fetching the currently logged-in customer cart and passing it onto a `checkout/index.html.twig` template, alongside several other variables needed for the shipment step. The `getAddressForm` method simply builds an address form for us. There is also a call toward our newly created the `foggyline_sales.shipment` service, which enables us to fetch a list of all available shipment methods.

We then create `src/Foggyline/SalesBundle/Resources/views/Default/checkout/index.html.twig` with content as follows:

```twig
{% extends 'base.html.twig' %}
{% block body %}
<h1>Checkout</h1>

<div class="row">
  <div class="large-8 columns">
    <form action="{{ path('foggyline_sales_checkout_payment') }}"
      method="post" id="shipping_form">
      <fieldset>
        <legend>Shipping Address</legend>
        {{ form_widget(shipping_address_form) }}
      </fieldset>

      <fieldset>
        <legend>Shipping Methods</legend>
        <ul>
          {% for method in shipping_methods %}
          {% set shipment = method.getInfo('street', 'city',
            'country', 'postcode', 'amount', 'qty')['shipment'] %}
          <li>
            <label>{{ shipment.title }}</label>
            <ul>
              {% for delivery_option in shipment.delivery_options %}
              <li>
                <input type="radio" name="shipment_method"
                  value="{{ shipment.code }}____
                  {{ delivery_option.code }}____
                  {{ delivery_option.price }}">
                  {{ delivery_option.title }}
                  ({{ delivery_option.price }})
                <br>
```

```
              </li>
            {% endfor %}
          </ul>
        </li>
      {% endfor %}
      </ul>
    </fieldset>
  </form>
</div>
<div class="large-4 columns">
  {% include
    'FoggylineSalesBundle:default:checkout/order_sumarry.html.twig'
  %}
  <div>Cart Subtotal: {{ cart_subtotal }}</div>
  <div><a id="shipping_form_submit" href="#"
    class="button">Next</a>
  </div>
</div>
</div>
</div>

<script type="text/javascript">
  var form = document.getElementById('shipping_form');
  document.getElementById('shipping_form_submit')
    .addEventListener('click', function () {
    form.submit();
  });
</script>
{% endblock %}
```

The template lists all of the address-related form fields, alongside available shipment methods. The JavaScript part handles the **Next** button click, which basically submits the form to the `foggyline_sales_checkout_payment` route.

We then define the `foggyline_sales_checkout_payment` route by adding the following entry under the `routes` element of the `src/Foggyline/SalesBundle/Resources/config/routing.xml` file:

```
<route id="foggyline_sales_checkout_payment"
  path="/checkout/payment">
  <default
    key="_controller">FoggylineSalesBundle:Checkout:payment</default>
</route>
```

The route entry expects to find a `paymentAction` within `CheckoutController`, which we define as follows:

```
public function paymentAction(Request $request)
{
  $addressForm = $this->getAddressForm();
  $addressForm->handleRequest($request);

  if ($addressForm->isSubmitted() && $addressForm->isValid() &&
    $customer = $this->getUser()) {

    $em = $this->getDoctrine()->getManager();
    $cart = $em->getRepository('FoggylineSalesBundle:Cart')->
      findOneBy(array('customer' => $customer));
    $items = $cart->getItems();
    $cartSubtotal = null;

    foreach ($items as $item) {
      $cartSubtotal += floatval($item->getQty() * $item->
        getUnitPrice());
    }

    $shipmentMethod = $_POST['shipment_method'];
    $shipmentMethod = explode('____', $shipmentMethod);
    $shipmentMethodCode = $shipmentMethod[0];
    $shipmentMethodDeliveryCode = $shipmentMethod[1];
    $shipmentMethodDeliveryPrice = $shipmentMethod[2];

    // Store relevant info into session
    $checkoutInfo = $addressForm->getData();
    $checkoutInfo['shipment_method'] = $shipmentMethodCode .
      '____' . $shipmentMethodDeliveryCode;
    $checkoutInfo['shipment_price'] =
      $shipmentMethodDeliveryPrice;
    $checkoutInfo['items_price'] = $cartSubtotal;
    $checkoutInfo['total_price'] = $cartSubtotal +
      $shipmentMethodDeliveryPrice;
    $this->get('session')->set('checkoutInfo', $checkoutInfo);

    return $this->render('FoggylineSalesBundle:default:
      checkout/payment.html.twig', array(
      'customer' => $customer,
      'items' => $items,
      'cart_subtotal' => $cartSubtotal,
```

```
        'delivery_subtotal' => $shipmentMethodDeliveryPrice,
        'delivery_label' =>'Delivery Label Here',
        'order_total' => $cartSubtotal +
          $shipmentMethodDeliveryPrice,
        'payment_methods' => $this->get
          ('foggyline_sales.payment')->getAvailableMethods()
    ));
  } else {
    $this->addFlash('warning', 'Only logged in customers can
      access checkout page.');
    return $this->redirectToRoute('foggyline_customer_login');
  }
}
```

The preceding code fetches the submission made from the shipment step of the checkout process, stores the relevant values into the session, fetches the variables required for the payment step and renders back the checkout/payment.html.twig template.

We define the src/Foggyline/SalesBundle/Resources/views/Default/checkout/payment.html.twig file with content as follows:

```
{% extends 'base.html.twig' %}
{% block body %}
<h1>Checkout</h1>
<div class="row">
  <div class="large-8 columns">
    <form action="{{ path('foggyline_sales_checkout_process') }}"
      method="post" id="payment_form">
      <fieldset>
        <legend>Payment Methods</legend>
        <ul>
          {% for method in payment_methods %}
          {% set payment = method.getInfo()['payment'] %}
          <li>
            <input type="radio" name="payment_method"
              value="{{ payment.code }}"> {{ payment.title }}
            {% if payment['form'] is defined %}
            <div id="{{ payment.code }}_form">
              {{ form_widget(payment['form']) }}
            </div>
            {% endif %}
          </li>
          {% endfor %}
        </ul>
```

```
          </fieldset>
        </form>
      </div>
      <div class="large-4 columns">
        {% include 'FoggylineSalesBundle:default:checkout/
          order_sumarry.html.twig' %}
        <div>Cart Subtotal: {{ cart_subtotal }}</div>
        <div>{{ delivery_label }}: {{ delivery_subtotal }}</div>
        <div>Order Total: {{ order_total }}</div>
        <div><a id="payment_form_submit" href="#" class="button">Place
          Order</a>
        </div>
      </div>
    </div>
    <script type="text/javascript">
      var form = document.getElementById('payment_form');
      document.getElementById('payment_form_submit').
        addEventListener('click', function () {
        form.submit();
      });
    </script>
  {% endblock %}
```

Similar to the shipment step, we have a rendering of available payment methods here, alongside a **Place Order** button which is handled by JavaScript as the button is located outside of the submission form. Once an order is placed, the POST submission is made onto the `foggyline_sales_checkout_process` route, which we defined under the `routes` element of the `src/Foggyline/SalesBundle/Resources/config/routing.xml` file as follows:

```
<route id="foggyline_sales_checkout_process"
  path="/checkout/process">
  <default
    key="_controller">FoggylineSalesBundle:Checkout:process</default>
</route>
```

The route points to the `processAction` function within `CheckoutController`, which we define as follows:

```
public function processAction()
{
  if ($customer = $this->getUser()) {

    $em = $this->getDoctrine()->getManager();
    // Merge all the checkout info, for SalesOrder
```

```php
$checkoutInfo = $this->get('session')->get
    ('checkoutInfo');
$now = new \DateTime();

// Create Sales Order
$salesOrder = new \Foggyline\SalesBundle\Entity
    \SalesOrder();
$salesOrder->setCustomer($customer);
$salesOrder->setItemsPrice($checkoutInfo['items_price']);
$salesOrder->setShipmentPrice
    ($checkoutInfo['shipment_price']);
$salesOrder->setTotalPrice($checkoutInfo['total_price']);
$salesOrder->setPaymentMethod($_POST['payment_method']);
$salesOrder->setShipmentMethod
    ($checkoutInfo['shipment_method']);
$salesOrder->setCreatedAt($now);
$salesOrder->setModifiedAt($now);
$salesOrder->setCustomerEmail($customer->getEmail());
$salesOrder->setCustomerFirstName
    ($customer->getFirstName());
$salesOrder->setCustomerLastName
    ($customer->getLastName());
$salesOrder->setAddressFirstName
    ($checkoutInfo['address_first_name']);
$salesOrder->setAddressLastName
    ($checkoutInfo['address_last_name']);
$salesOrder->setAddressCountry
    ($checkoutInfo['address_country']);
$salesOrder->setAddressState
    ($checkoutInfo['address_state']);
$salesOrder->setAddressCity
    ($checkoutInfo['address_city']);
$salesOrder->setAddressPostcode
    ($checkoutInfo['address_postcode']);
$salesOrder->setAddressStreet
    ($checkoutInfo['address_street']);
$salesOrder->setAddressTelephone
    ($checkoutInfo['address_telephone']);
$salesOrder->setStatus(\Foggyline\SalesBundle\Entity\
    SalesOrder::STATUS_PROCESSING);

$em->persist($salesOrder);
$em->flush();

// Foreach cart item, create order item, and delete cart
    item
```

```
$cart = $em->getRepository('FoggylineSalesBundle:Cart')->
  findOneBy(array('customer' => $customer));
$items = $cart->getItems();

foreach ($items as $item) {
  $orderItem = new \Foggyline\SalesBundle\Entity
    \SalesOrderItem();

  $orderItem->setSalesOrder($salesOrder);
  $orderItem->setTitle($item->getProduct()->getTitle());
  $orderItem->setQty($item->getQty());
  $orderItem->setUnitPrice($item->getUnitPrice());
  $orderItem->setTotalPrice($item->getQty() * $item-
>getUnitPrice());
  $orderItem->setModifiedAt($now);
  $orderItem->setCreatedAt($now);
  $orderItem->setProduct($item->getProduct());

  $em->persist($orderItem);
  $em->remove($item);
}

$em->remove($cart);
$em->flush();

$this->get('session')->set('last_order', $salesOrder->
getId());
  return $this->redirectToRoute
    ('foggyline_sales_checkout_success');
} else {
  $this->addFlash('warning', 'Only logged in customers can
    access checkout page.');
  return $this->redirectToRoute('foggyline_customer_login');
  }
}
```

Once the POST submission hits the controller, a new order with all of the related items gets created. At the same time, the cart and cart items are cleared. Finally, the customer is redirected to the order success page.

Creating the order success page

The order success page has an important role in full-blown web shop applications. This is where we get to thank the customer for their purchase and possibly present some more related or cross-related shopping options, alongside some optional discounts. Though our application is simple, it's worth building a simple order success page.

We start by adding the following route definition under the `routes` element of the `src/Foggyline/SalesBundle/Resources/config/routing.xml` file:

```
<route id="foggyline_sales_checkout_success"
  path="/checkout/success">
  <default
    key="_controller">FoggylineSalesBundle:Checkout:success</default>
</route>
```

The route points to a `successAction` function within `CheckoutController`, which we define as follows:

```
public function successAction()
{

  return $this->render('FoggylineSalesBundle:default:
    checkout/success.html.twig', array(
    'last_order' => $this->get('session')->get('last_order')
  ));
}
```

Here, we are simply fetching the last created order ID for the currently logged-in customer and passing the full order object to the `src/Foggyline/SalesBundle/Resources/views/Default/checkout/success.html.twig` template as follows:

```
{% extends 'base.html.twig' %}
{% block body %}
<h1>Checkout Success</h1>
<div class="row">
  <p>Thank you for placing your order #{{ last_order }}.</p>
  <p>You can see order details <a href="{{
    path('customer_account') }}">here</a>.</p>
</div>
{% endblock %}
```

With this, we finalize the entire checkout process for our web shop. Though it is an absolutely simplistic one, it sets the foundation for more robust implementations.

Creating a store manager dashboard

Now that we have finalized the checkout `Sales` module, let's revert quickly to our core module, `AppBundle`. As per our application requirements, let's go ahead and create a simple store manager dashboard.

We start by adding the `src/AppBundle/Controller/StoreManagerController.php` file with content as follows:

```php
namespace AppBundle\Controller;

use Sensio\Bundle\FrameworkExtraBundle\Configuration\Route;
use Symfony\Bundle\FrameworkBundle\Controller\Controller;

class StoreManagerController extends Controller
{
  /**
  * @Route("/store_manager", name="store_manager")
  */
  public function indexAction()
  {
    return $this->render
      ('AppBundle:default:store_manager.html.twig');
  }
}
```

The `indexAction` function simply returns the `src/AppBundle/Resources/views/default/store_manager.html.twig` file, whose content we define as follows:

```twig
{% extends 'base.html.twig' %}
{% block body %}
<h1>Store Manager</h1>
<div class="row">
  <div class="large-6 columns">
    <div class="stacked button-group">
      <a href="{{ path('category_new') }}" class="button">Add new
        Category</a>
      <a href="{{ path('product_new') }}" class="button">Add new
        Product</a>
      <a href="{{ path('customer_new') }}" class="button">Add new
        Customer</a>
    </div>
  </div>
  <div class="large-6 columns">
    <div class="stacked button-group">
      <a href="{{ path('category_index') }}" class="button">List &
        Manage Categories</a>
      <a href="{{ path('product_index') }}" class="button">List &
        Manage Products</a>
      <a href="{{ path('customer_index') }}" class="button">List &
        Manage Customers</a>
```

```
    <a href="{{ path('salesorder_index') }}" class="button">List
      & Manage Orders</a>
    </div>
  </div>
</div>
{% endblock %}
```

The template merely renders the category, product, customer, and order management links. The actual access to these links is controlled by the firewall, as explained in previous chapters.

Unit testing

The `Sales` module is far more robust than any of the previous modules. There are several things we can unit test. However, we won't be covering full unit testing as part of this chapter. We will simply turn our attention to a single unit test, the one for the `CustomerOrders` service.

We start off by adding the following line under the `testsuites` element of our `phpunit.xml.dist` file:

```
<directory>src/Foggyline/SalesBundle/Tests</directory>
```

With that in place, running the `phpunit` command from the root of our shop should pick up any test we have defined under the `src/Foggyline/SalesBundle/Tests/` directory.

Now, let's go ahead and create a test for our `CustomerOrders` service. We do so by defining the `src/Foggyline/SalesBundle/Tests/Service/CustomerOrdersTest.php` file with content as follows:

```
namespace Foggyline\SalesBundle\Test\Service;

use Symfony\Bundle\FrameworkBundle\Test\KernelTestCase;
use Symfony\Component\Security\Core\Authentication\
  Token\UsernamePasswordToken;

class CustomerOrdersTest extends KernelTestCase
{
  private $container;

  public function setUp()
  {
    static::bootKernel();
    $this->container = static::$kernel->getContainer();
```

```
    }

    public function testGetOrders()
    {
        $firewall = 'foggyline_customer';

        $em = $this->container->get
            ('doctrine.orm.entity_manager');

        $user = $em->getRepository
            ('FoggylineCustomerBundle:Customer')->findOneByUsername
            ('ajzele@gmail.com');
        $token = new UsernamePasswordToken($user, null, $firewall,
            array('ROLE_USER'));

        $tokenStorage = $this->container->get
            ('security.token_storage');
        $tokenStorage->setToken($token);

        $orders = new \Foggyline\SalesBundle\Service
            \CustomerOrders(
            $em,
            $tokenStorage,
            $this->container->get('router')
        );

        $this->assertNotEmpty($orders->getOrders());
    }
}
```

Here, we are using the UsernamePasswordToken function in order to simulate a customer login. The password token is then passed on to the CustomerOrders service. The CustomerOrders service then internally checks whether token storage has a token assigned, flagging it as a logged-in user and returning the list of its orders. Being able to simulate customer login is essential for any other tests we might be writing for our sales module.

Functional testing

Similar to unit testing, we will only focus on a single functional test, as doing anything more robust would be out of the scope of this chapter. We will write a simple code that adds a product to the cart and accesses the checkout page. In order to add an item to the cart, here we also need to simulate the user login.

We write the `src/Foggyline/SalesBundle/Tests/Controller/`
`CartControllerTest.php` **test as follows:**

```php
namespace Foggyline\SalesBundle\Tests\Controller;

use Symfony\Bundle\FrameworkBundle\Test\WebTestCase;
use Symfony\Component\BrowserKit\Cookie;
use Symfony\Component\Security\Core\Authentication\
Token\UsernamePasswordToken;

class CartControllerTest extends WebTestCase
{
  private $client = null;

  public function setUp()
  {
    $this->client = static::createClient();
  }

  public function testAddToCartAndAccessCheckout()
  {
    $this->logIn();

    $crawler = $this->client->request('GET', '/');
    $crawler = $this->client->click($crawler->selectLink('Add
      to Cart')->link());
    $crawler = $this->client->followRedirect();

    $this->assertTrue($this->client->getResponse()->
      isSuccessful());
    $this->assertGreaterThan(0, $crawler->filter
      ('html:contains("added to cart")')->count());

    $crawler = $this->client->request('GET', '/sales/cart/');
    $crawler = $this->client->click($crawler->selectLink('Go
      to Checkout')->link());


    $this->assertTrue($this->client->getResponse()->
      isSuccessful());
    $this->assertGreaterThan(0, $crawler->filter
      ('html:contains("Checkout")')->count());
  }
```

```
private function logIn()
{
  $session = $this->client->getContainer()->get('session');
  $firewall = 'foggyline_customer'; // firewall name
  $em = $this->client->getContainer()->get('doctrine')->
    getManager();
  $user = $em->getRepository
    ('FoggylineCustomerBundle:Customer')->findOneByUsername
    ('ajzele@gmail.com');

  $token = new UsernamePasswordToken($user, null, $firewall,
    array('ROLE_USER'));
  $session->set('_security_' . $firewall,
    serialize($token));
  $session->save();

  $cookie = new Cookie($session->getName(), $session->
    getId());
  $this->client->getCookieJar()->set($cookie);
 }
}
```

Once run, the test will simulate the customer login, add an item to the cart, and try to access the checkout page. Depending on the actual customers we have in our database, we might need to change the customer e-mail provided in the preceding test.

Running the phpunit command now should successfully execute our tests.

Summary

In this chapter, we built a simple yet functional `Sales` module. With just four simple entities (`Cart`, `CartItem`, `SalesOrder`, and `SalesOrderItem`), we managed to implement simple cart and checkout features. By doing so, we empowered customers to actually make a purchase, instead of just browsing the product catalog. The sales module made use of the payment and shipment services defined in previous chapters. While the payment and shipment services are implemented as imaginary, dummy ones, they do provide a basic skeleton that we can use for real payment and shipment API implementations.

Furthermore, in this chapter, we addressed the admin dashboard, by making a simple interface that merely aggregates a few of the existing CRUD interfaces. Access to the dashboard and the management links is protected by entries in `app/config/security.yml`, and allowed only for `ROLE_ADMIN`.

Together, the modules written so far make up a simplified application. Writing robust web shop applications would normally include tens of other features found in modern e-commerce platforms such as Magento. These include multiple language, currency, and website support; robust category, product, and product inventory management; shopping cart and catalog sales rules; and many others. Modularizing our application makes development and maintenance processes easier.

Moving forward, in the final chapter, we will look into distributing our modules.

12
Integrating and Distributing Modules

Throughout a few of the previous chapters, we built a simple web shop application in a modular manner. Each of the modules play a special role in handling individual bits and pieces, which add to the overall application. The application itself, though written in modular, was kept in a Git single version control repository. It would be a far cleaner separation if each of the modules was provided in its own repository. This way, we will be able to keep the different module developments as completely different projects while still being able to use them together. As we move forward, we will see how we can achieve this via GIT and Composer in two different manners.

In this chapter, we will cover the following tools and services:

- Understanding Git
- Understanding GitHub
- Understanding Composer
- Understanding Packagist

Understanding Git

Originally started by Linus Torvalds, Git version control is currently one of the most popular version control systems. Overall speed and efficiency with large projects, alongside a great branching system, has made it popular among developers.

Learning about Git version control itself is out of the scope of this book, for which recommended reading is the *Pro Git* book.

The *Pro Git* book, written by Scott Chacon and Ben Straub, and published by Apress, is available for free at `https://git-scm.com/book/en/v2`.

One neat feature of Git, which we are interested in as part of this chapter, is its submodules. They enable us to slice larger modular projects, such as our web shop app, into a series of smaller submodules, whereas each submodule is a Git repository on its own.

Understanding GitHub

Within three years of Git's appearance, GitHub emerged. GitHub is basically a web service built on top of the Git version control system. It enables developers to easily post their code online, where others can simply clone their repository and use their code. Creating an account on GitHub is free and can be done by following instructions on their official homepage (`https://github.com`).

Currently, our application is structured as per the following image:

What we want to do is to split it into six different Git repositories, as follows:

* `core`
* `catalog`
* `customer`

- payment
- sales
- shipment

The `core` repository is to contain everything except the content of the `src/Foggyline` directory.

Assuming we created an empty `core` repository on GitHub, and our local *all-in-one* app is currently held in the `shop` directory, we initialize the following commands on our computer:

```
cp -R shop core-repository
rm -Rfcore-repository/.git/
rm -Rfcore-repository/src/Foggyline/*
touch core-repository/src/Foggyline/.gitkeep
cd core-repository
git init
git remote add origin git@github.com:<user>/<core-repository>.git
git add --all
git commit -m "Initial commit of core application"
git push origin master
```

At this point, we merely pushed the core application part of our all-in-one web shop app into the `core` repository on GitHub. The `src/Foggyline/` directory does not contain any modules in it.

Now, let's go back to GitHub and create an appropriate empty repository for each of the five modules, that is, `catalog`, `customer`, `payment`, `sales`, and `shipment`. We can now execute a set of console commands for each of the modules, as shown in the following `CatalogBundle` example:

```
cp -R shop/src/Foggyline/CatalogBundle catalog-repository
cd catalog-repository
git init
git remote add origin git@github.com:<user>/<catalog-repository>.git
git add --all
git commit -m "Initial commit of catalog module"
git push origin master
```

Once all of the five modules are pushed to a repository, we can finally treat them as submodules, as shown here:

```
cd core-repository
git submodule add git@github.com:/<catalog-repository>.git
src/Foggyline/CatalogBundle
git submodule add git@github.com:/<customer-repository>.git
src/Foggyline/CustomerBundle
git submodule add git@github.com:<user>/<payment-repository>.git
src/Foggyline/PaymentBundle
git submodule add git@github.com:<user>/<sales-repository>.git
src/Foggyline/SalesBundle
git submodule add git@github.com:<user>/<shipment-repository>.git
src/Foggyline/ShipmentBundle
```

If we were to run the `ls-al` command within the `core` repository directory now, we should be able to see a `.gitmodules` file in there with the following content:

```
[submodule "src/Foggyline/CatalogBundle"]
        path = src/Foggyline/CatalogBundle
url = git@github.com:<user>/<catalog-repository>.git


[submodule "src/Foggyline/CustomerBundle"]
        path = src/Foggyline/CustomerBundle
url = git@github.com:<user>/<customer-repository>.git


[submodule "src/Foggyline/PaymentBundle"]
        path = src/Foggyline/PaymentBundle
url = git@github.com:<user>/<payment-repository>.git


[submodule "src/Foggyline/SalesBundle"]
        path = src/Foggyline/SalesBundle
url = git@github.com:<user>/<sales-repository>.git


[submodule "src/Foggyline/ShipmentBundle"]
        path = src/Foggyline/ShipmentBundle
        url = git@github.com:<user>/<shipment-repository>.git
```

The `.gitmodules` file, basically, contains the list of all of the submodules added to our core project, that is, core application. We should commit and push this file to the `core` repository now. Assuming that the `.gitmodules` file is pushed to the `core` repository, we can easily delete all directories created so far and initiate the project with one simple command, as follows:

```
git clone --recursive git@github.com:<user>/<core-repository>.git
```

The `--recursive` argument to the `git clone` command automatically initializes and updates each submodule in the repository based on the `.gitmodules` file.

Understanding Composer

Composer is a dependency management tool for PHP. By default, it does not install anything global but rather on a per-project basis. We can use it to redistribute our project in order to define which libraries and packages it needs for it to be successfully executed. Using Composer is quite simple. All it creating is to create a `composer.json` file in the root directory of our project with similar content, as follows:

```
{
"require": {
"twig/twig": "~1.0"
    }
}
```

If we were to create the preceding `composer.json` file in some empty directory and execute the `composer install` command within that directory, Composer will pickup the `composer.json` file and install the defined dependencies for our project. The actual `install` action implies on downloading the required code from a remote repository to our machine. In doing so, the `install` command creates the `composer.lock` file, which writes a list of the exact versions of dependencies installed.

We can also simply execute the command `twig/twig:~1.0` that a Composer requires, which does the same thing but with a different approach. It does not require us to write a `composer.json` file, and if one exists, it will update it.

Learning about Composer itself is out of the scope of this book, for which the recommended official documentation is available at `https://getcomposer.org/doc`.

Composer allows packaging and formal dependency management, making it a great choice to slice our all-in-one modular application into a series of Composer packages. These packages need a repository.

Understanding Packagist

The main repository, when it comes to Composer packages, is **Packagist** (https://packagist.org). It is a web service that we can access through our browser, open an account on for free, and start submitting our packages to the repository. We can also use it to search through already existing packages.

Packagist is generally used for free open source packages, though we can attach **privateGitHub** and **BitBucket** repositories to it in the same manner, the only difference being that the private repositories require SSH keys in order to work.

There are more convenient commercial installations of the Composer packager, such as **Toran Proxy** (https://toranproxy.com). This allows easier hosting of private packages, higher bandwidth for faster package installations, and commercial support.

Up to this point, we sliced our applications into six different Git repositories, one for core application and the remaining five for each module (catalog, customer, payment, sales, and shipment) individually. Now, let's take the final step and see how we can move away from the Git submodules to the Composer packages.

Assuming we created an account on https://packagist.org and successfully logged in, we will start by clicking on the **Submit** button, which should land us on a screen similar to the following screenshot:

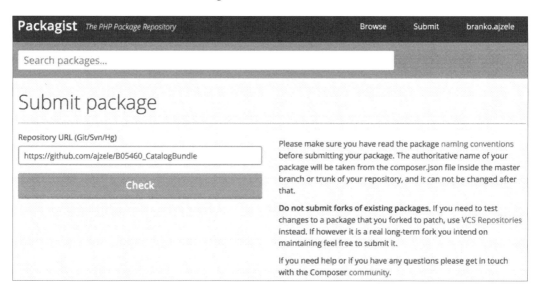

Here, we need to provide a link to our existing Git, SVN, or Mercurial (HG) repository. The preceding example provides a link (`https://github.com/ajzele/B05460_CatalogBundle`) to the Git repository. Before we press the **Check** button, we will need to make sure that our repository has a `composer.json` file defined in its root, otherwise an error similar to the one shown in the following screenshot will be thrown.

Submit package

The package name was not found in the composer.json, make sure there is a name present.

We will then create the `composer.json` file for our `CatalogBundle` with the following content:

```
{
"name": "foggyline/catalogbundle",
"version" : "1.0.0",
"type": "library",
"description": "Just a test module for web shop application.",
"keywords": [
"catalog"
  ],
"homepage": "https://github.com/ajzele/B05460_CatalogBundle",
"license": "MIT",
"authors": [
    {
"name": "Branko Ajzele",
"email": "ajzele@gmail.com",
"homepage": "http://foggyline.net",
"role": "Developer"
    }
  ],
"minimum-stability": "dev",
"prefer-stable": true,
"autoload": {
"psr-0": {
"Foggyline\\CatalogBundle\\": ""
    }
  },
"target-dir": "Foggyline/CatalogBundle"
}
```

There are quite a lot of attributes here, all of which are fully documented over on the `https://getcomposer.org/doc/04-schema.md` page.

With the preceding `composer.json` file in place, running the `composer install` command on console will pull in the code under the `vendor/foggyline/catalogbundle` directory, making for a full path of our bundle file under `vendor/foggyline/catalogbundle/Foggyline/CatalogBundle/FoggylineCatalogBundle.php`.

Once we add the preceding `composer.json` file to our Git repository, we can go back to Packagist and proceed with clicking the **Check** button, which should result in a screen similar to the following screenshot:

Finally, when we click the **Submit** button, a screen similar to the following screenshot should appear:

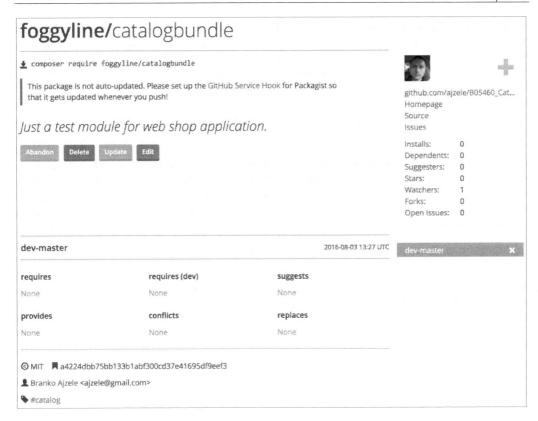

Our package is now added to Packagist, and running the following command on console will install it to into the project:

```
composer require foggyline/catalogbundle:dev-master
```

Similarly, we can just add the proper entry to the existing project's composer.json file, as shown in the following code block:

```
{
"require": {
"foggyline/catalogbundle": "dev-master"
    },
}
```

Now that we know how to slice out the application across several Git repositories and Composer packages, we need to do the same for the remaining modules within the src/Foggyline/ directory, as only those modules will be registered as the Composer packages.

During the sales module development, we noticed that it depends on several other modules, such as catalog and customer. We can use the require attribute of the composer.json file to outline this dependency.

Once all of the Git repositories for the src/Foggyline/ modules are updated with the proper composer.json definitions, we can go back to our core application repository and update the require attribute in its composer.json file, as follows:

```
{
"require": {
// ...
"foggyline/catalogbundle": "dev-master"
"foggyline/customerbundle": "dev-master"
"foggyline/paymentbundle": "dev-master"
"foggyline/salesbundle": "dev-master"
"foggyline/shipmentbundle": "dev-master"
        // ...
    },
}
```

The difference between using submodules and packages might not be that obvious at this point. However, packages, unlike submodules, allow versioning. Though all of our packages are pulled in from dev-master, we could have easily targeted specific versions of packages, if any.

Summary

Throughout this chapter, we took a quick look at Git and Composer and how we can integrate and distribute our modules via GitHub and Packagist as their respectful services. Publishing packages under Packagist has been shown to be a pretty straightforward and easy process. All it took was a public link to the version control system repository and a `composer.json` file definition within the root of our project.

Writing our own applications from ground up does not necessarily mean we need to use the Git submodules or the Composer packages, as presented in this chapter. The Symfony application, on its own, is structured modularly via bundles. The version control system, when used on a Symfony project, is supposed to save only our code, which means all of the Symfony libraries and other dependencies are to be pulled in via Composer when the project is being set. The examples shown in this chapter merely show what can be accomplished if we are after writing modular components that are to be shared with others. As an example, if we were really working on a robust `catalog` module, others interested in coding their own web shop might find it interesting to require and use it in their project.

This book started by looking into the current state of the PHP ecosystem. We then touched upon design patterns and principles, as a foundation of professional programming. Then we moved onto writing a brief, more visual, specification for our web shop application. Finally, we split our application into core and several other smaller modules, which we then coded following the specification. Along the way, we familiarized ourselves with some of the most commonly used Symfony features. The overall application we wrote is far from being robust. It is a web shop in its simplest form, which leaves much to be desired on a feature side. However, the concepts applied showcase how easy and quick it can be to write modular applications in PHP.

Index

Made in the USA
Middletown, DE
10 November 2018